GREAT POWER

GREAT POWER

TOM TAYLOR
WRITER

JORGE MOLINA
PENCILER

ADRIANO DI BENEDETTO
WITH ROBERTO POGGI
INKERS

DAVID CURIEL
COLORIST

VC's CORY PETIT
LETTERER

JORGE MOLINA
COVER ART

THE THRESHING PLACE

JEFF LEMIRE
WRITER

MIKE DEL MUNDO
ARTIST

MIKE DEL MUNDO &
MARCO D'ALFONSO
COLORISTS

VC's CORY PETIT
LETTERER

JORGE MOLINA
COVER ART

FLATLINE

DECLAN SHALVEY
WRITER/ARTIST/COLORIST/COVER

VC's CORY PETIT
LETTERER

TIME OF MONSTERS – "A LITTLE FIRE"

DAVID VAUGHN
WRITER

KEVIN NOWLAN
ARTIST/COLORIST/LETTERER

JUAN FERREYRA
COVER ART

SARAH BRUNSTAD
ASSOCIATE EDITOR

WIL MOSS
EDITOR

TOM BREVOORT
EXECUTIVE EDITOR

COLLECTION EDITOR: JENNIFER GRÜNWALD
ASSISTANT EDITOR: DANIEL KIRCHHOFFER
ASSISTANT MANAGING EDITOR: MAIA LOY
ASSISTANT MANAGING EDITOR: LISA MONTALBANO

VP PRODUCTION & SPECIAL PROJECTS: JEFF YOUNGQUIST
BOOK DESIGNER: ADAM DEL RE
SVP PRINT, SALES & MARKETING: DAVID GABRIEL
EDITOR IN CHIEF: C.B. CEBULSKI

HULK
CREATED BY
STAN LEE &
JACK KIRBY

…TAL HULK: GREAT POWER. Contains material originally published in magazine form as IMMORTAL HULK: GREAT POWER (2020) #1, IMMORTAL HULK: THE THRESHING PLACE (2020) #1, IMMORTAL HULK: FLATLINE (2021) #1 and IMMORTAL HULK: … MONSTERS (2021) #1. First printing 2021. ISBN 978-1-302-93117-9. Published by MARVEL WORLDWIDE, INC., a subsidiary of MARVEL ENTERTAINMENT, LLC. OFFICE OF PUBLICATION: 1290 Avenue of the Americas, New York, NY 10104. © 2021 … No similarity between any of the names, characters, persons, and/or institutions in this magazine with those of any living or dead person or institution is intended, and any such similarity which may exist is purely coincidental. **Printed in Canada.** …EIGE, Chief Creative Officer; DAN BUCKLEY, President, Marvel Entertainment; JOE QUESADA, EVP & Creative Director; DAVID BOGART, Associate Publisher & SVP of Talent Affairs; TOM BREVOORT, VP, Executive Editor; NICK LOWE, Executive Editor, VP …nt, Digital Publishing; DAVID GABRIEL, VP of Print & Digital Publishing; JEFF YOUNGQUIST, VP of Production & Special Projects; ALEX MORALES, Director of Publishing Operations; DAN EDINGTON, Managing Editor; RICKEY PURDIN, Director of Talent …s; JENNIFER GRÜNWALD, Senior Editor, Special Projects; SUSAN CRESPI, Production Manager; STAN LEE, Chairman Emeritus. For information regarding advertising in Marvel Comics or on Marvel.com, please contact Vit DeBellis, Custom Solutions & …

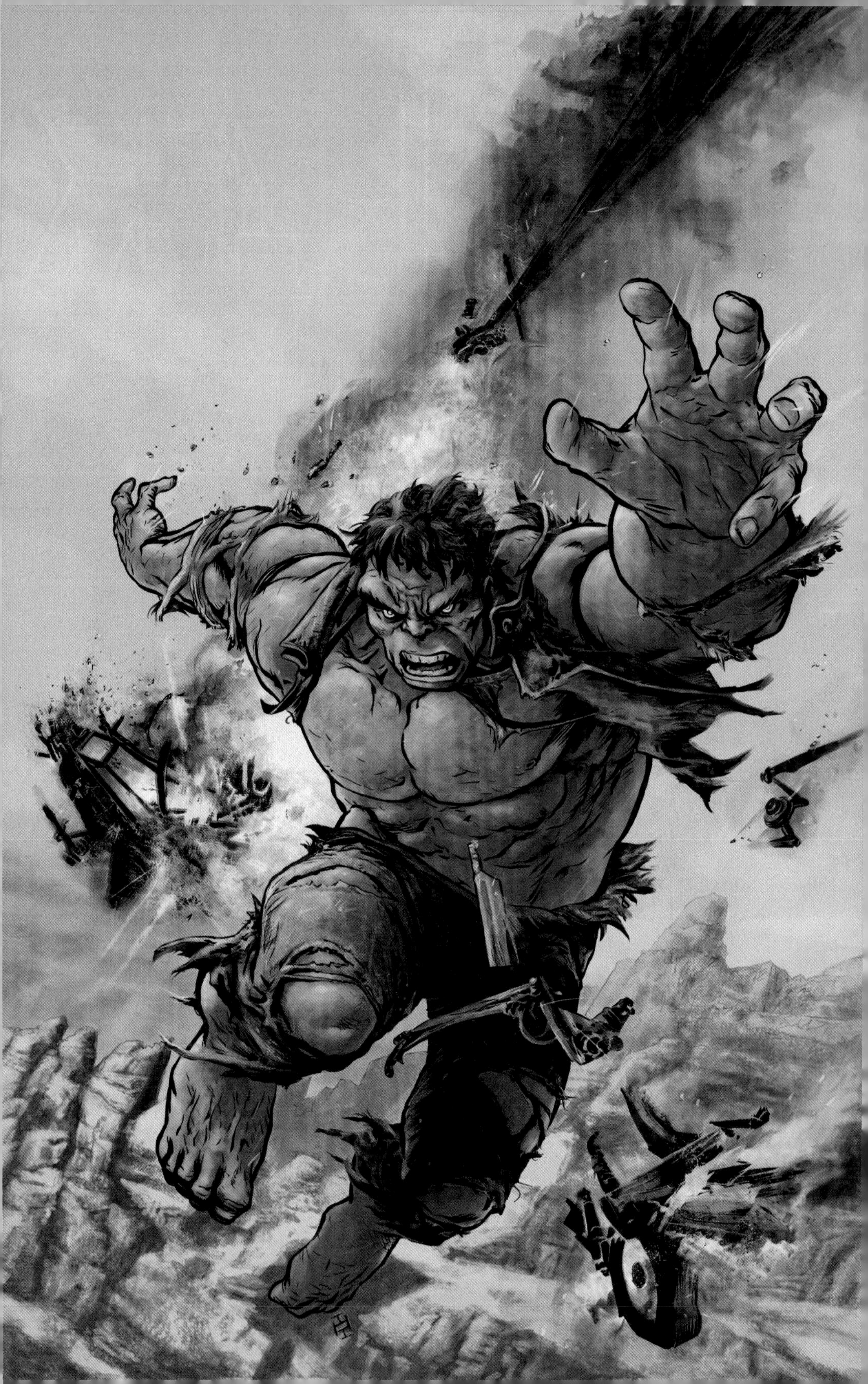

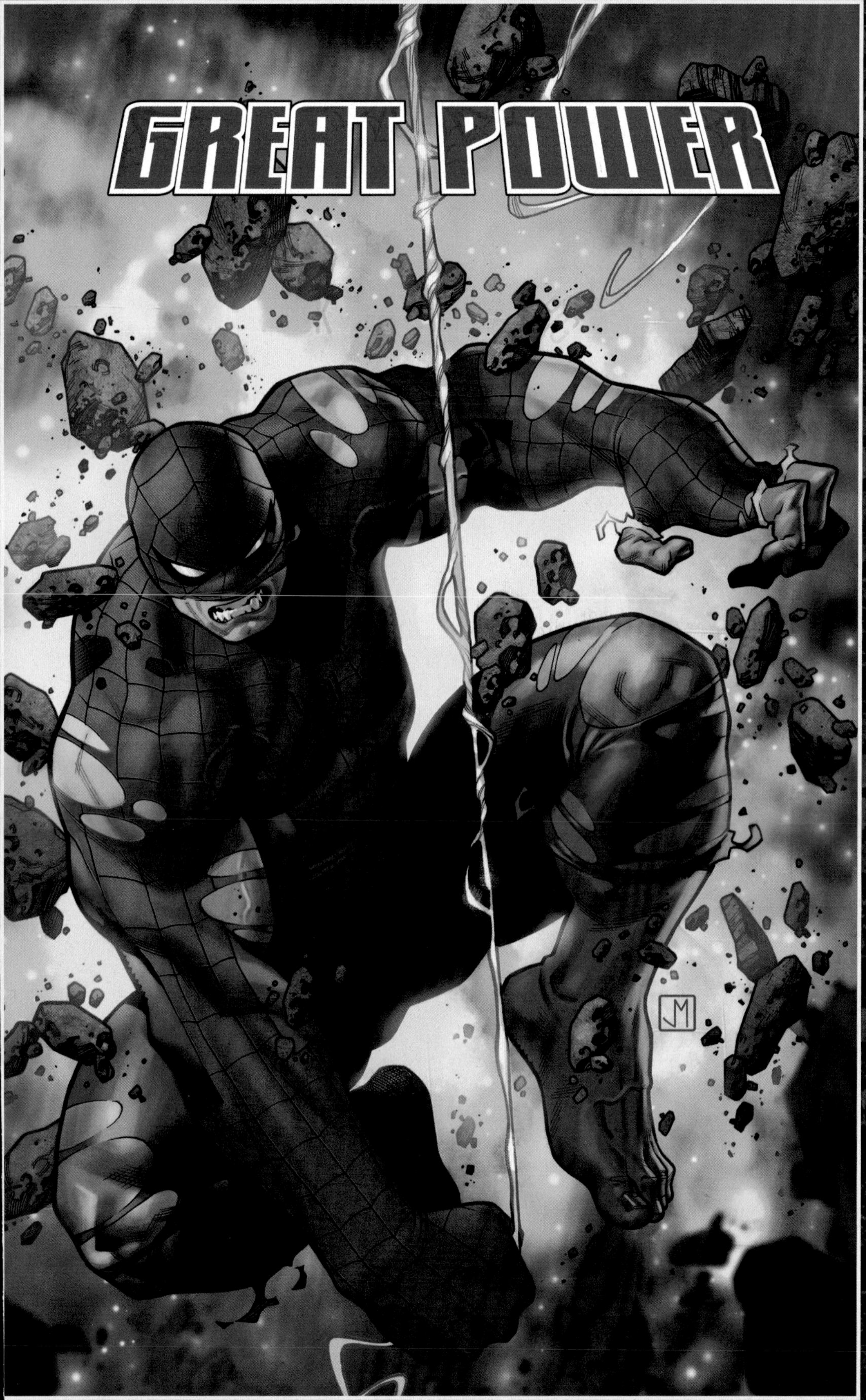
GREAT POWER
JM

"**WITH GREAT POWER, THERE MUST ALSO COME GREAT RESPONSIBILITY.**"

– BEN PARKER

[NOTE: THIS STORY TAKES PLACE BEFORE *IMMORTAL HULK #14* AND *FANTASTIC FOUR #12.*]

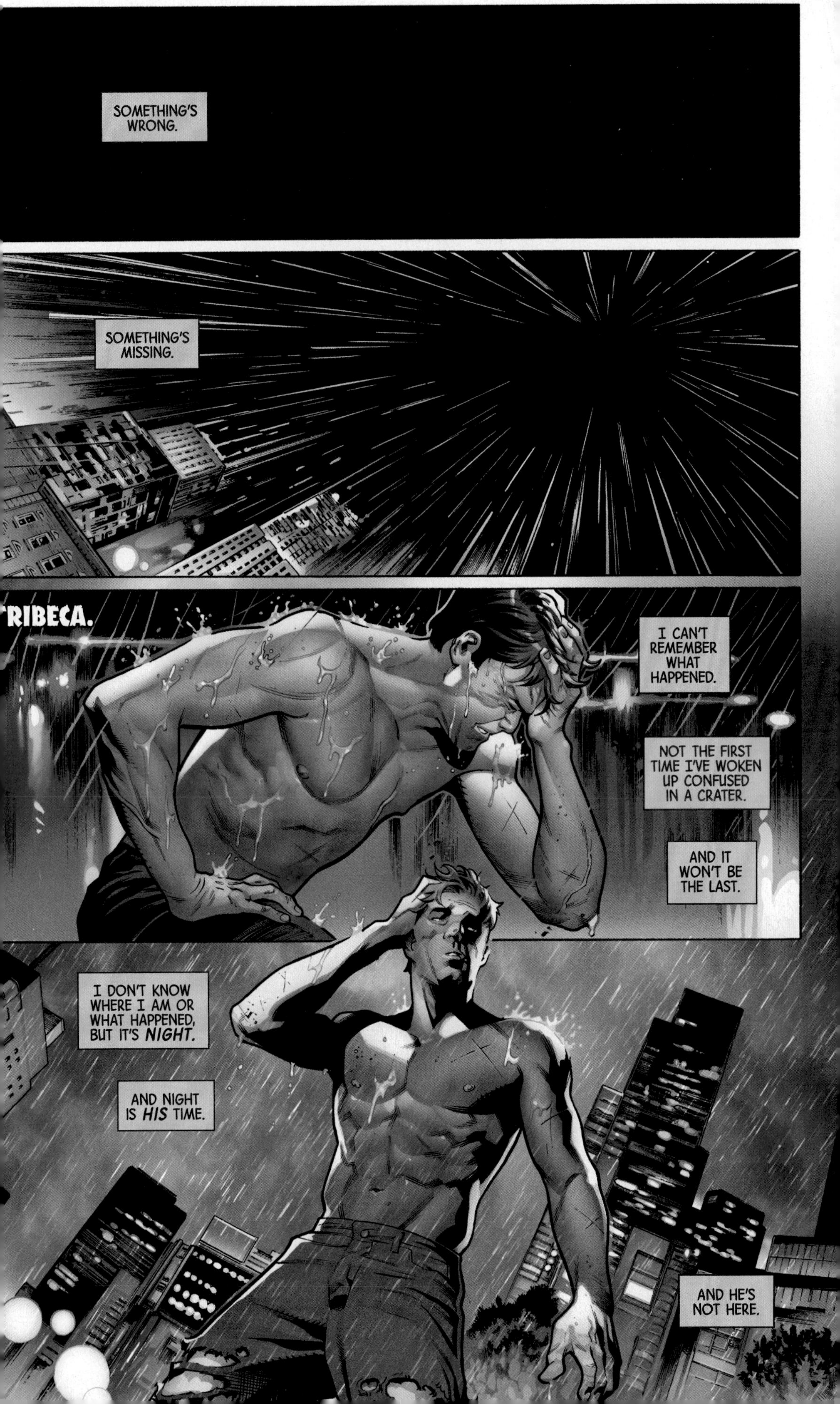
SOMETHING'S WRONG.
SOMETHING'S MISSING.
TRIBECA.
I CAN'T REMEMBER WHAT HAPPENED.
NOT THE FIRST TIME I'VE WOKEN UP CONFUSED IN A CRATER.
AND IT WON'T BE THE LAST.
I DON'T KNOW WHERE I AM OR WHAT HAPPENED, BUT IT'S NIGHT.
AND NIGHT IS HIS TIME.
AND HE'S NOT HERE.

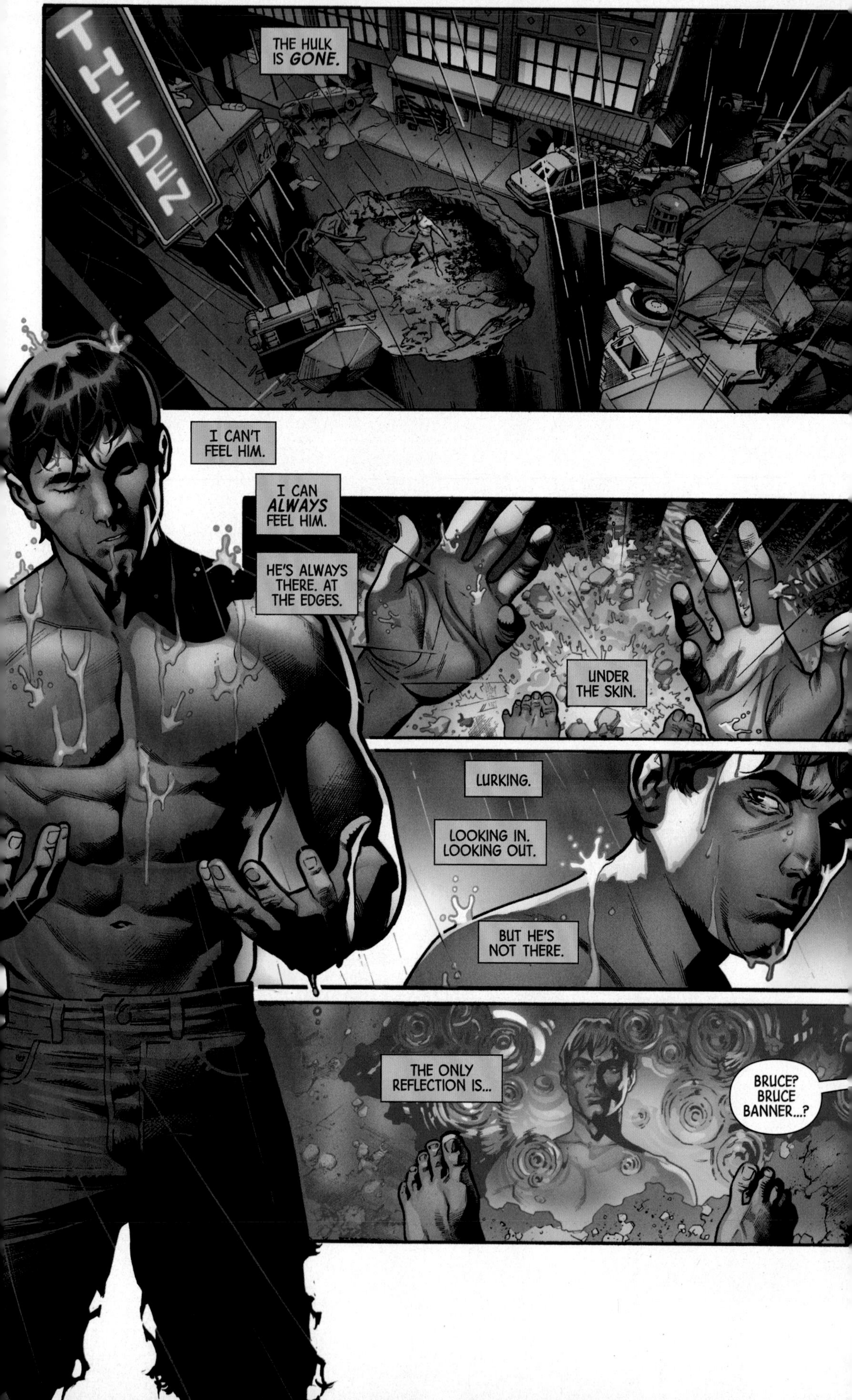
THE DEN
THE HULK IS *GONE.*
I CAN'T FEEL HIM.
I CAN *ALWAYS* FEEL HIM.
HE'S ALWAYS THERE. AT THE EDGES.
UNDER THE SKIN.
LURKING.
LOOKING IN. LOOKING OUT.
BUT HE'S NOT THERE.
THE ONLY REFLECTION IS...
BRUCE? BRUCE BANNER...?

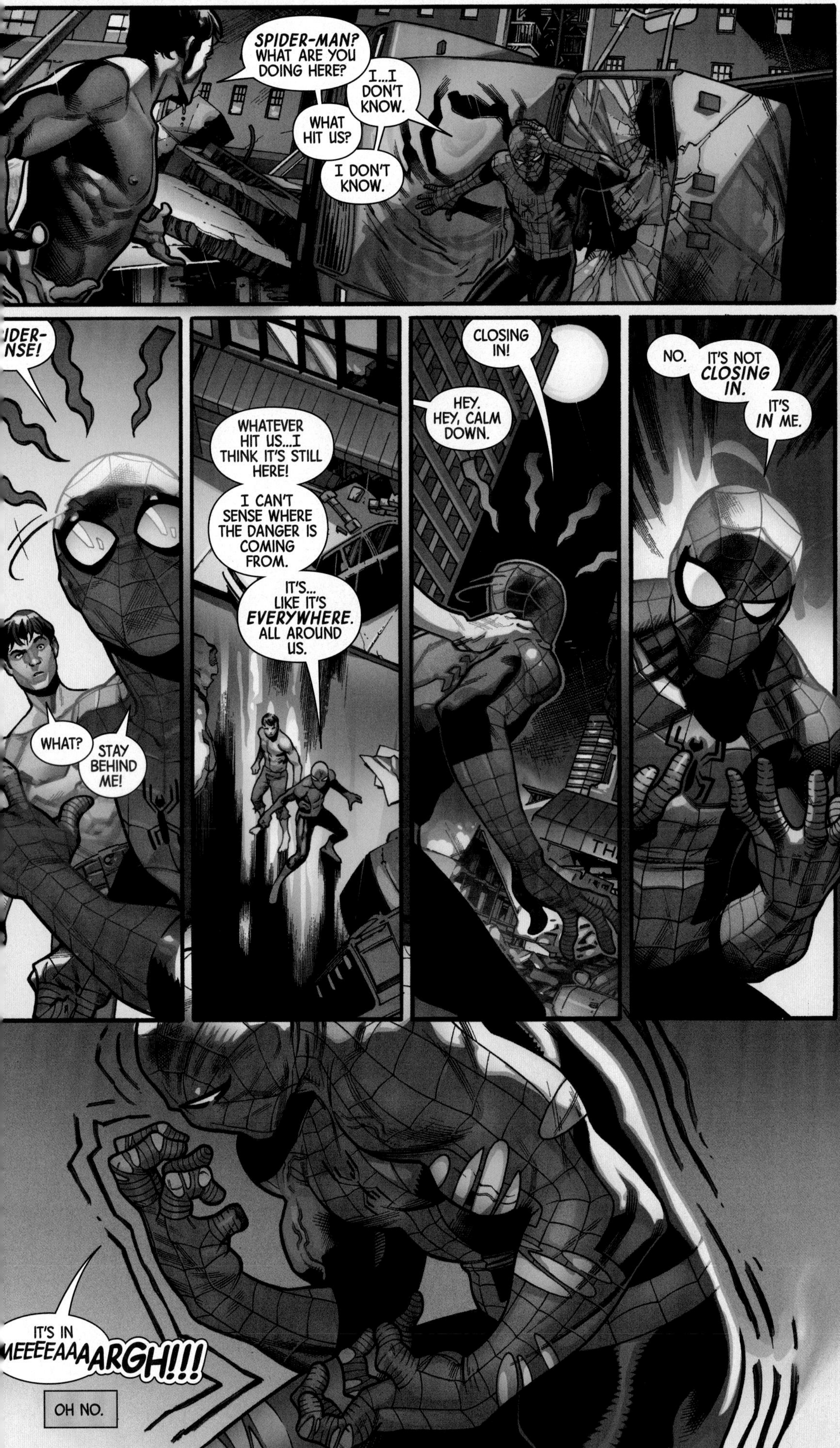

SPIDER-MAN? WHAT ARE YOU DOING HERE?
I...I DON'T KNOW.
WHAT HIT US?
I DON'T KNOW.
IDER-NSE!
WHAT?
STAY BEHIND ME!
WHATEVER HIT US...I THINK IT'S STILL HERE!
I CAN'T SENSE WHERE THE DANGER IS COMING FROM.
IT'S... LIKE IT'S EVERYWHERE. ALL AROUND US.
CLOSING IN!
HEY. HEY, CALM DOWN.
NO.
IT'S NOT CLOSING IN.
IT'S IN ME.
IT'S IN MEEEEAAAARGH!!!
OH NO.

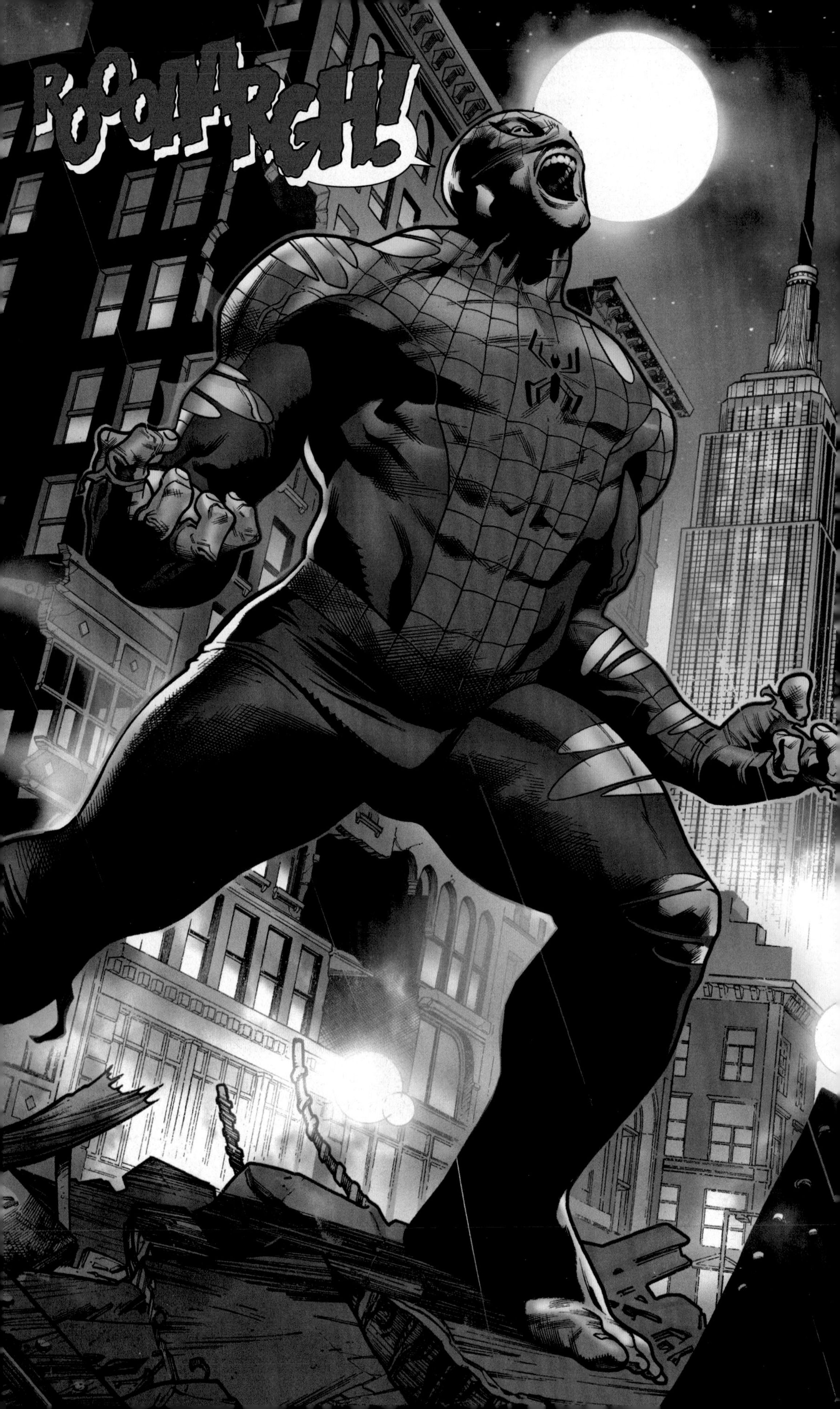
ROOOWARGH!

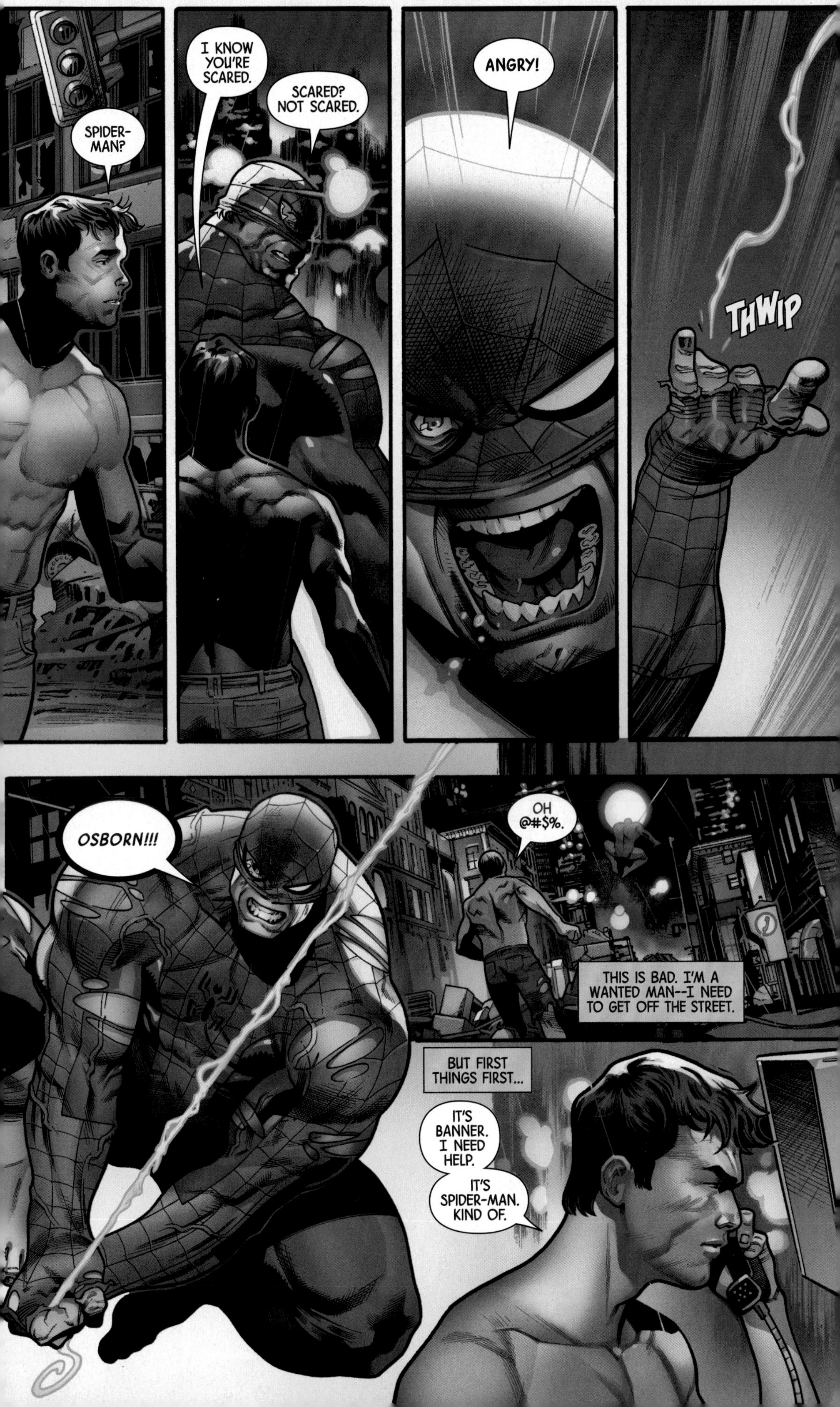
SPIDER-MAN?
I KNOW YOU'RE SCARED.
SCARED? NOT SCARED.
ANGRY!
THWIP
OSBORN!!!
OH @#$%.
THIS IS BAD. I'M A WANTED MAN--I NEED TO GET OFF THE STREET.
BUT FIRST THINGS FIRST...
IT'S BANNER. I NEED HELP.
IT'S SPIDER-MAN. KIND OF.

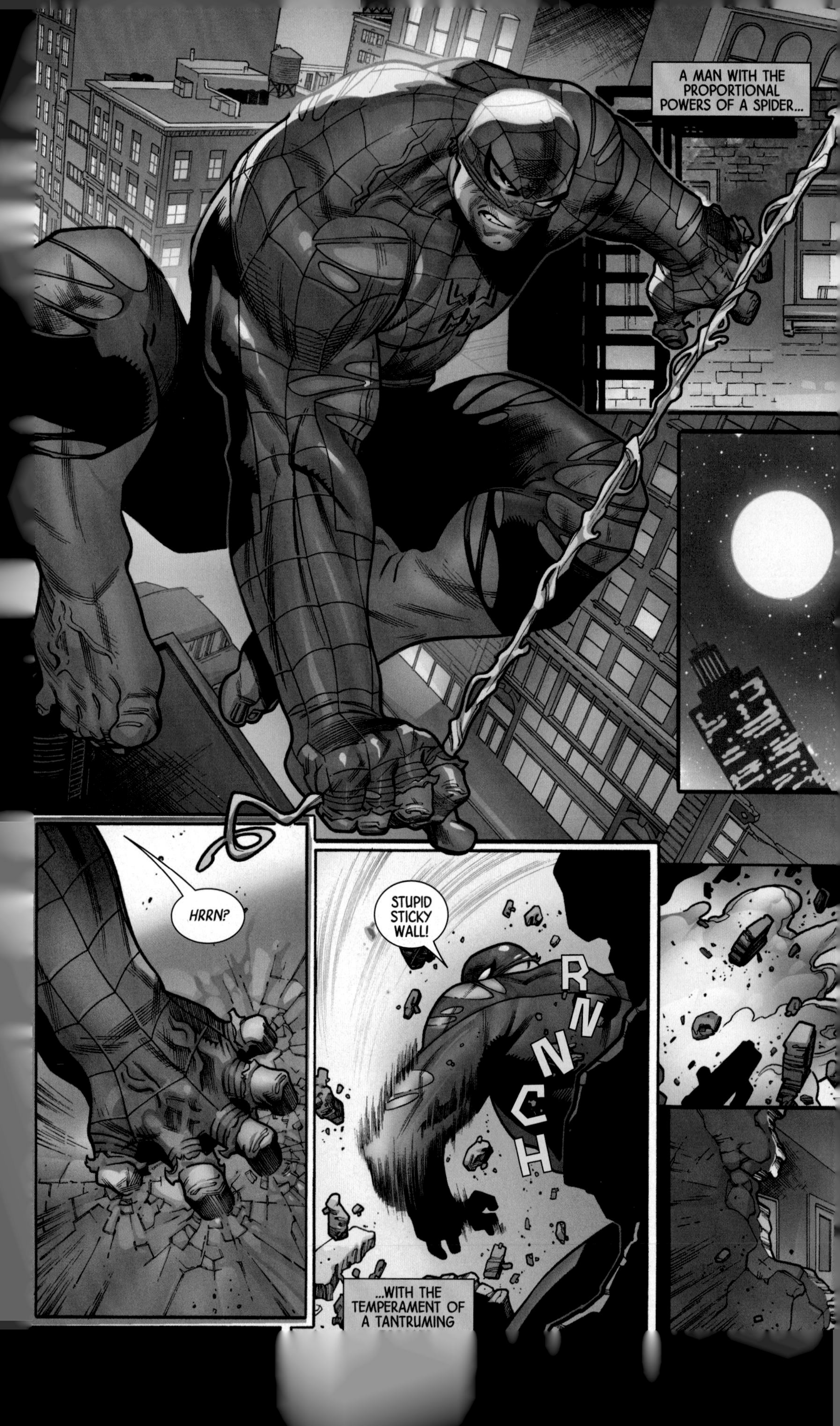
A MAN WITH THE PROPORTIONAL POWERS OF A SPIDER...
HRRN?
STUPID STICKY WALL!
RNNCH
...WITH THE TEMPERAMENT OF A TANTRUMING

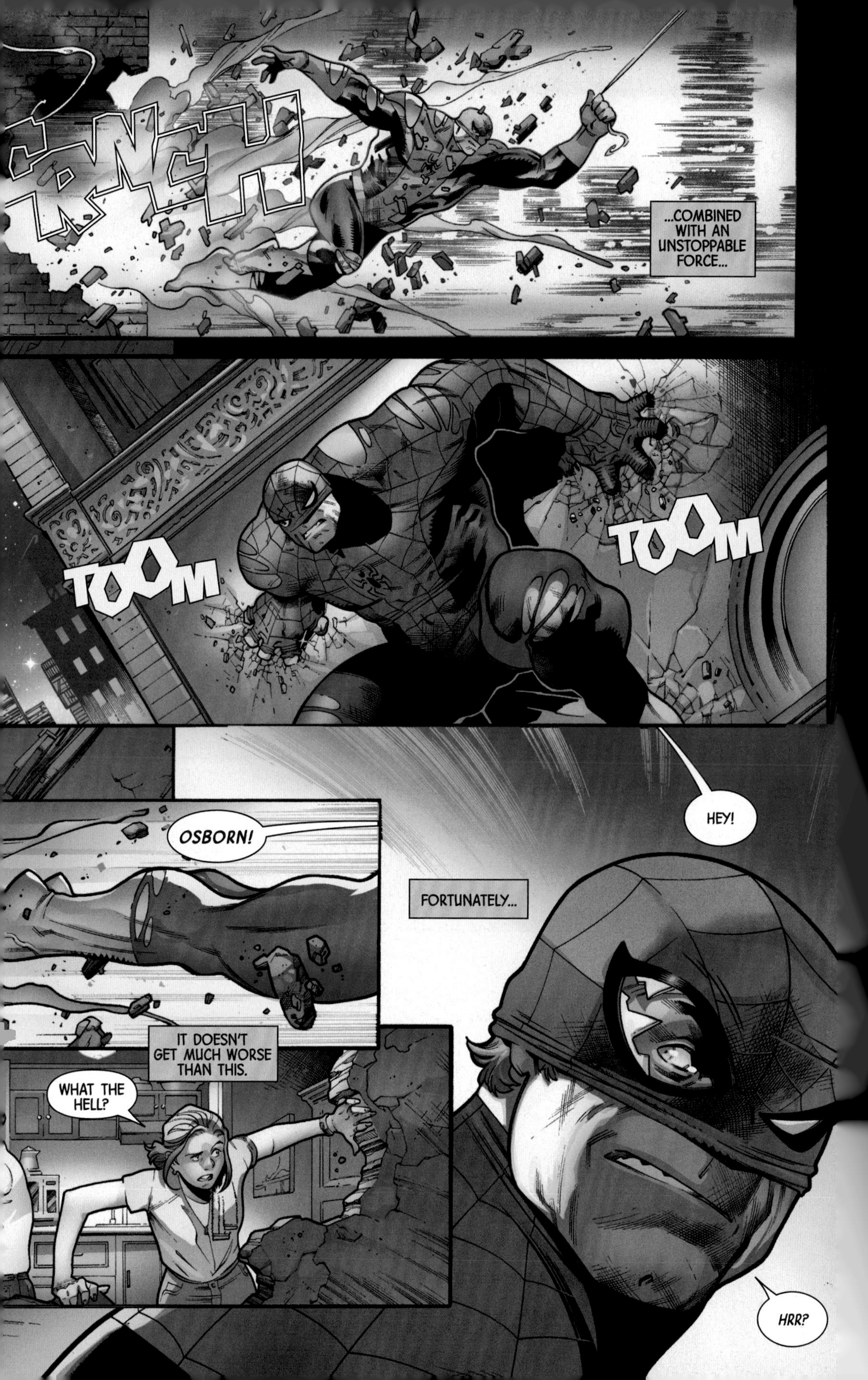
...COMBINED WITH AN UNSTOPPABLE FORCE...
TOOM
TOOM
HEY!
OSBORN!
FORTUNATELY...
IT DOESN'T GET MUCH WORSE THAN THIS.
WHAT THE HELL?
HRR?

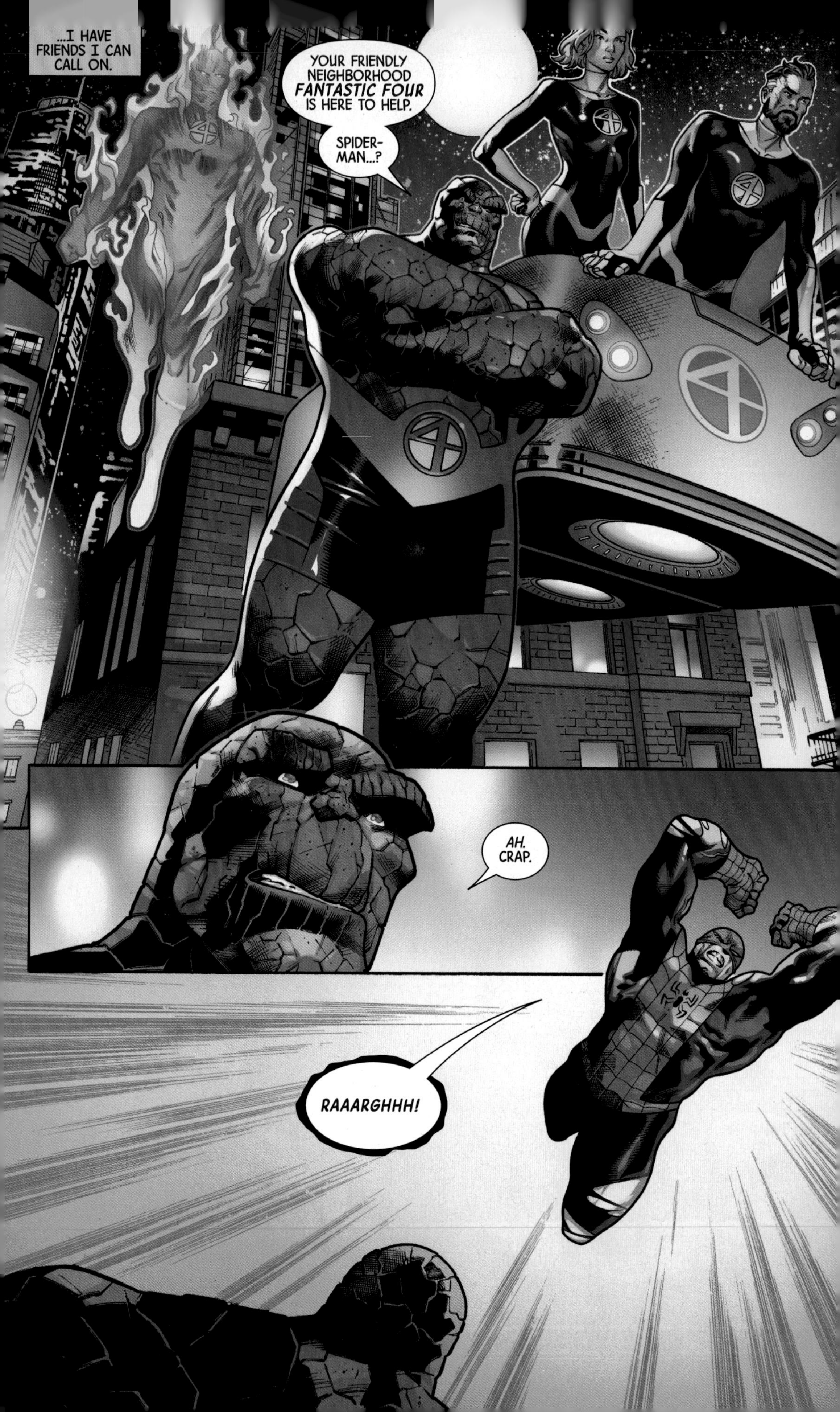
...I HAVE FRIENDS I CAN CALL ON.
YOUR FRIENDLY NEIGHBORHOOD *FANTASTIC FOUR* IS HERE TO HELP.
SPIDER-MAN...?
AH. CRAP.
RAAARGHHH!

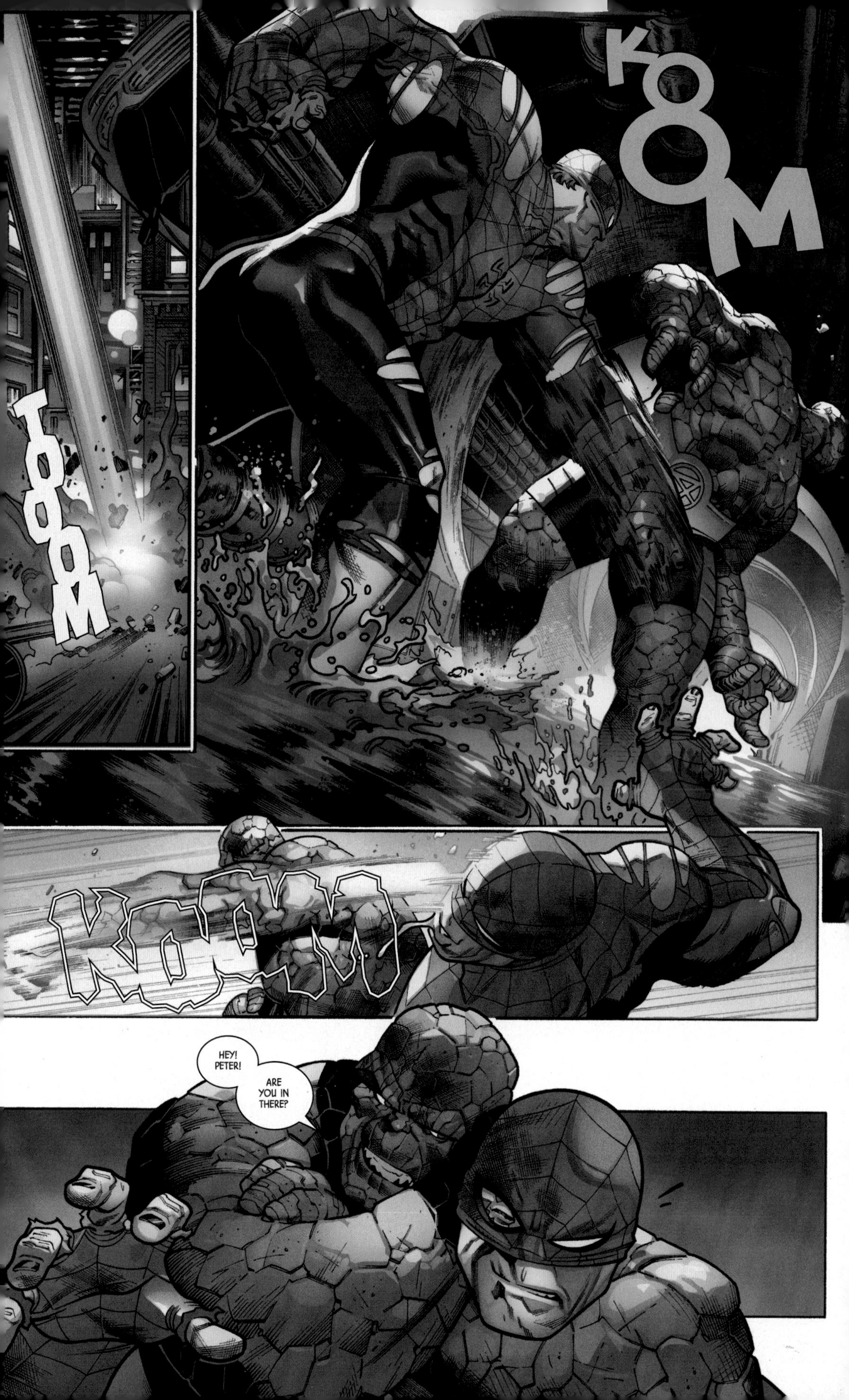

KOOM
TOOOM
KROOM
HEY! PETER!
ARE YOU IN THERE?

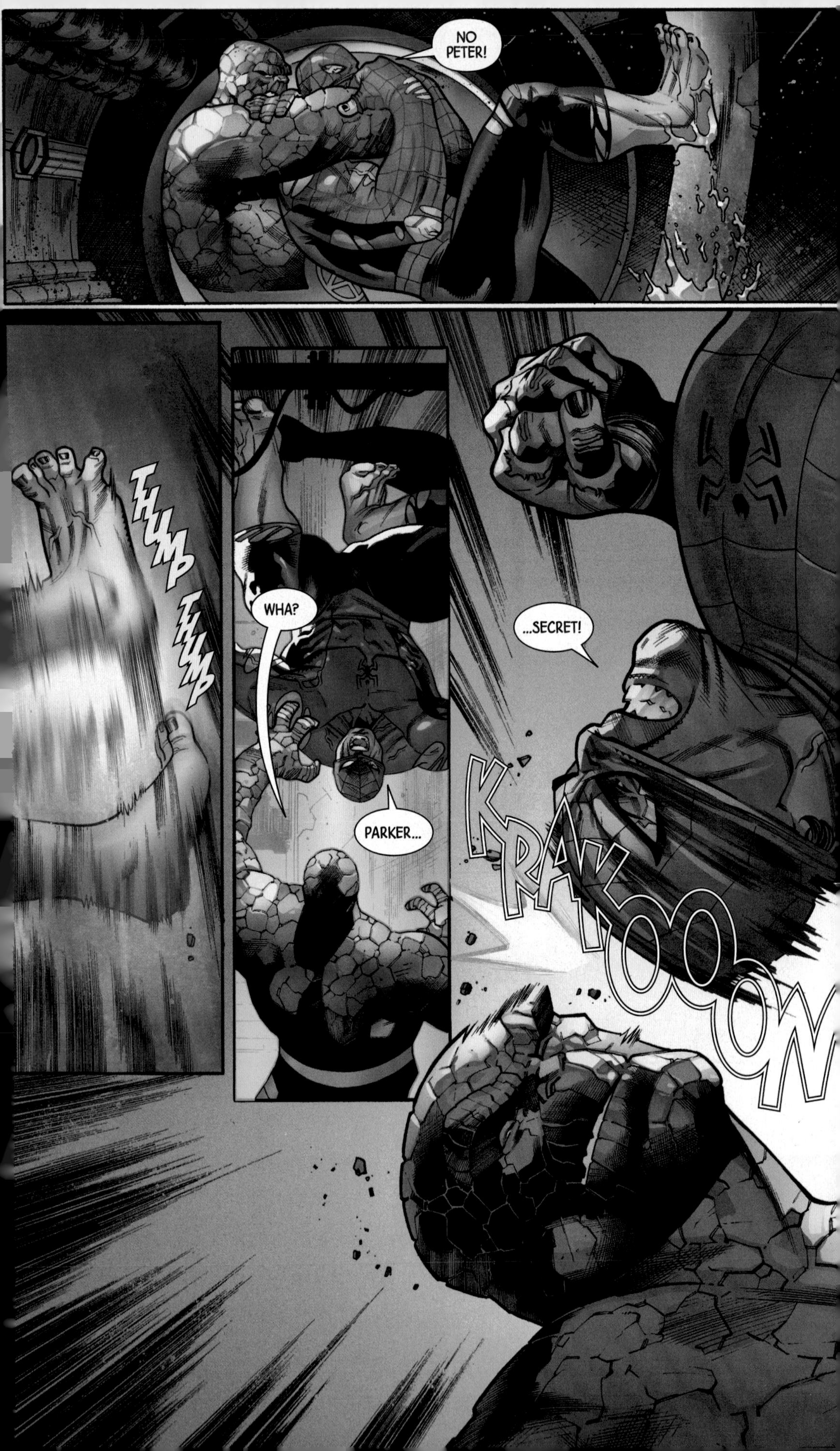
NO PETER!
THUMP THUMP THUMP
WHA?
PARKER...
...SECRET!
KRAKOOOOM

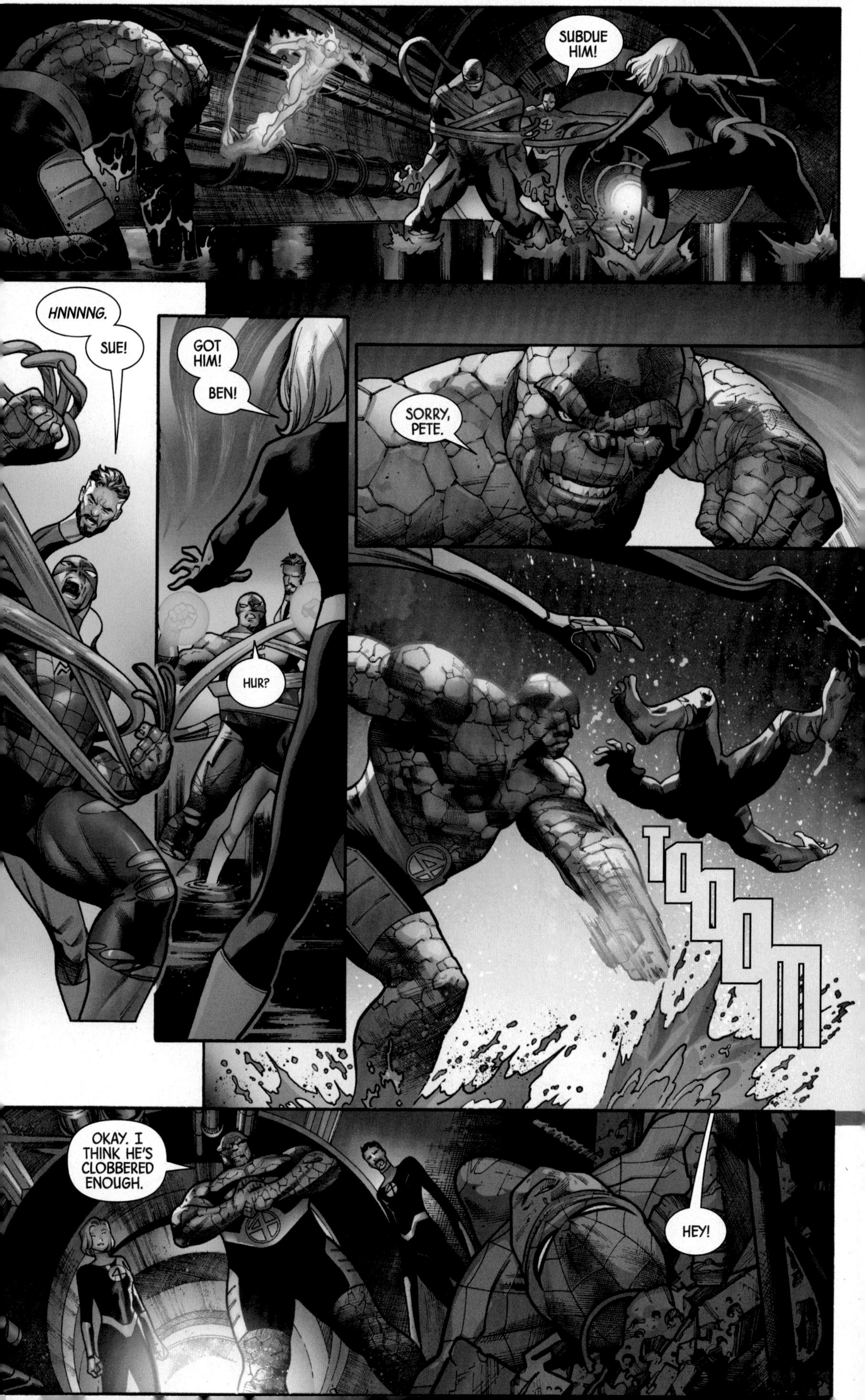
SUBDUE HIM!
HNNNNG.
SUE!
GOT HIM!
BEN!
HUR?
SORRY, PETE.
TOOOOM
OKAY. I THINK HE'S CLOBBERED ENOUGH.
HEY!

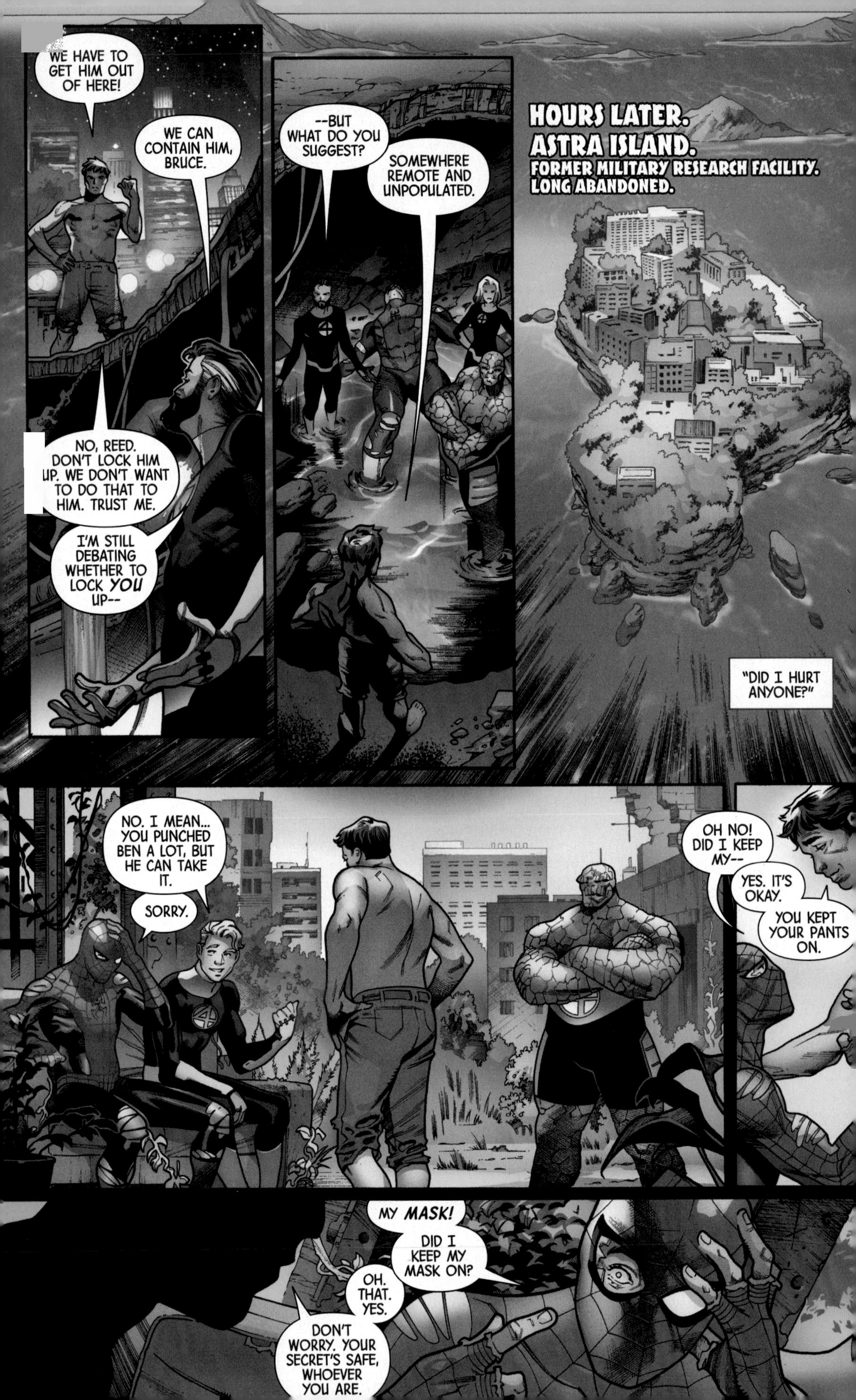
WE HAVE TO GET HIM OUT OF HERE!
WE CAN CONTAIN HIM, BRUCE.
NO, REED. DON'T LOCK HIM UP. WE DON'T WANT TO DO THAT TO HIM. TRUST ME.
I'M STILL DEBATING WHETHER TO LOCK YOU UP--
--BUT WHAT DO YOU SUGGEST?
SOMEWHERE REMOTE AND UNPOPULATED.
HOURS LATER. ASTRA ISLAND.
FORMER MILITARY RESEARCH FACILITY. LONG ABANDONED.
"DID I HURT ANYONE?"
NO. I MEAN... YOU PUNCHED BEN A LOT, BUT HE CAN TAKE IT.
SORRY.
OH NO! DID I KEEP MY--
YES. IT'S OKAY.
YOU KEPT YOUR PANTS ON.
MY MASK!
DID I KEEP MY MASK ON?
OH. THAT. YES.
DON'T WORRY. YOUR SECRET'S SAFE, WHOEVER YOU ARE.

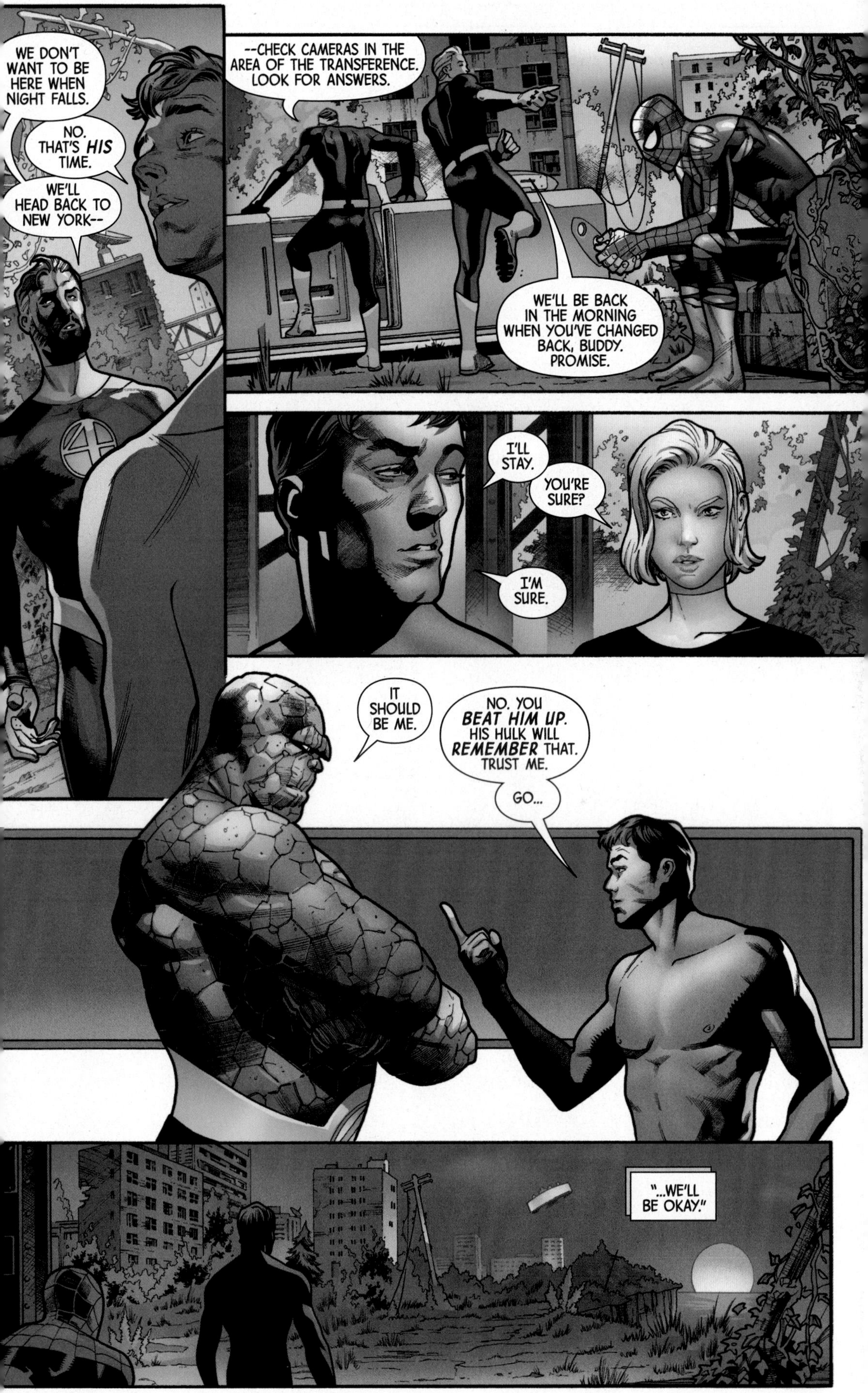
WE DON'T WANT TO BE HERE WHEN NIGHT FALLS.
NO. THAT'S *HIS* TIME.
WE'LL HEAD BACK TO NEW YORK--
--CHECK CAMERAS IN THE AREA OF THE TRANSFERENCE. LOOK FOR ANSWERS.
WE'LL BE BACK IN THE MORNING WHEN YOU'VE CHANGED BACK, BUDDY. PROMISE.
I'LL STAY.
YOU'RE SURE?
I'M SURE.
IT SHOULD BE ME.
NO. YOU ***BEAT HIM UP***. HIS HULK WILL ***REMEMBER*** THAT. TRUST ME.
GO...
"...WE'LL BE OKAY."

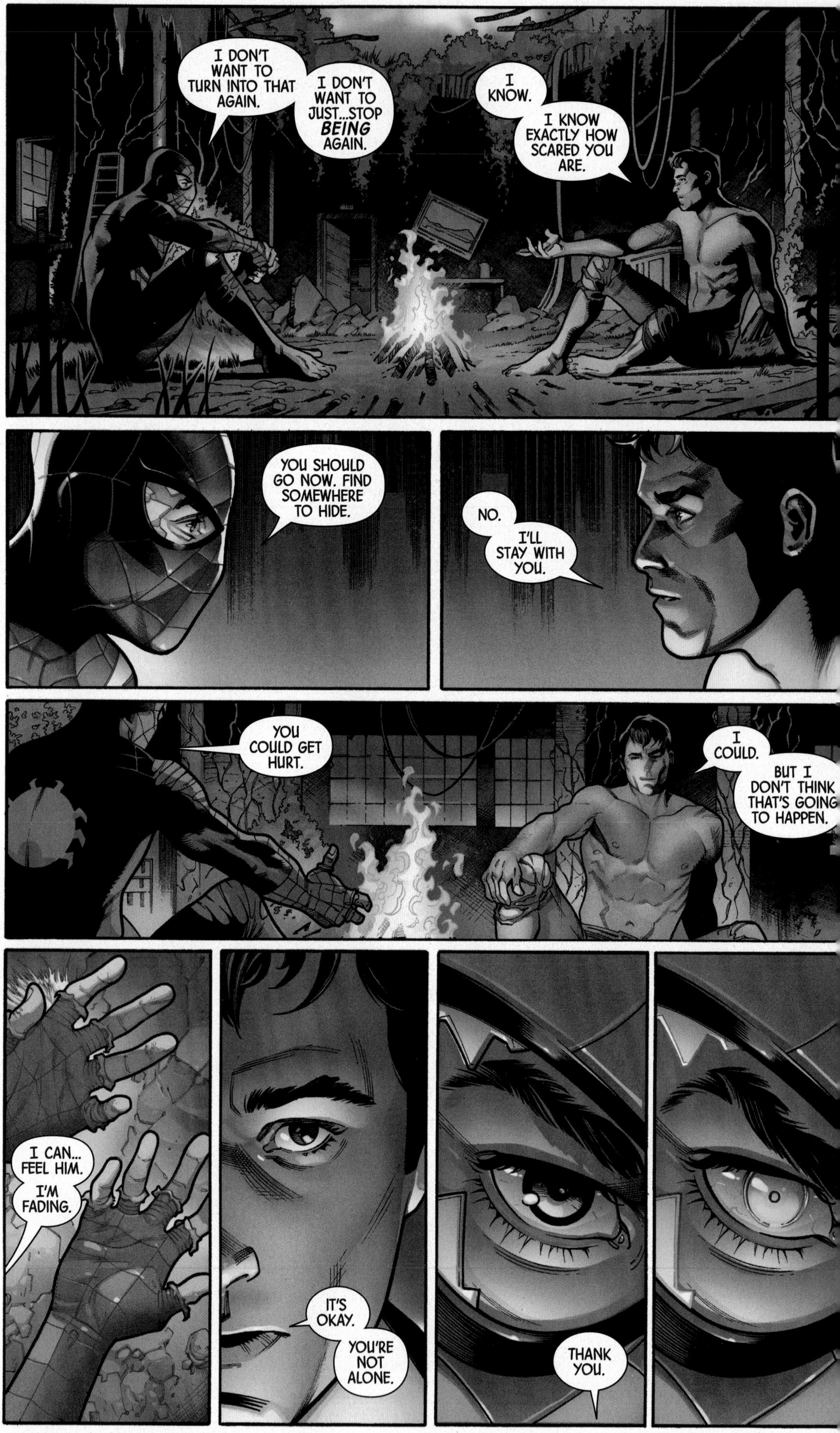
I DON'T WANT TO TURN INTO THAT AGAIN.
I DON'T WANT TO JUST...STOP *BEING* AGAIN.
I KNOW.
I KNOW EXACTLY HOW SCARED YOU ARE.
YOU SHOULD GO NOW. FIND SOMEWHERE TO HIDE.
NO.
I'LL STAY WITH YOU.
YOU COULD GET HURT.
I COULD.
BUT I DON'T THINK THAT'S GOING TO HAPPEN.
I CAN... FEEL HIM.
I'M FADING.
IT'S OKAY.
YOU'RE NOT ALONE.
THANK YOU.

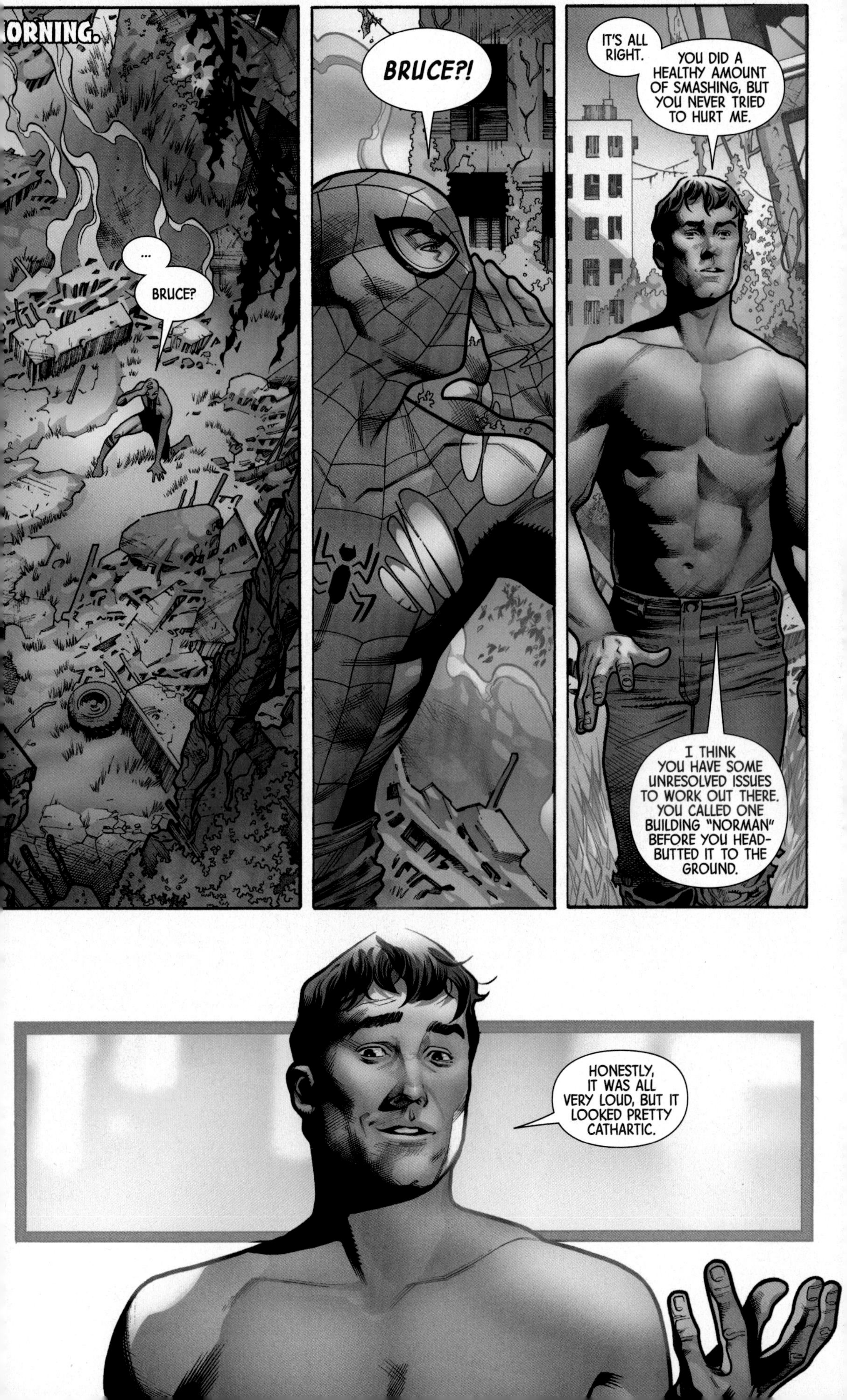
ORNING.
...
BRUCE?
BRUCE?!
IT'S ALL RIGHT.
YOU DID A HEALTHY AMOUNT OF SMASHING, BUT YOU NEVER TRIED TO HURT ME.
I THINK YOU HAVE SOME UNRESOLVED ISSUES TO WORK OUT THERE. YOU CALLED ONE BUILDING "NORMAN" BEFORE YOU HEAD-BUTTED IT TO THE GROUND.
HONESTLY, IT WAS ALL VERY LOUD, BUT IT LOOKED PRETTY CATHARTIC.

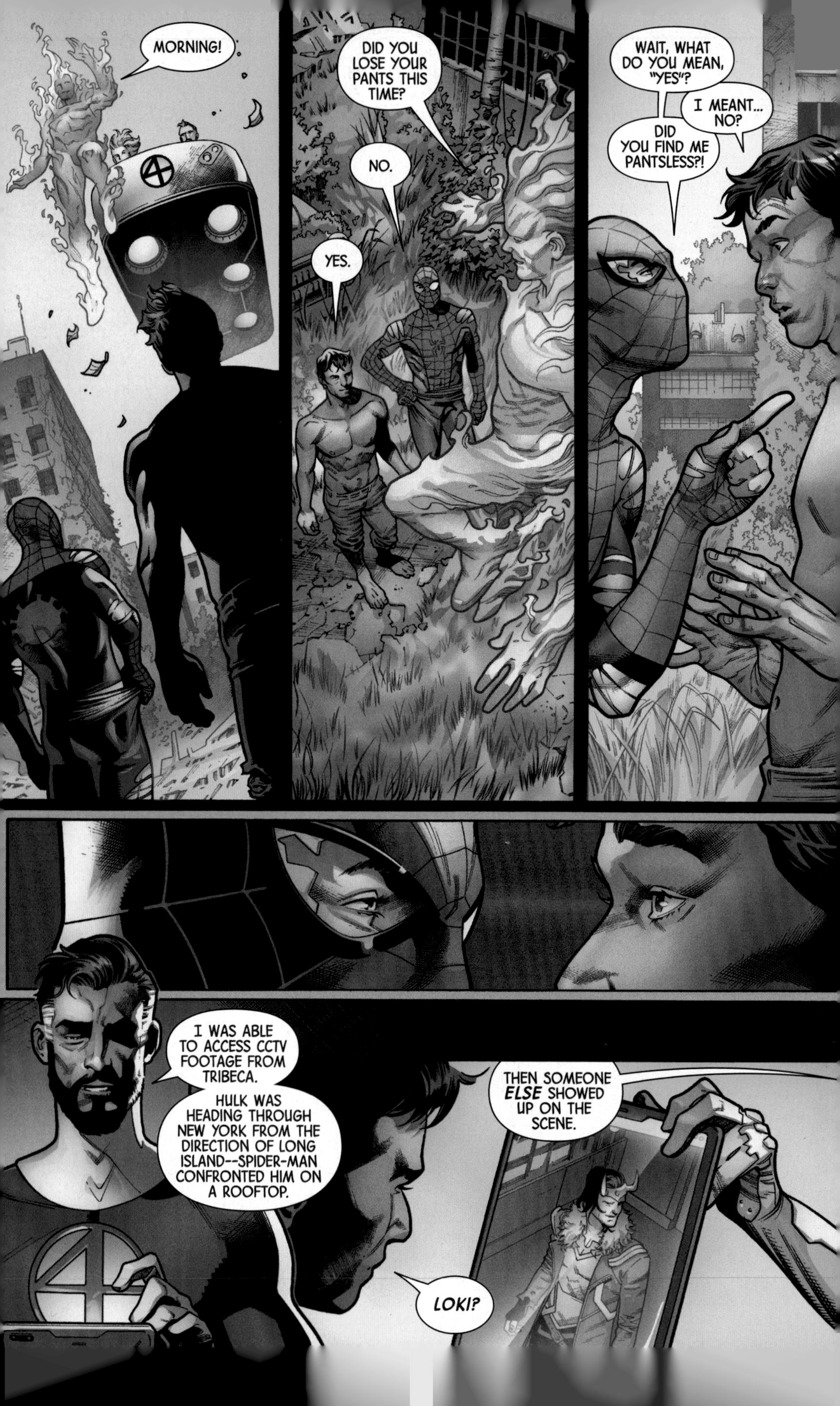

MORNING!
DID YOU LOSE YOUR PANTS THIS TIME?
NO.
YES.
WAIT, WHAT DO YOU MEAN, "YES"?
DID YOU FIND ME PANTSLESS?!
I MEANT... NO?
I WAS ABLE TO ACCESS CCTV FOOTAGE FROM TRIBECA.
HULK WAS HEADING THROUGH NEW YORK FROM THE DIRECTION OF LONG ISLAND--SPIDER-MAN CONFRONTED HIM ON A ROOFTOP.
THEN SOMEONE *ELSE* SHOWED UP ON THE SCENE.
LOKI?

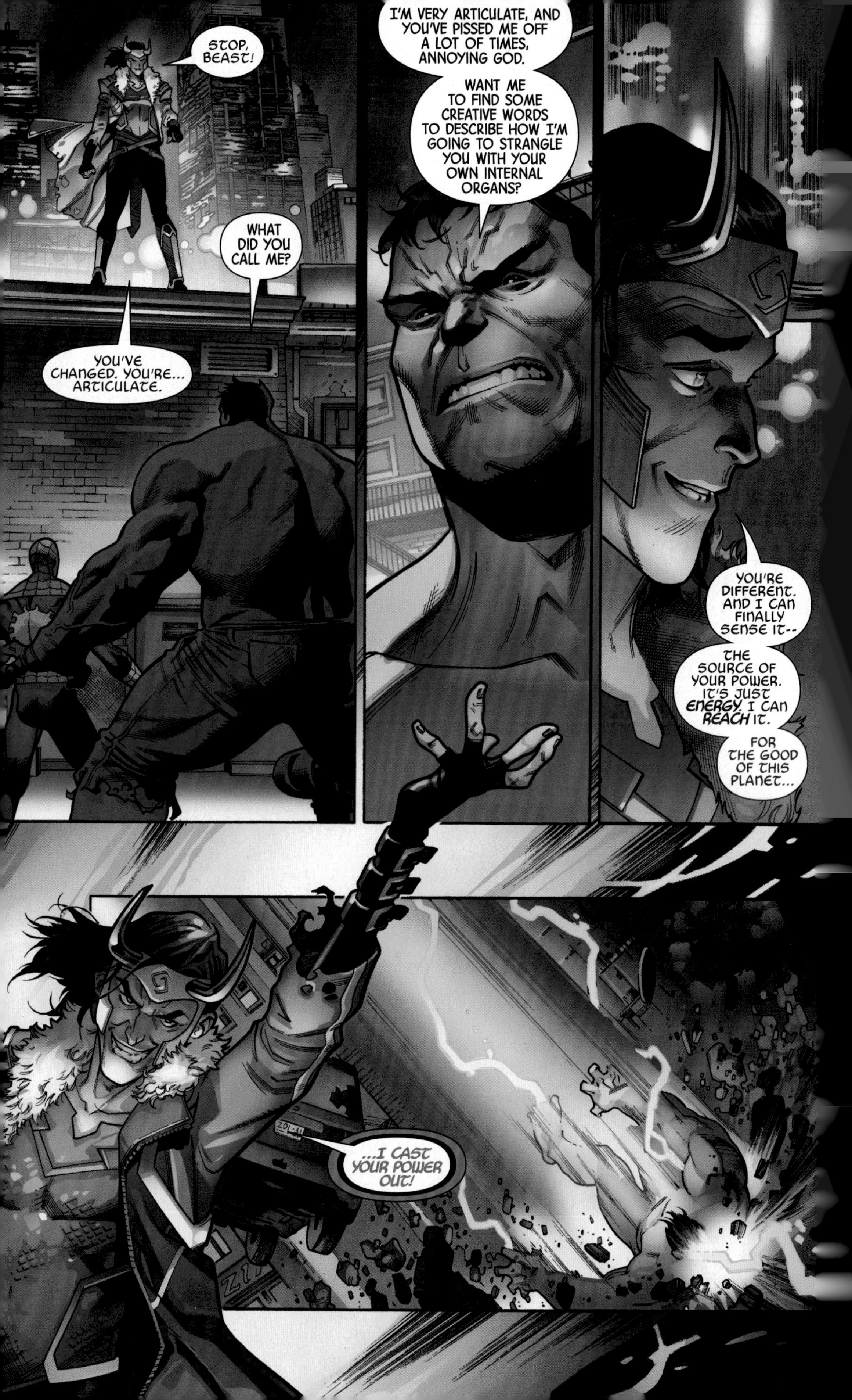
STOP, BEAST!
WHAT DID YOU CALL ME?
YOU'VE CHANGED. YOU'RE... ARTICULATE.
I'M VERY ARTICULATE, AND YOU'VE PISSED ME OFF A LOT OF TIMES, ANNOYING GOD.
WANT ME TO FIND SOME CREATIVE WORDS TO DESCRIBE HOW I'M GOING TO STRANGLE YOU WITH YOUR OWN INTERNAL ORGANS?
YOU'RE DIFFERENT. AND I CAN FINALLY SENSE IT--
THE SOURCE OF YOUR POWER. IT'S JUST ENERGY. I CAN REACH IT.
FOR THE GOOD OF THIS PLANET...
...I CAST YOUR POWER OUT!

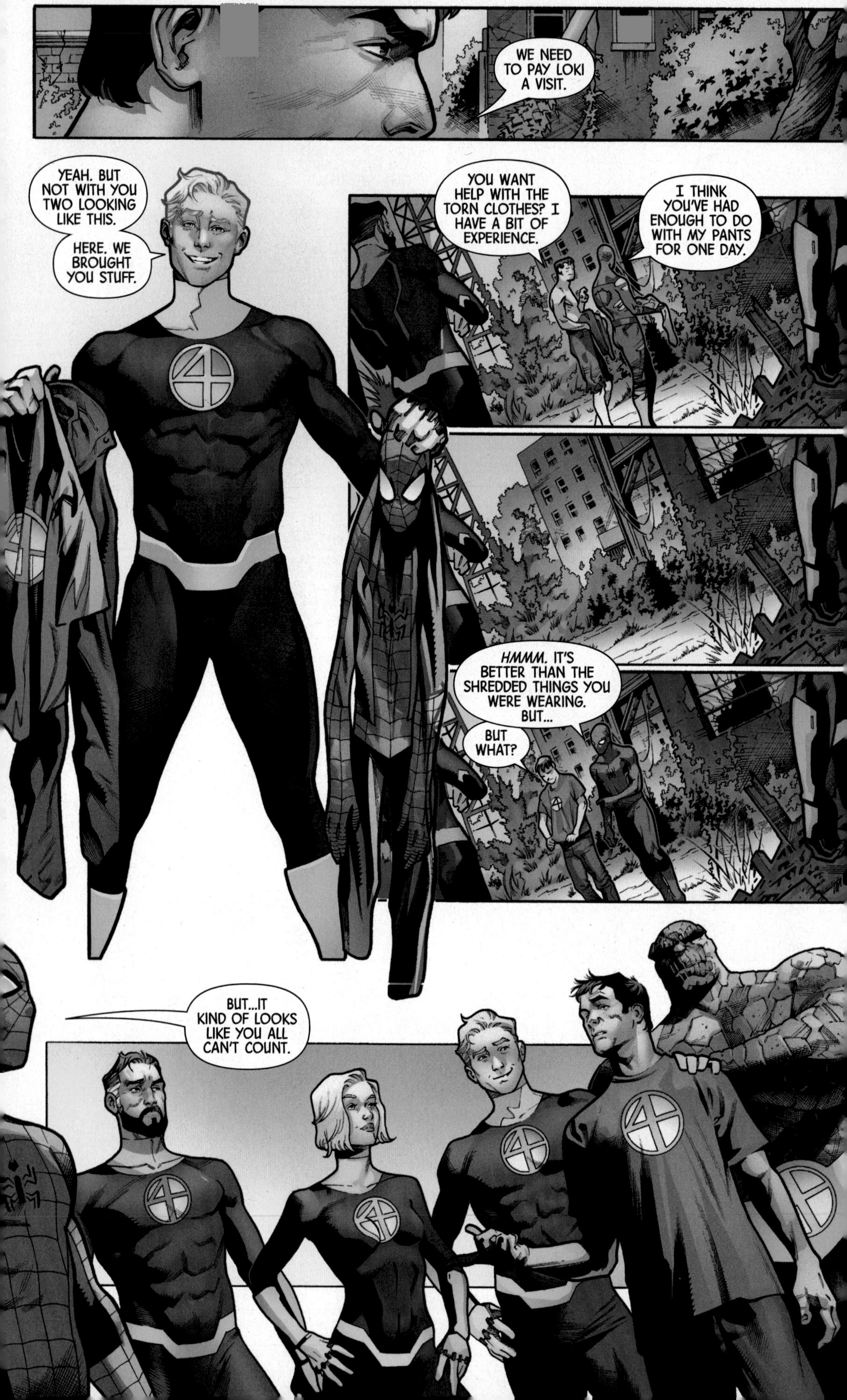
WE NEED TO PAY LOKI A VISIT.
YEAH. BUT NOT WITH YOU TWO LOOKING LIKE THIS.
HERE. WE BROUGHT YOU STUFF.
YOU WANT HELP WITH THE TORN CLOTHES? I HAVE A BIT OF EXPERIENCE.
I THINK YOU'VE HAD ENOUGH TO DO WITH MY PANTS FOR ONE DAY.
HMMM. IT'S BETTER THAN THE SHREDDED THINGS YOU WERE WEARING. BUT...
BUT WHAT?
BUT...IT KIND OF LOOKS LIKE YOU ALL CAN'T COUNT.

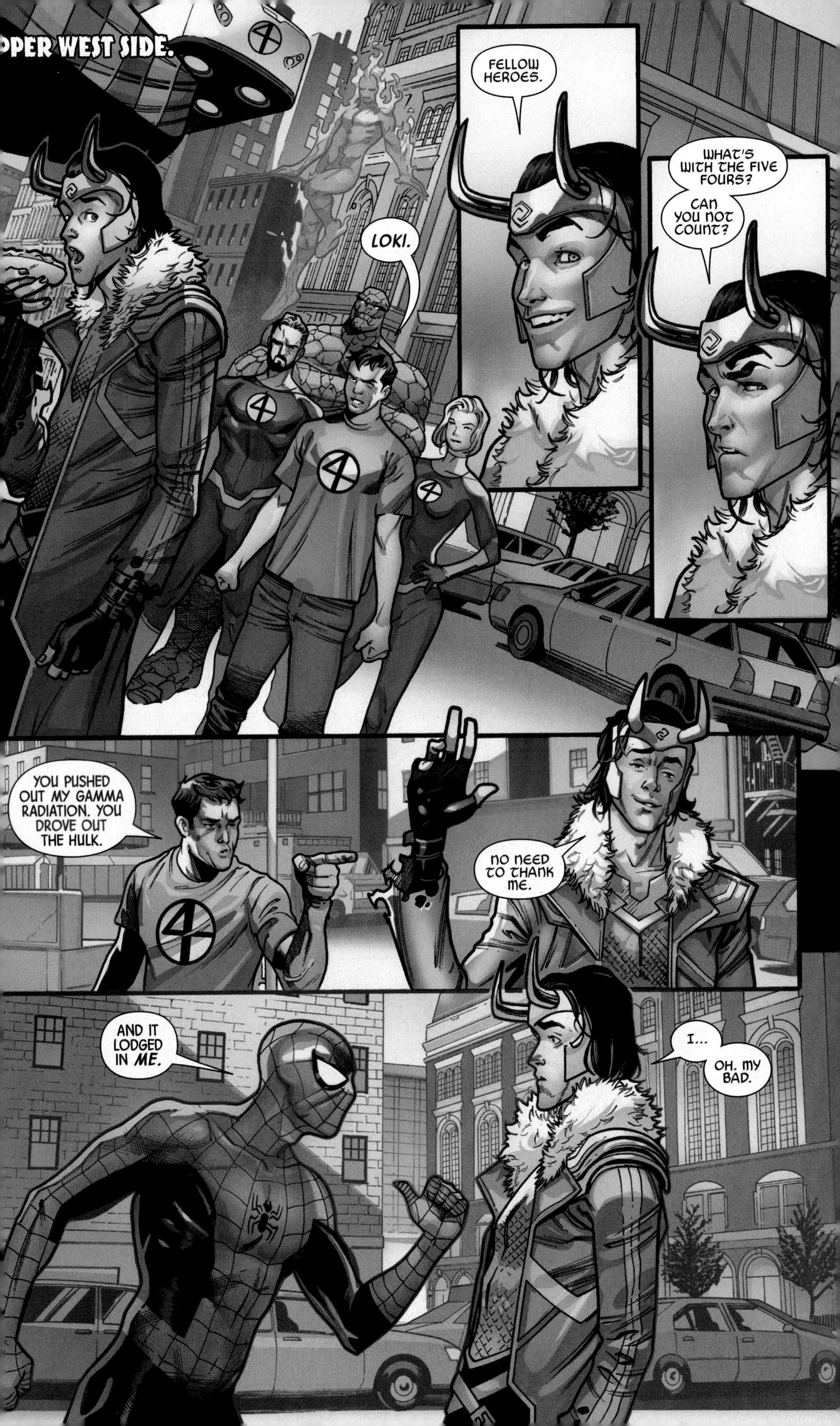

PPER WEST SIDE.
LOKI.
FELLOW HEROES.
WHAT'S WITH THE FIVE FOURS?
CAN YOU NOT COUNT?
YOU PUSHED OUT MY GAMMA RADIATION. YOU DROVE OUT THE HULK.
NO NEED TO THANK ME.
AND IT LODGED IN *ME*.
I...
OH. MY BAD.

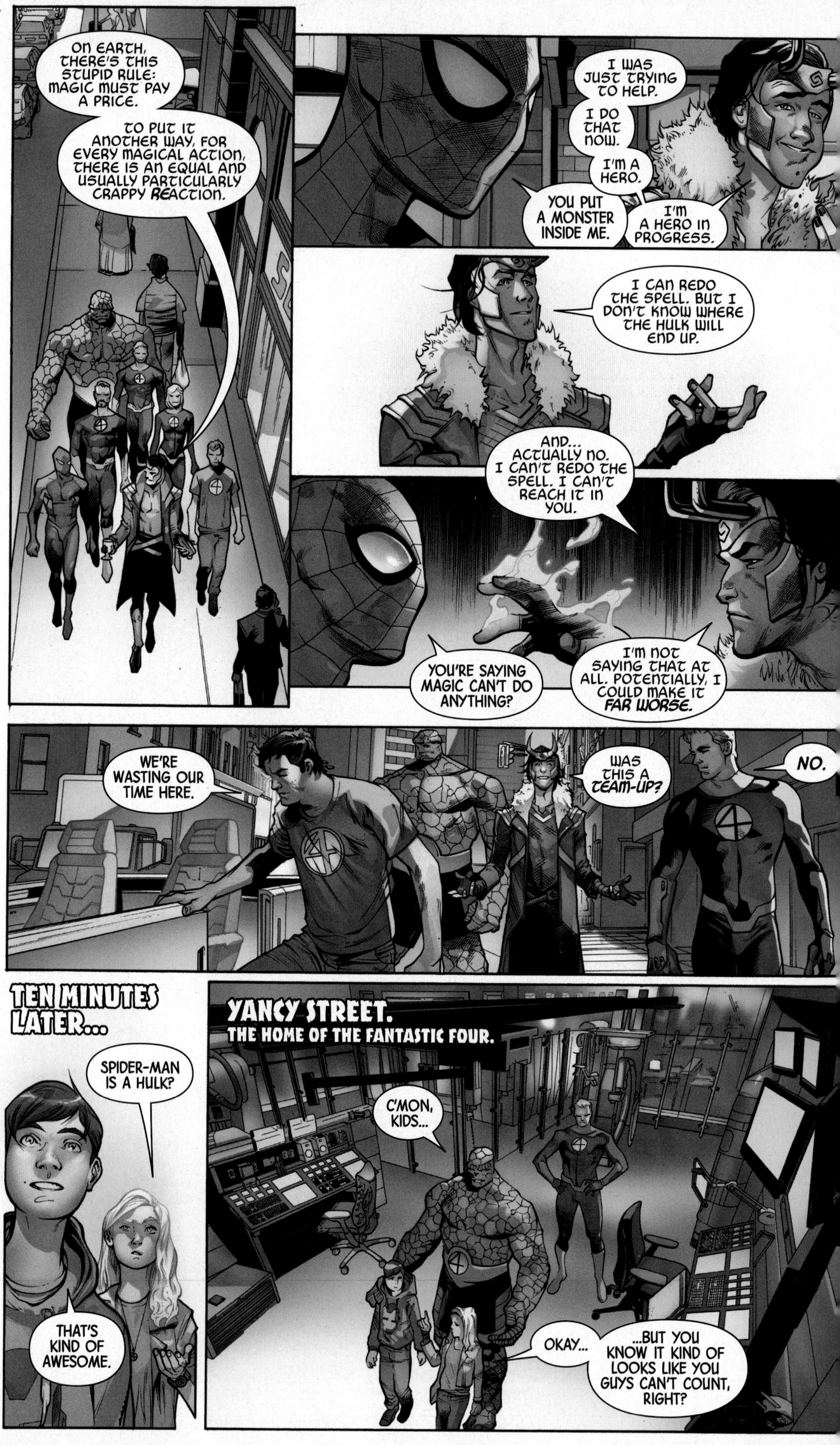
ON EARTH, THERE'S THIS STUPID RULE: MAGIC MUST PAY A PRICE.
TO PUT IT ANOTHER WAY, FOR EVERY MAGICAL ACTION, THERE IS AN EQUAL AND USUALLY PARTICULARLY CRAPPY REACTION.
I WAS JUST TRYING TO HELP.
I DO THAT NOW.
I'M A HERO.
YOU PUT A MONSTER INSIDE ME.
I'M A HERO IN PROGRESS.
I CAN REDO THE SPELL. BUT I DON'T KNOW WHERE THE HULK WILL END UP.
AND... ACTUALLY NO. I CAN'T REDO THE SPELL. I CAN'T REACH IT IN YOU.
YOU'RE SAYING MAGIC CAN'T DO ANYTHING?
I'M NOT SAYING THAT AT ALL. POTENTIALLY, I COULD MAKE IT FAR WORSE.
WE'RE WASTING OUR TIME HERE.
WAS THIS A TEAM-UP?
NO.
TEN MINUTES LATER...
YANCY STREET.
THE HOME OF THE FANTASTIC FOUR.
SPIDER-MAN IS A HULK?
THAT'S KIND OF AWESOME.
C'MON, KIDS...
OKAY...
...BUT YOU KNOW IT KIND OF LOOKS LIKE YOU GUYS CAN'T COUNT, RIGHT?

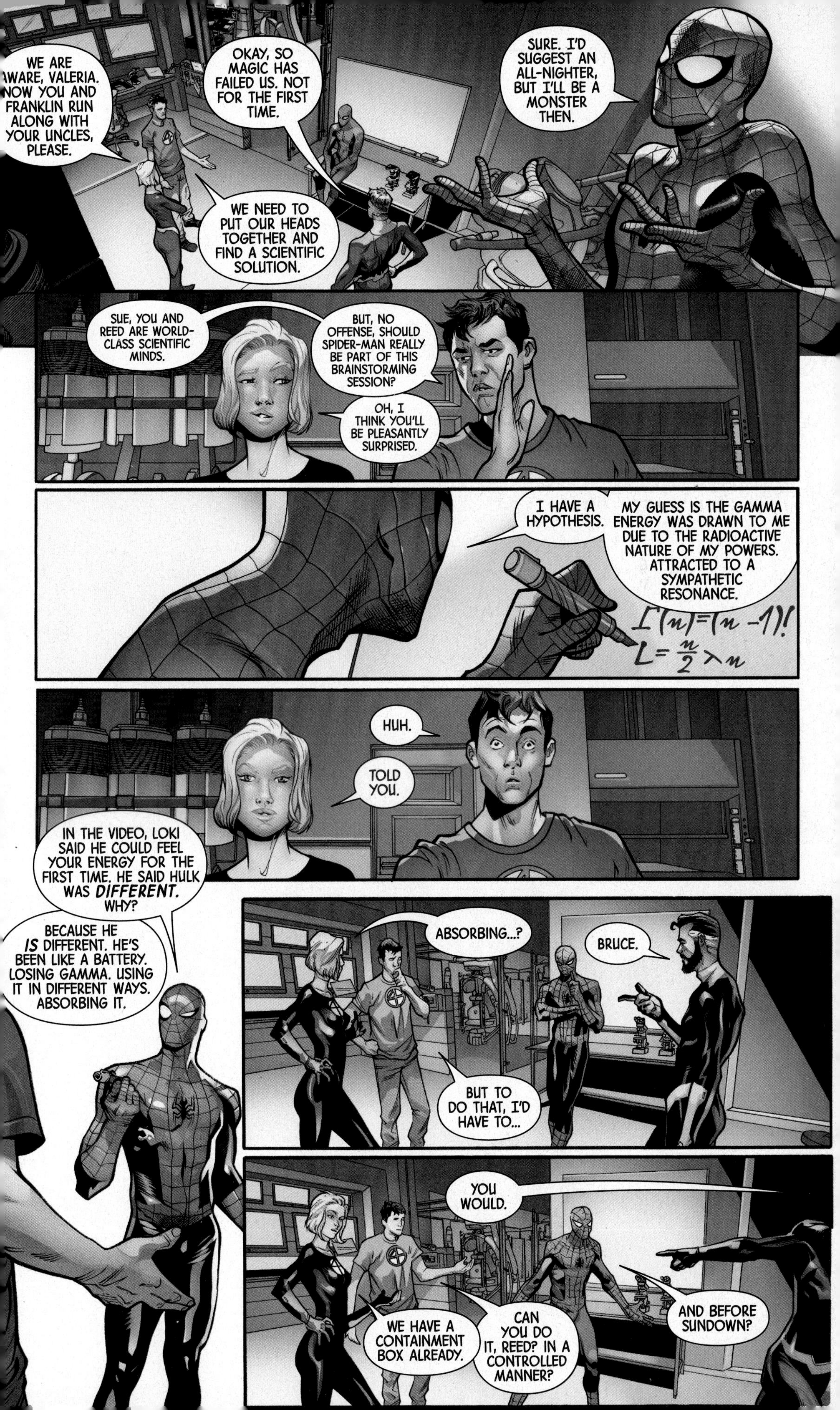
WE ARE AWARE, VALERIA. NOW YOU AND FRANKLIN RUN ALONG WITH YOUR UNCLES, PLEASE.
OKAY, SO MAGIC HAS FAILED US. NOT FOR THE FIRST TIME.
WE NEED TO PUT OUR HEADS TOGETHER AND FIND A SCIENTIFIC SOLUTION.
SURE. I'D SUGGEST AN ALL-NIGHTER, BUT I'LL BE A MONSTER THEN.
SUE, YOU AND REED ARE WORLD-CLASS SCIENTIFIC MINDS.
BUT, NO OFFENSE, SHOULD SPIDER-MAN REALLY BE PART OF THIS BRAINSTORMING SESSION?
OH, I THINK YOU'LL BE PLEASANTLY SURPRISED.
I HAVE A HYPOTHESIS.
MY GUESS IS THE GAMMA ENERGY WAS DRAWN TO ME DUE TO THE RADIOACTIVE NATURE OF MY POWERS. ATTRACTED TO A SYMPATHETIC RESONANCE.
Γ(n)=(n-1)!
L= n/2 λn
HUH.
TOLD YOU.
IN THE VIDEO, LOKI SAID HE COULD FEEL YOUR ENERGY FOR THE FIRST TIME. HE SAID HULK WAS DIFFERENT. WHY?
BECAUSE HE IS DIFFERENT. HE'S BEEN LIKE A BATTERY. LOSING GAMMA. USING IT IN DIFFERENT WAYS. ABSORBING IT.
ABSORBING...?
BRUCE.
BUT TO DO THAT, I'D HAVE TO...
YOU WOULD.
WE HAVE A CONTAINMENT BOX ALREADY.
CAN YOU DO IT, REED? IN A CONTROLLED MANNER?
AND BEFORE SUNDOWN?

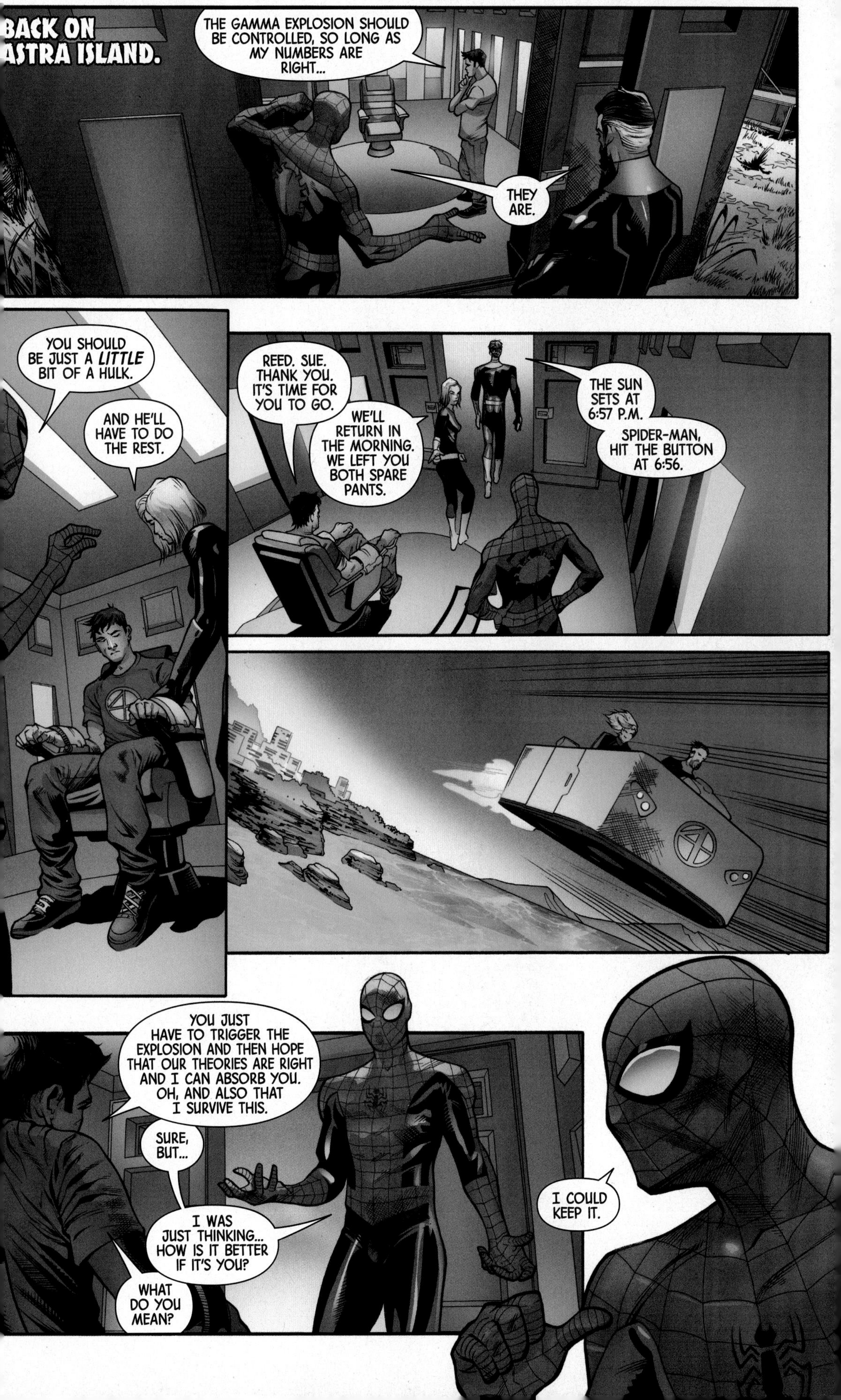
BACK ON ASTRA ISLAND.
THE GAMMA EXPLOSION SHOULD BE CONTROLLED, SO LONG AS MY NUMBERS ARE RIGHT...
THEY ARE.
YOU SHOULD BE JUST A LITTLE BIT OF A HULK.
AND HE'LL HAVE TO DO THE REST.
REED. SUE. THANK YOU. IT'S TIME FOR YOU TO GO.
WE'LL RETURN IN THE MORNING. WE LEFT YOU BOTH SPARE PANTS.
THE SUN SETS AT 6:57 P.M.
SPIDER-MAN, HIT THE BUTTON AT 6:56.
YOU JUST HAVE TO TRIGGER THE EXPLOSION AND THEN HOPE THAT OUR THEORIES ARE RIGHT AND I CAN ABSORB YOU. OH, AND ALSO THAT I SURVIVE THIS.
SURE, BUT...
I WAS JUST THINKING... HOW IS IT BETTER IF IT'S YOU?
WHAT DO YOU MEAN?
I COULD KEEP IT.

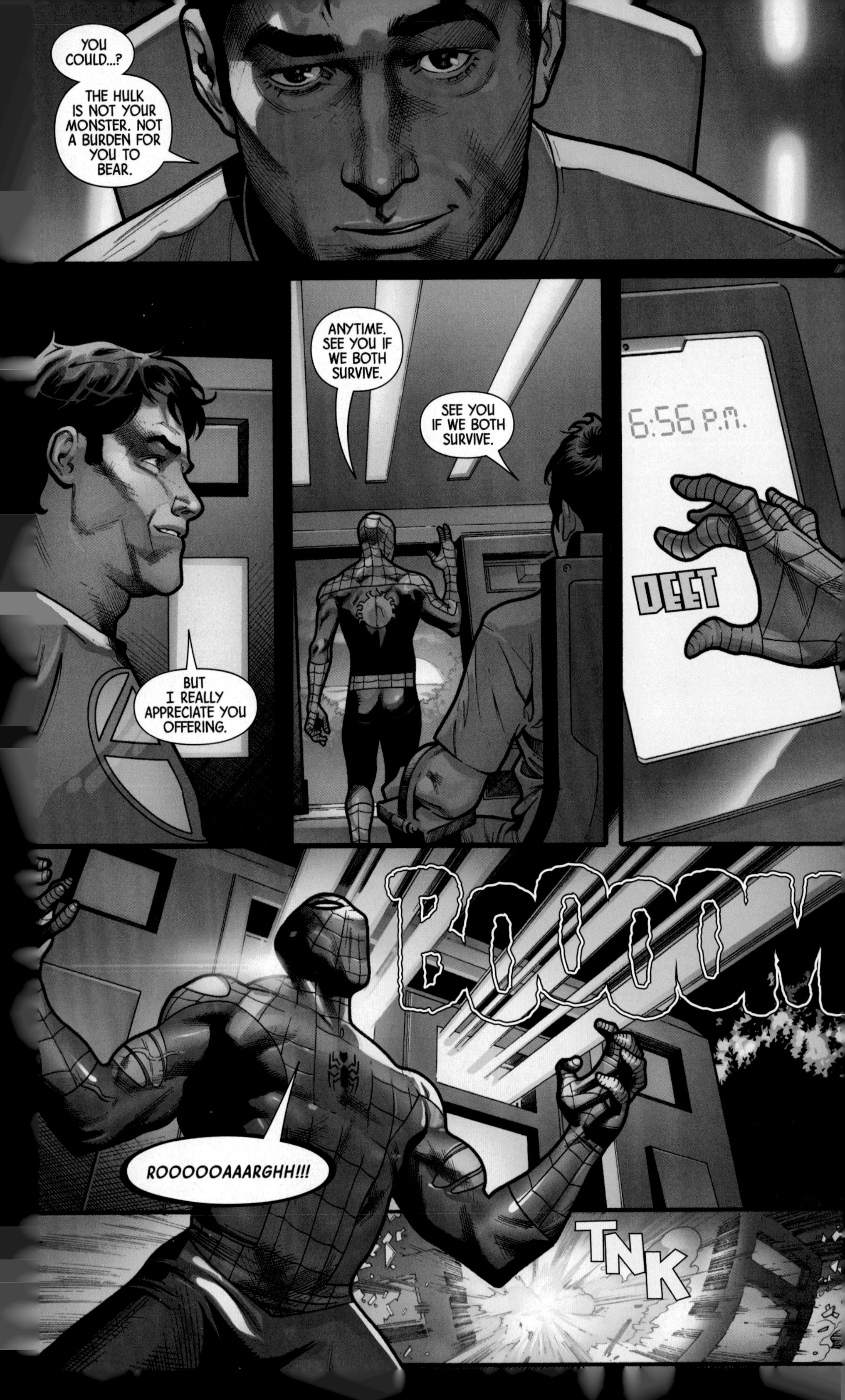
YOU COULD...?
THE HULK IS NOT YOUR MONSTER. NOT A BURDEN FOR YOU TO BEAR.
BUT I REALLY APPRECIATE YOU OFFERING.
ANYTIME. SEE YOU IF WE BOTH SURVIVE.
SEE YOU IF WE BOTH SURVIVE.
6:56 P.M.
DEET
BOOOOM
ROOOOOAAARGHH!!!
TNK

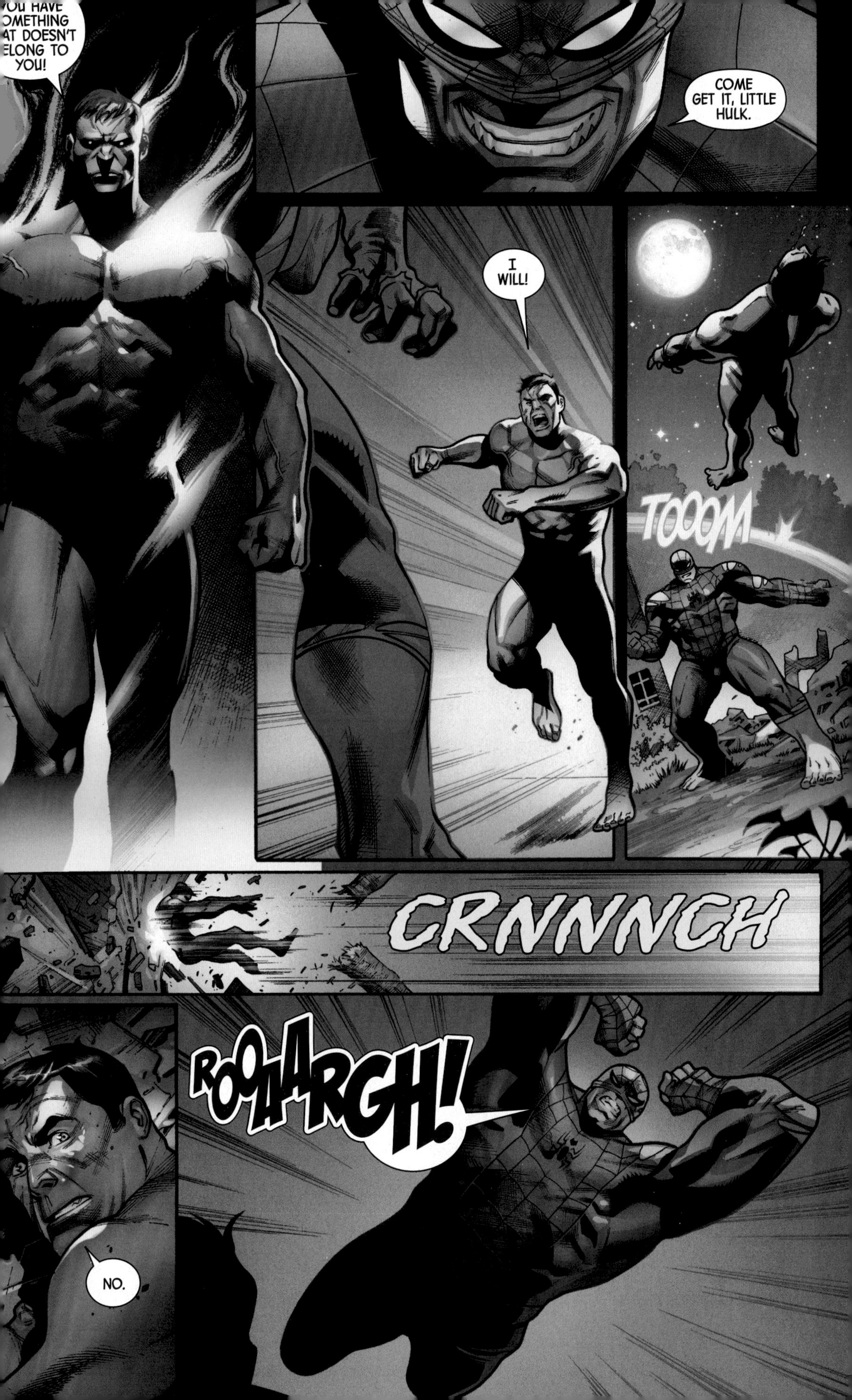

YOU HAVE SOMETHING THAT DOESN'T BELONG TO YOU!
COME GET IT, LITTLE HULK.
I WILL!
TOOOM
CRNNNCH
ROOAARGH!
NO.

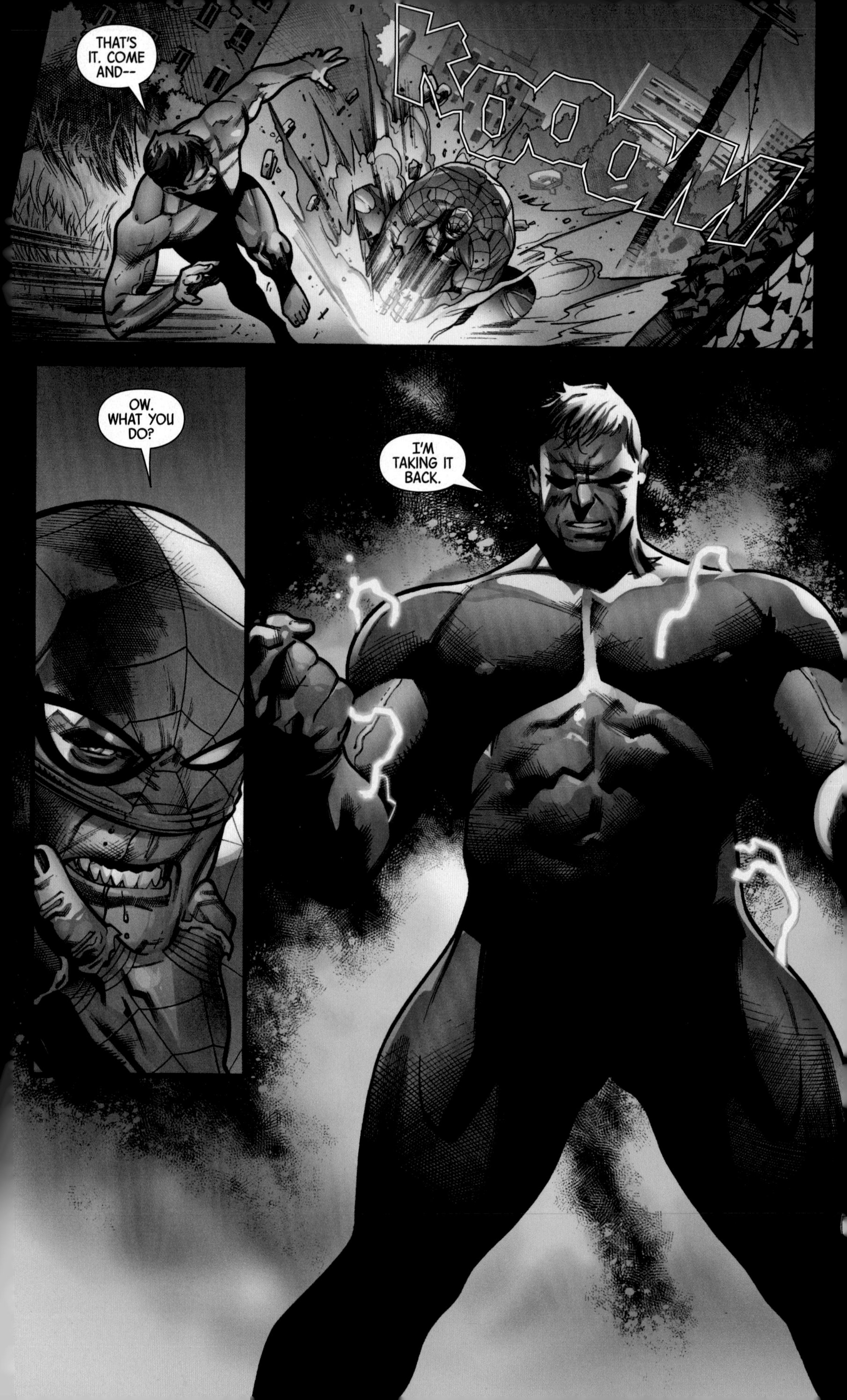
THAT'S IT. COME AND--
KROOOM
OW. WHAT YOU DO?
I'M TAKING IT BACK.

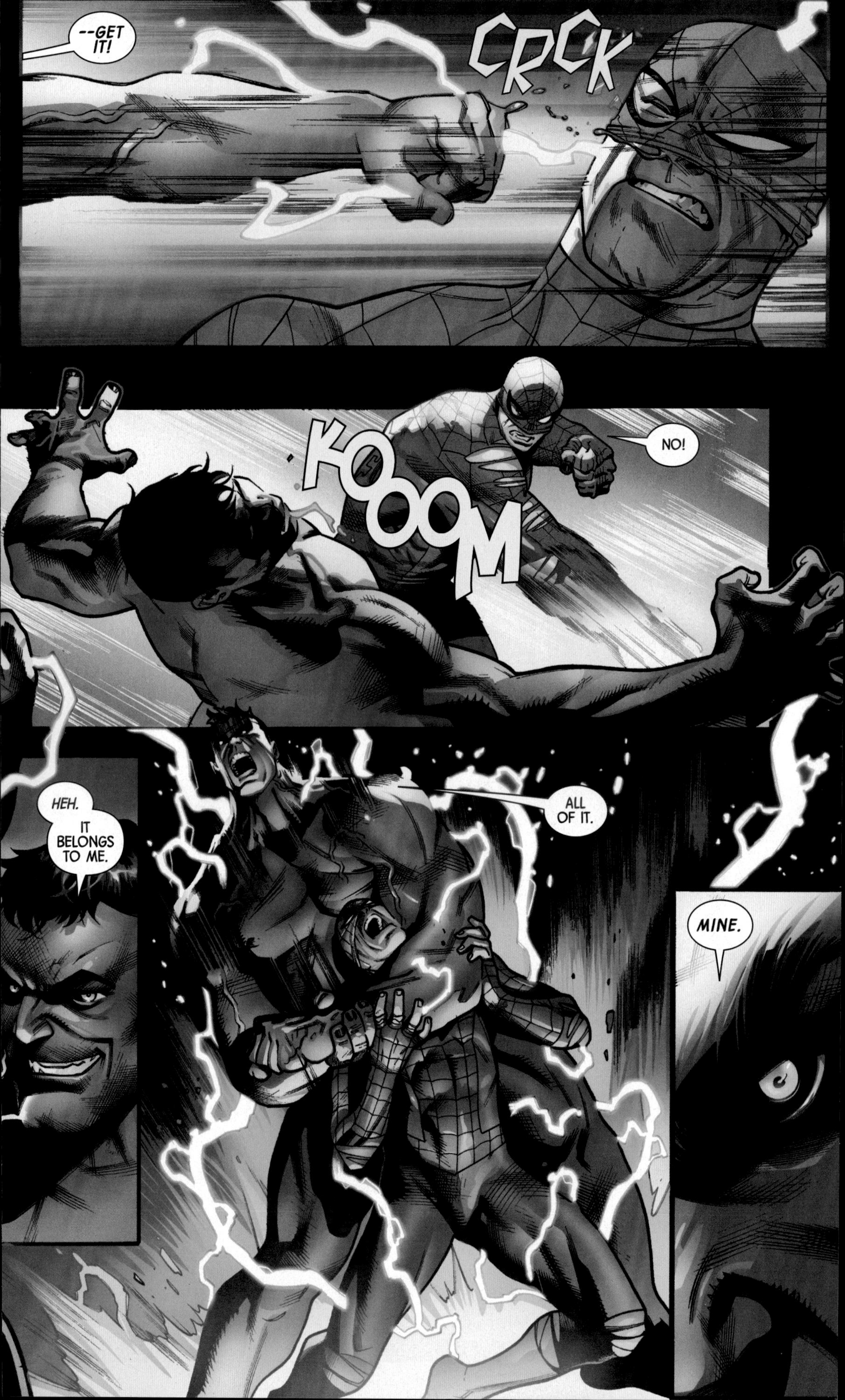
--GET IT!
CRCK
KOOOM
NO!
HEH.
IT BELONGS TO ME.
ALL OF IT.
MINE.

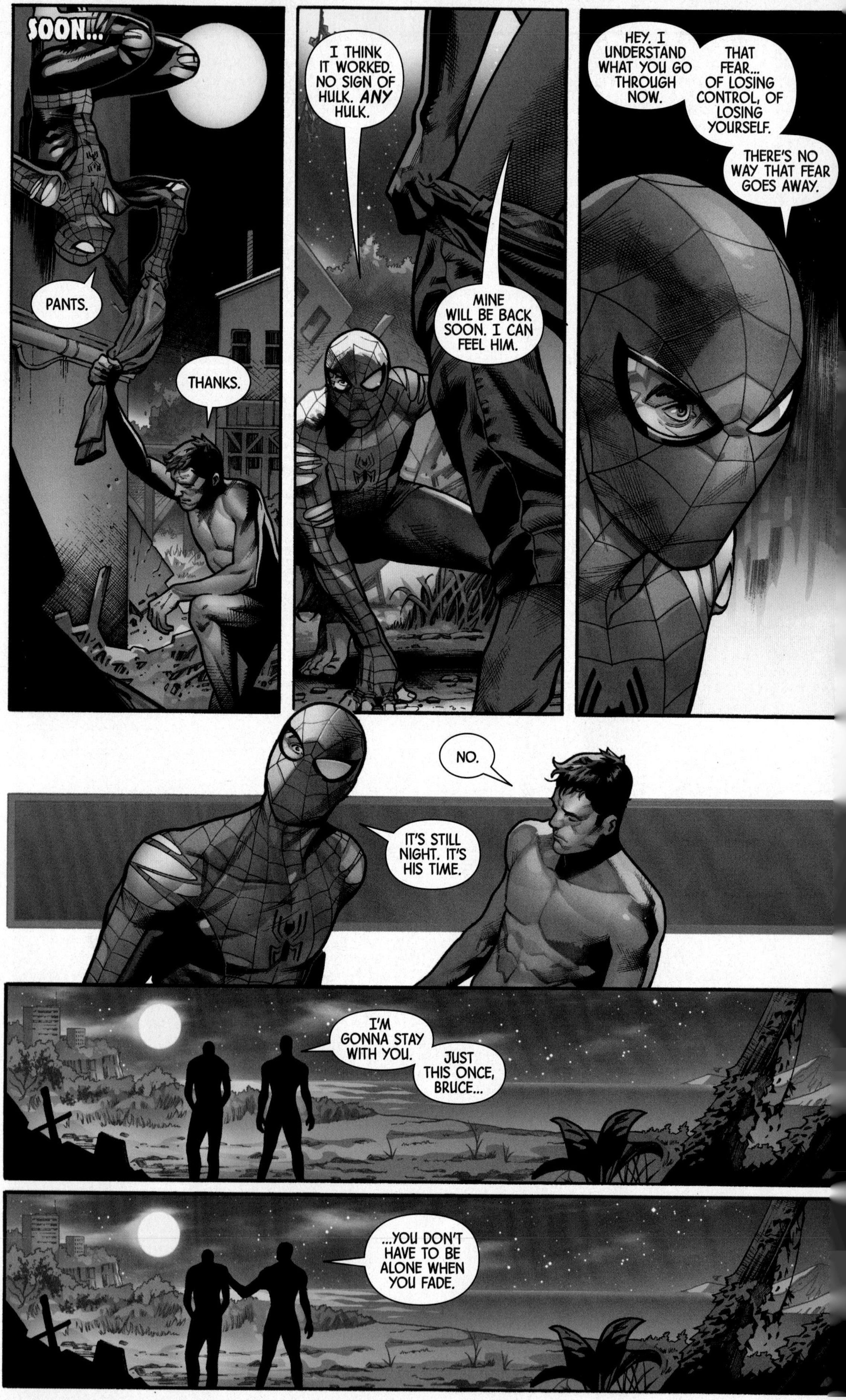
SOON...!
PANTS.
THANKS.
I THINK IT WORKED. NO SIGN OF HULK. *ANY* HULK.
MINE WILL BE BACK SOON. I CAN FEEL HIM.
HEY. I UNDERSTAND WHAT YOU GO THROUGH NOW.
THAT FEAR... OF LOSING CONTROL, OF LOSING YOURSELF.
THERE'S NO WAY THAT FEAR GOES AWAY.
NO.
IT'S STILL NIGHT. IT'S HIS TIME.
I'M GONNA STAY WITH YOU.
JUST THIS ONCE, BRUCE...
...YOU DON'T HAVE TO BE ALONE WHEN YOU FADE.

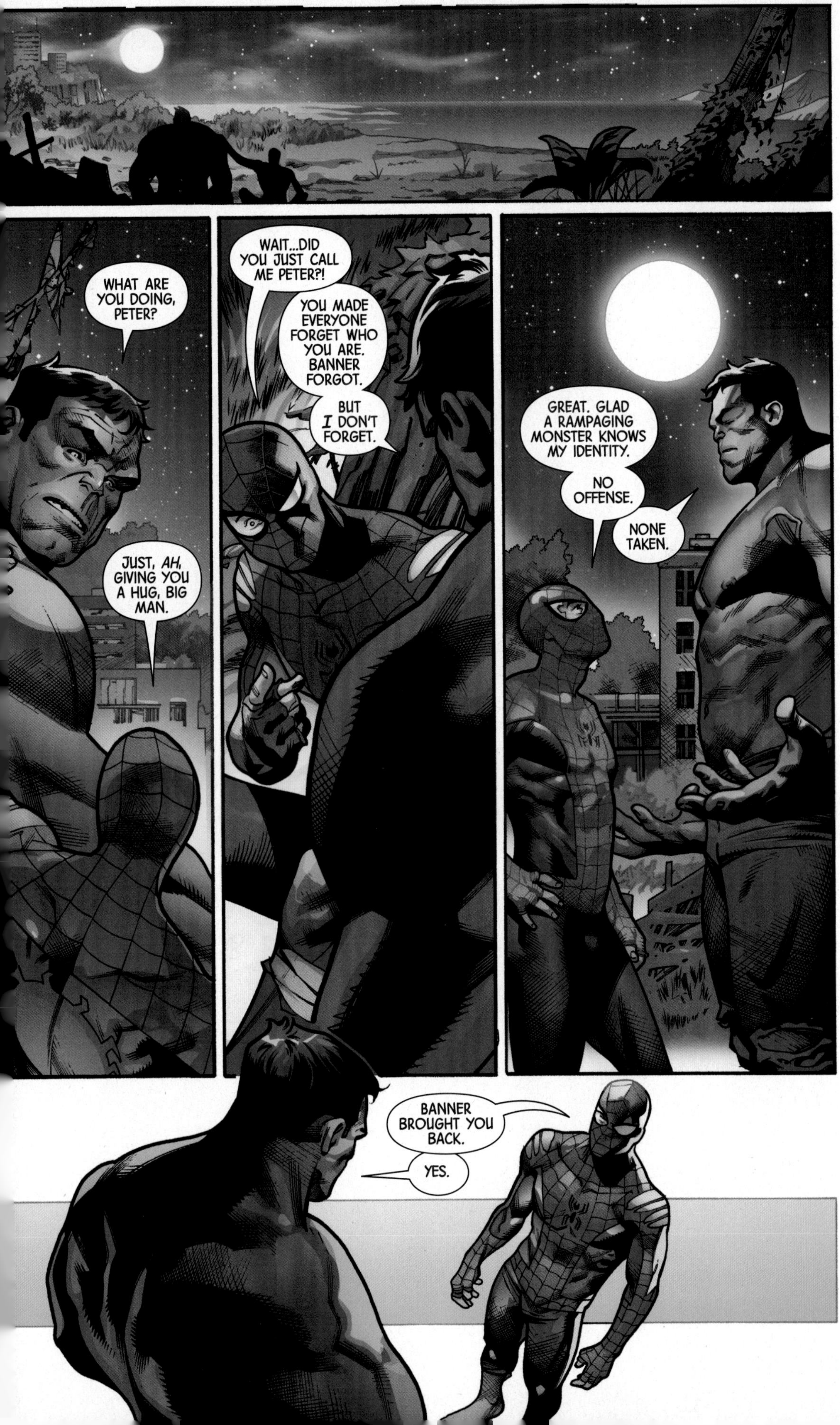
WHAT ARE YOU DOING, PETER?
JUST, *AH*, GIVING YOU A HUG, BIG MAN.
WAIT...DID YOU JUST CALL ME PETER?!
YOU MADE EVERYONE FORGET WHO YOU ARE. BANNER FORGOT.
BUT *I* DON'T FORGET.
GREAT. GLAD A RAMPAGING MONSTER KNOWS MY IDENTITY.
NO OFFENSE.
NONE TAKEN.
BANNER BROUGHT YOU BACK.
YES.

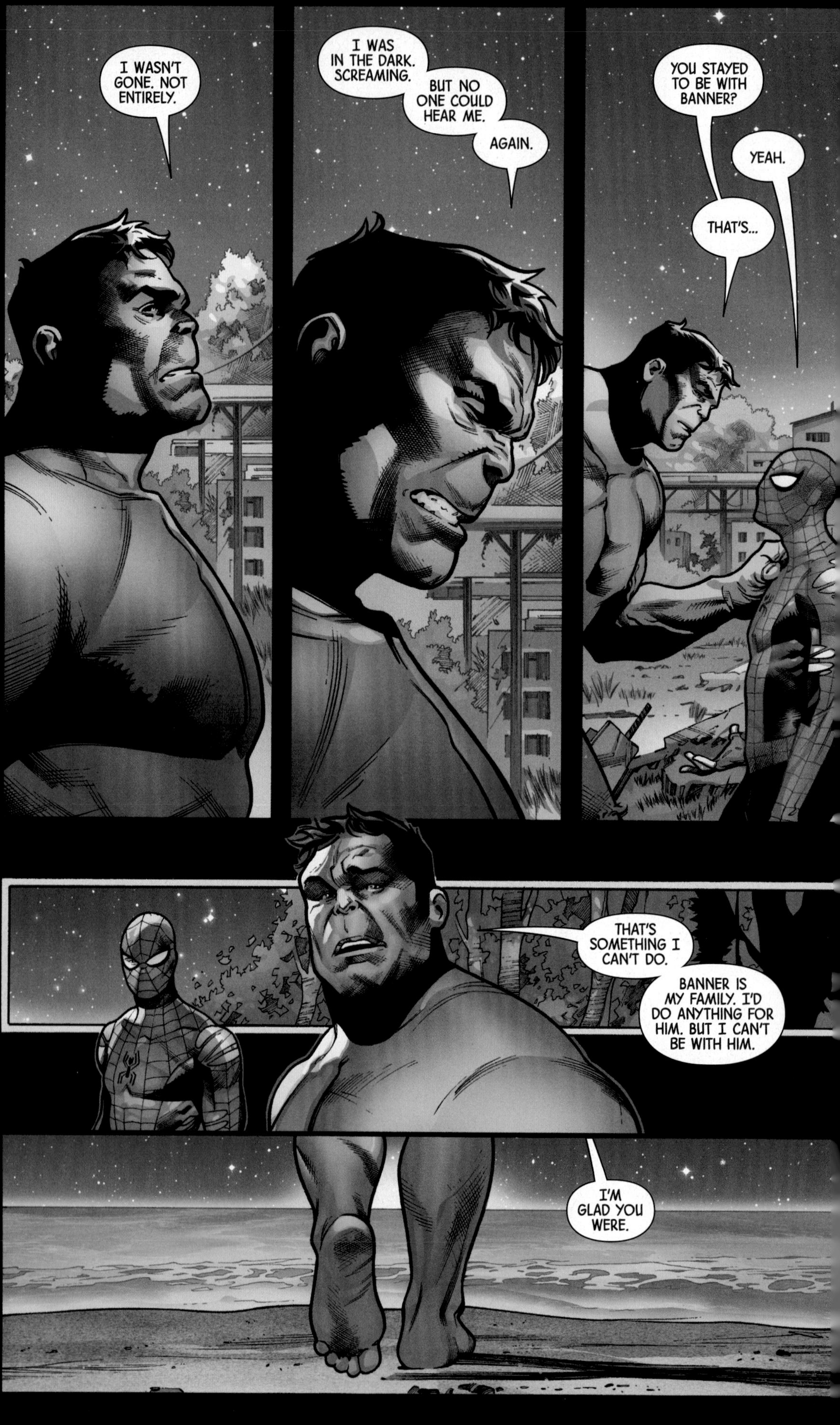
I WASN'T GONE. NOT ENTIRELY.
I WAS IN THE DARK. SCREAMING.
BUT NO ONE COULD HEAR ME.
AGAIN.
YOU STAYED TO BE WITH BANNER?
THAT'S...
YEAH.
THAT'S SOMETHING I CAN'T DO.
BANNER IS MY FAMILY. I'D DO ANYTHING FOR HIM. BUT I CAN'T BE WITH HIM.
I'M GLAD YOU WERE.

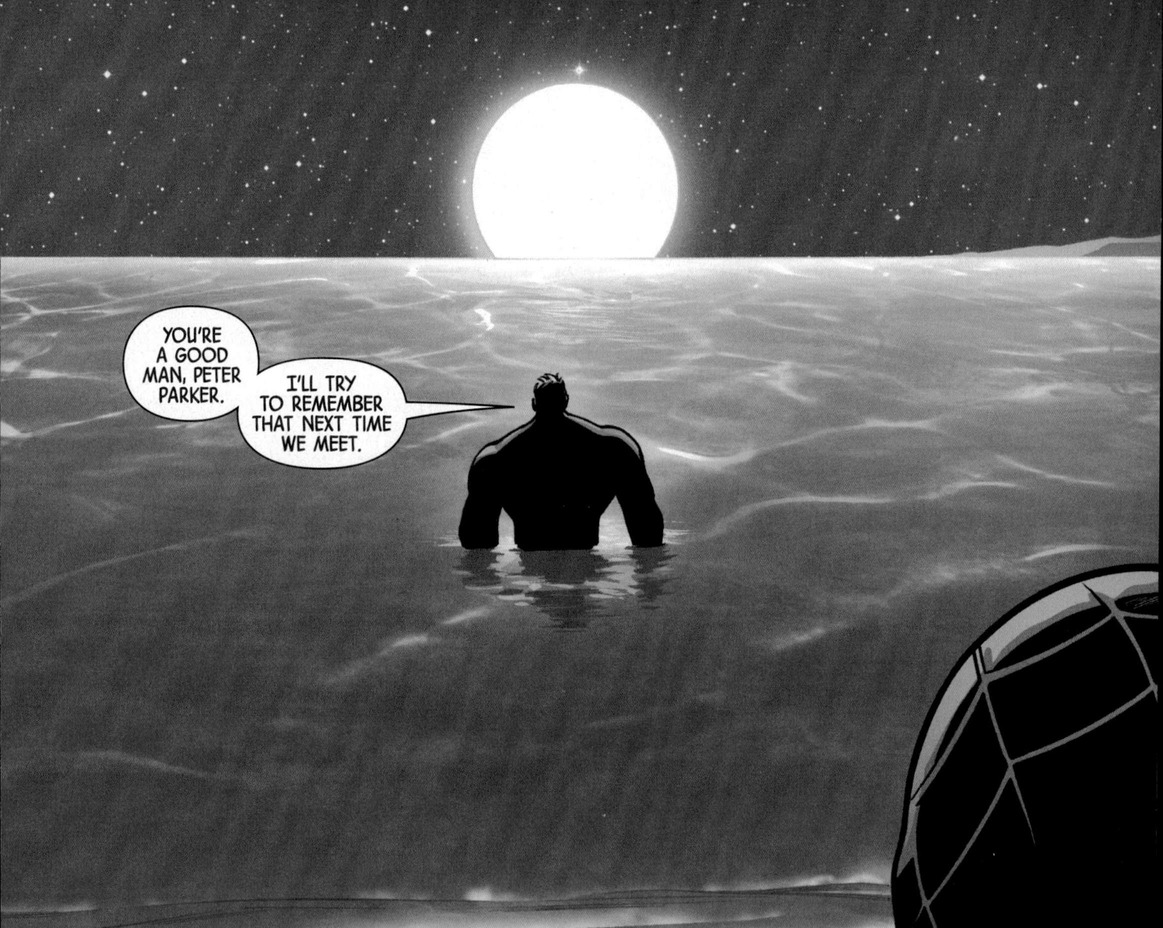
YOU'RE A GOOD MAN, PETER PARKER.
I'LL TRY TO REMEMBER THAT NEXT TIME WE MEET.

GREAT POWER

TOM TAYLOR WRITER
JORGE MOLINA PENCILER
ADRIANO DI BENEDETTO WITH **ROBERTO POGGI** INKERS
DAVID CURIEL COLORIST
VC'S CORY PETIT LETTERER
JORGE MOLINA COVER ARTIST
MAX FIUMARA VARIANT COVER ARTIST
SARAH BRUNSTAD ASSOCIATE EDITOR
WIL MOSS EDITOR
TOM BREVOORT EXECUTIVE EDITOR
C.B. CEBULSKI EDITOR IN CHIEF

HULK CREATED BY **STAN LEE & JACK KIRBY**

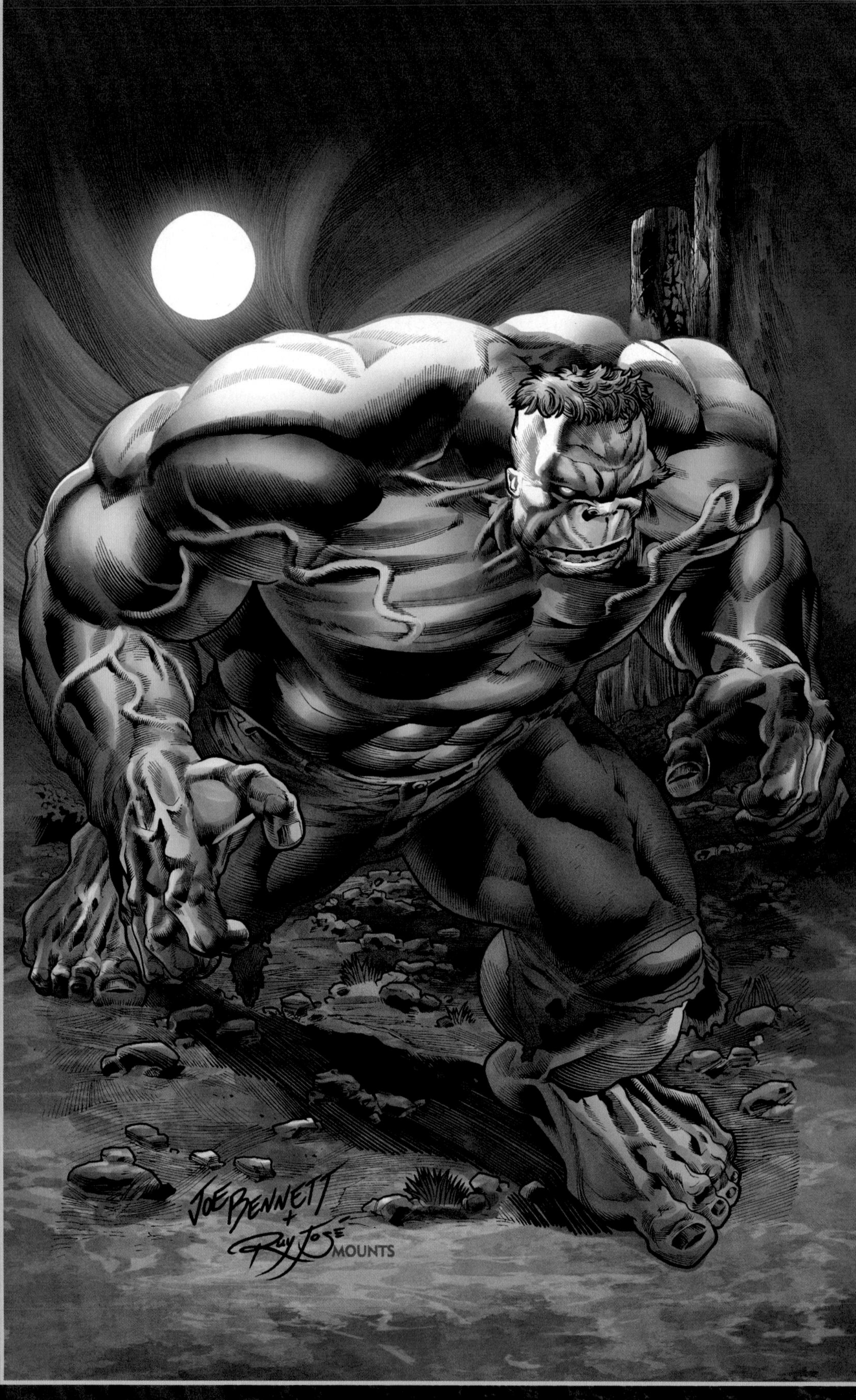
JOE BENNETT
+
RUY JOSE
MOUNTS

JOE BENNETT, RUY JOSÉ & PAUL MOUNTS
THRESHING PLACE VARIANT

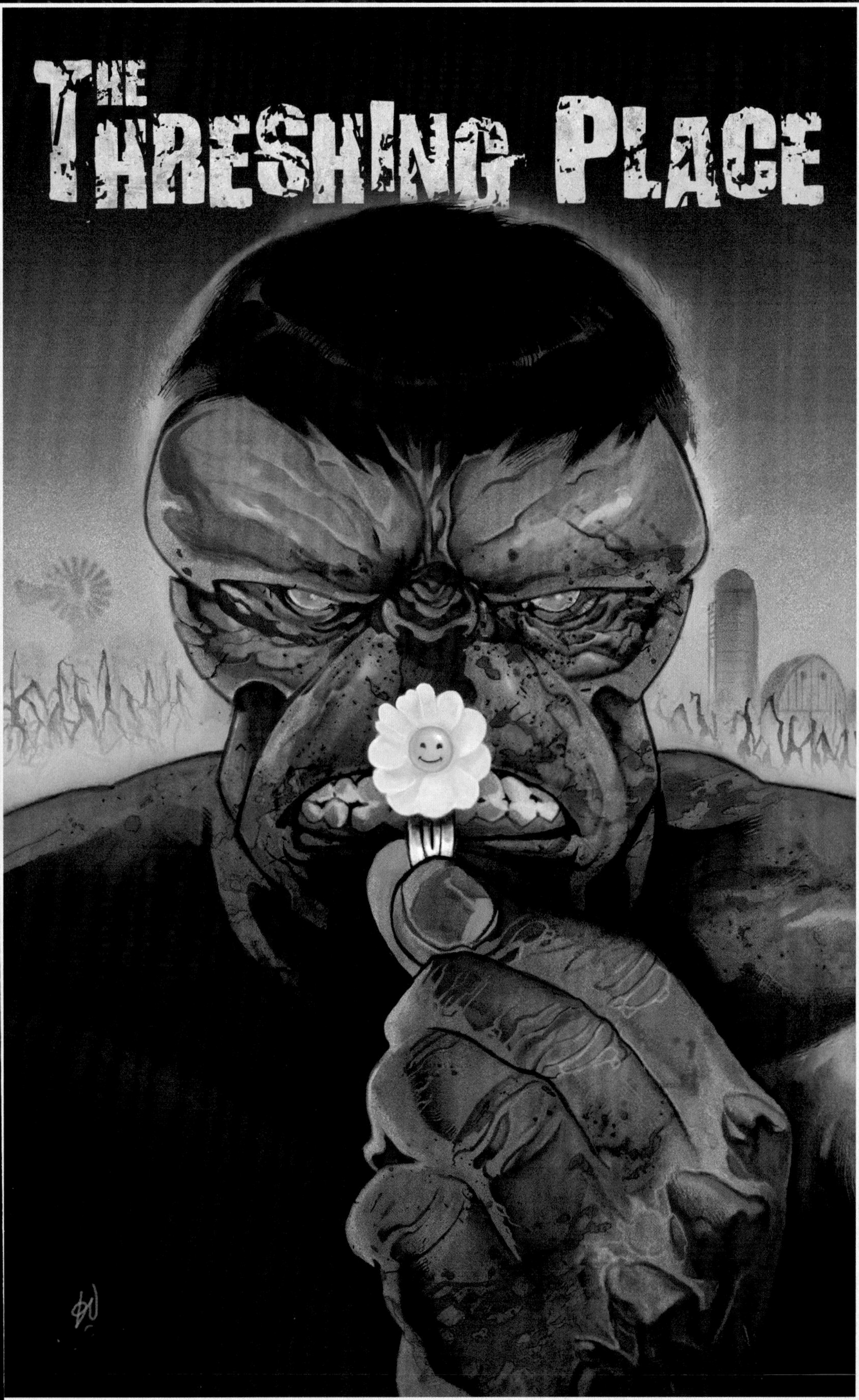
THE THRESHING PLACE

"The threshing places will be full of grain; the pits beside the presses will overflow with wine and olive oil. I will give you back what you lost in the years when swarms of locusts ate your crops."

– JOEL 2:24-25

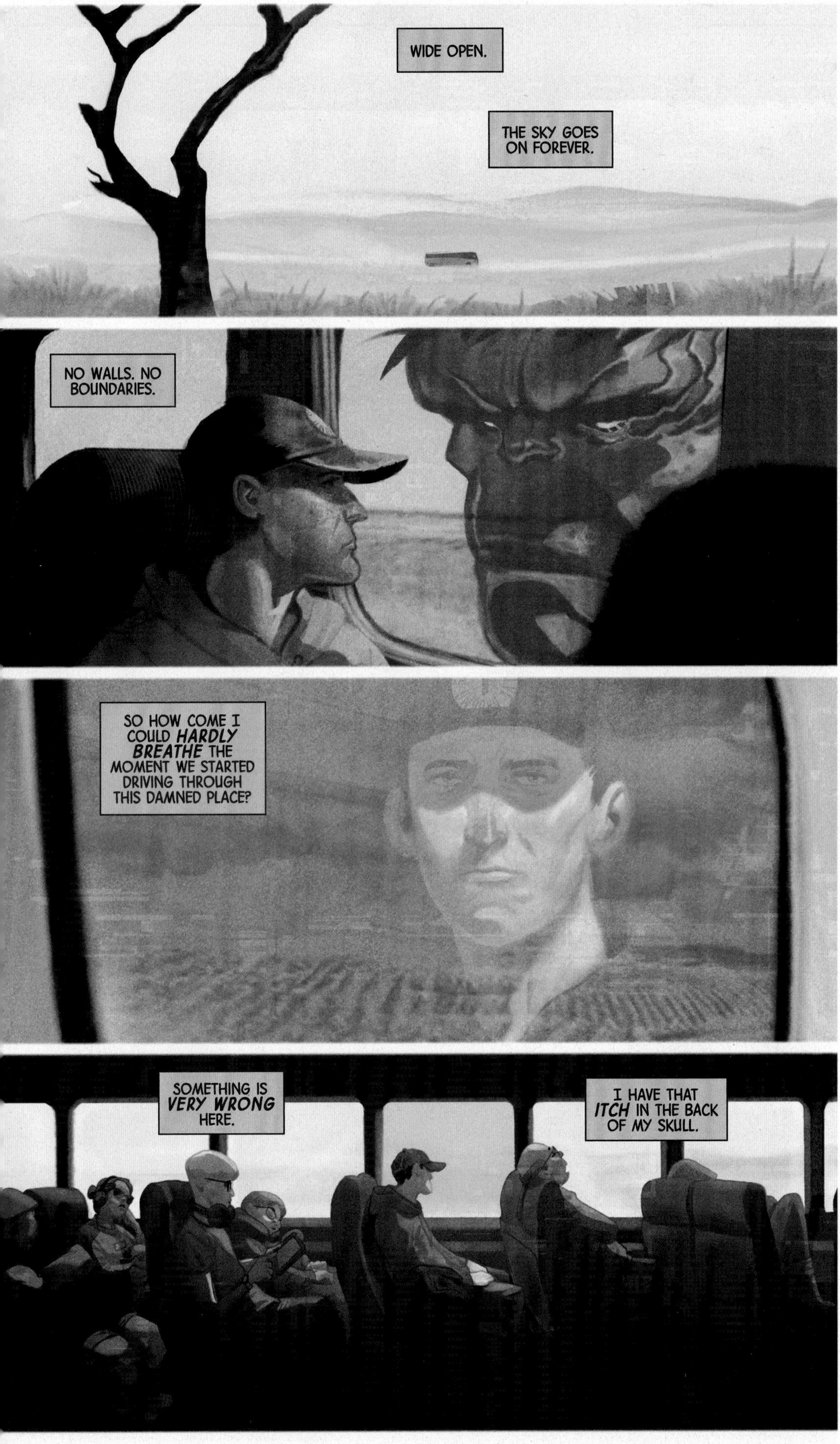
WIDE OPEN.
THE SKY GOES ON FOREVER.
NO WALLS. NO BOUNDARIES.
SO HOW COME I COULD HARDLY BREATHE THE MOMENT WE STARTED DRIVING THROUGH THIS DAMNED PLACE?
SOMETHING IS VERY WRONG HERE.
I HAVE THAT ITCH IN THE BACK OF MY SKULL.

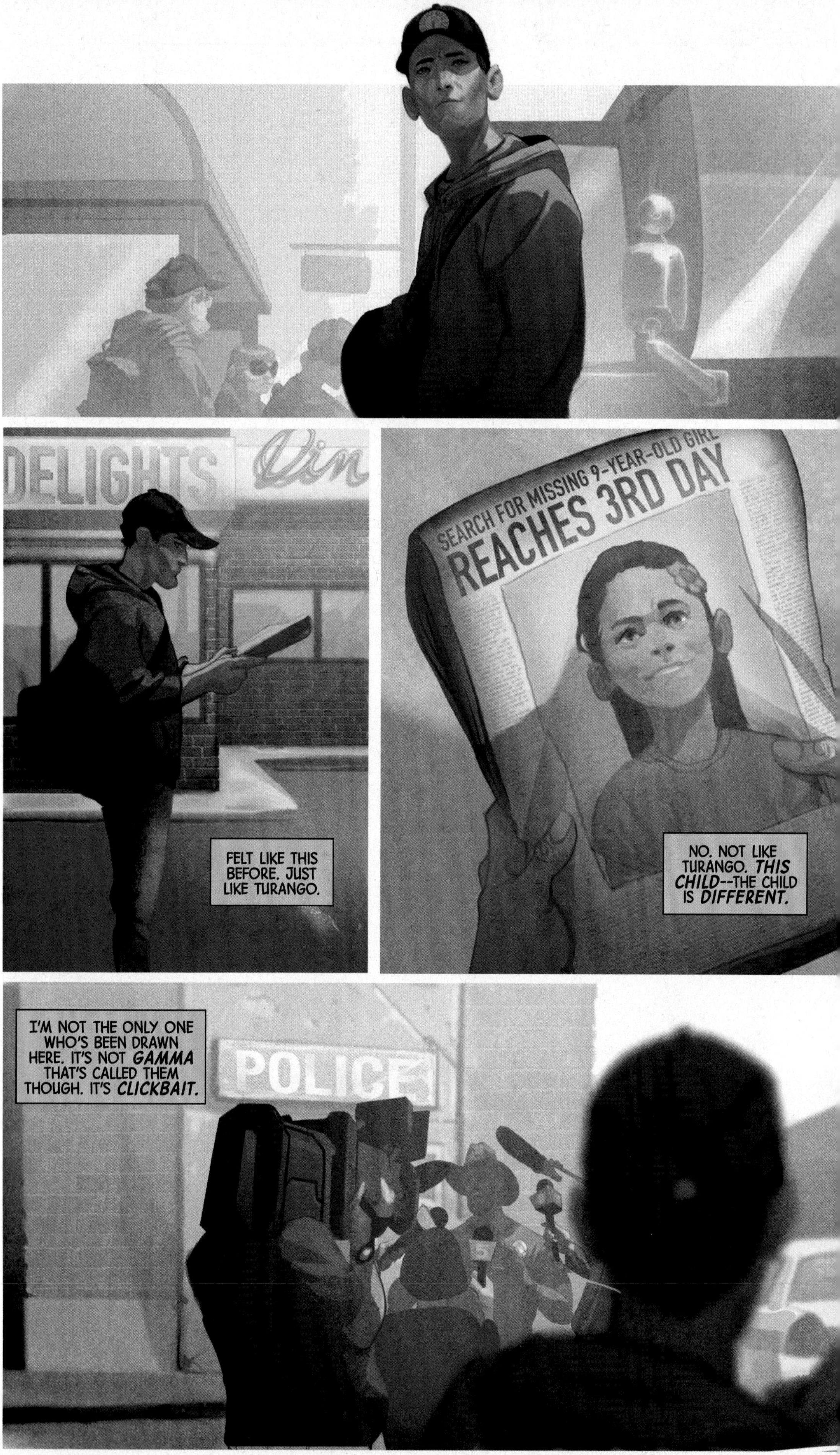
DELIGHTS
FELT LIKE THIS BEFORE. JUST LIKE TURANGO.
SEARCH FOR MISSING 9-YEAR-OLD GIRL REACHES 3RD DAY
NO. NOT LIKE TURANGO. *THIS CHILD*--THE CHILD IS *DIFFERENT.*
I'M NOT THE ONLY ONE WHO'S BEEN DRAWN HERE. IT'S NOT *GAMMA* THAT'S CALLED THEM THOUGH. IT'S *CLICKBAIT.*
POLICE

THREE DAYS AGO, 9-YEAR-OLD *REBECCA GREEN* (YES, GREEN) WAS PLAYING OUT BEHIND HER HOUSE.

WHEN HER DAD CALLED HER IN FOR DINNER, SHE NEVER CAME.

THE FATHER AND HIS CLOSEST NEIGHBORS LOOKED THROUGH THE NIGHT. THEY DIDN'T FIND HER, BUT THEY FOUND *SOMETHING ELSE...*

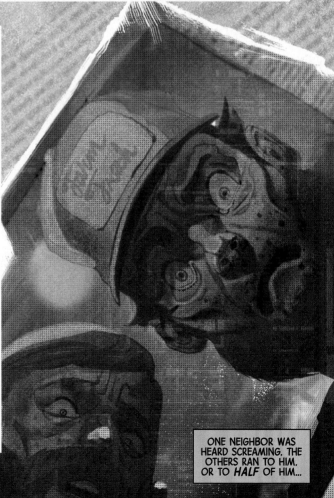

ONE NEIGHBOR WAS HEARD SCREAMING. THE OTHERS RAN TO HIM. OR TO *HALF* OF HIM...

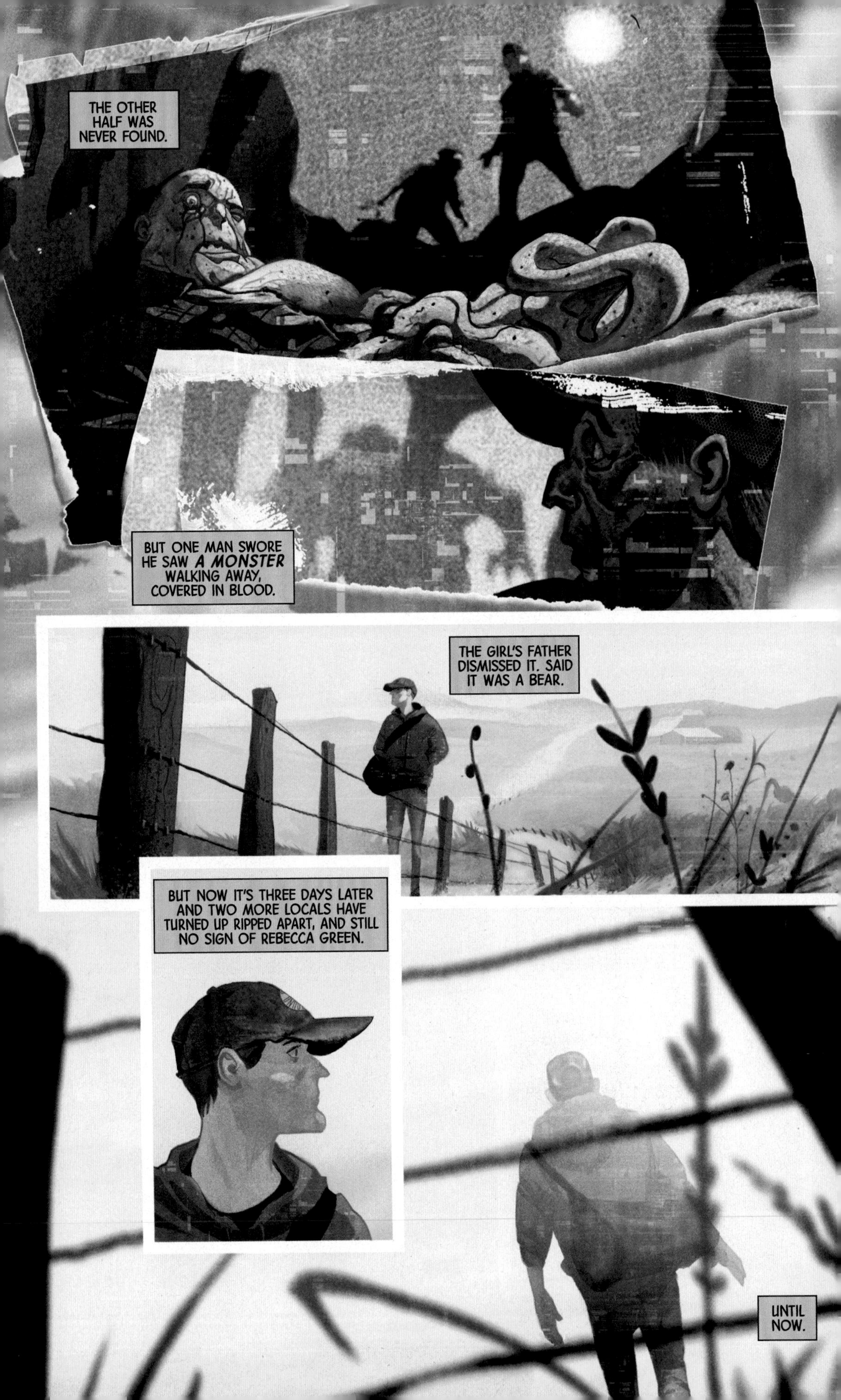
THE OTHER HALF WAS NEVER FOUND.
BUT ONE MAN SWORE HE SAW A MONSTER WALKING AWAY, COVERED IN BLOOD.
THE GIRL'S FATHER DISMISSED IT. SAID IT WAS A BEAR.
BUT NOW IT'S THREE DAYS LATER AND TWO MORE LOCALS HAVE TURNED UP RIPPED APART, AND STILL NO SIGN OF REBECCA GREEN.
UNTIL NOW.

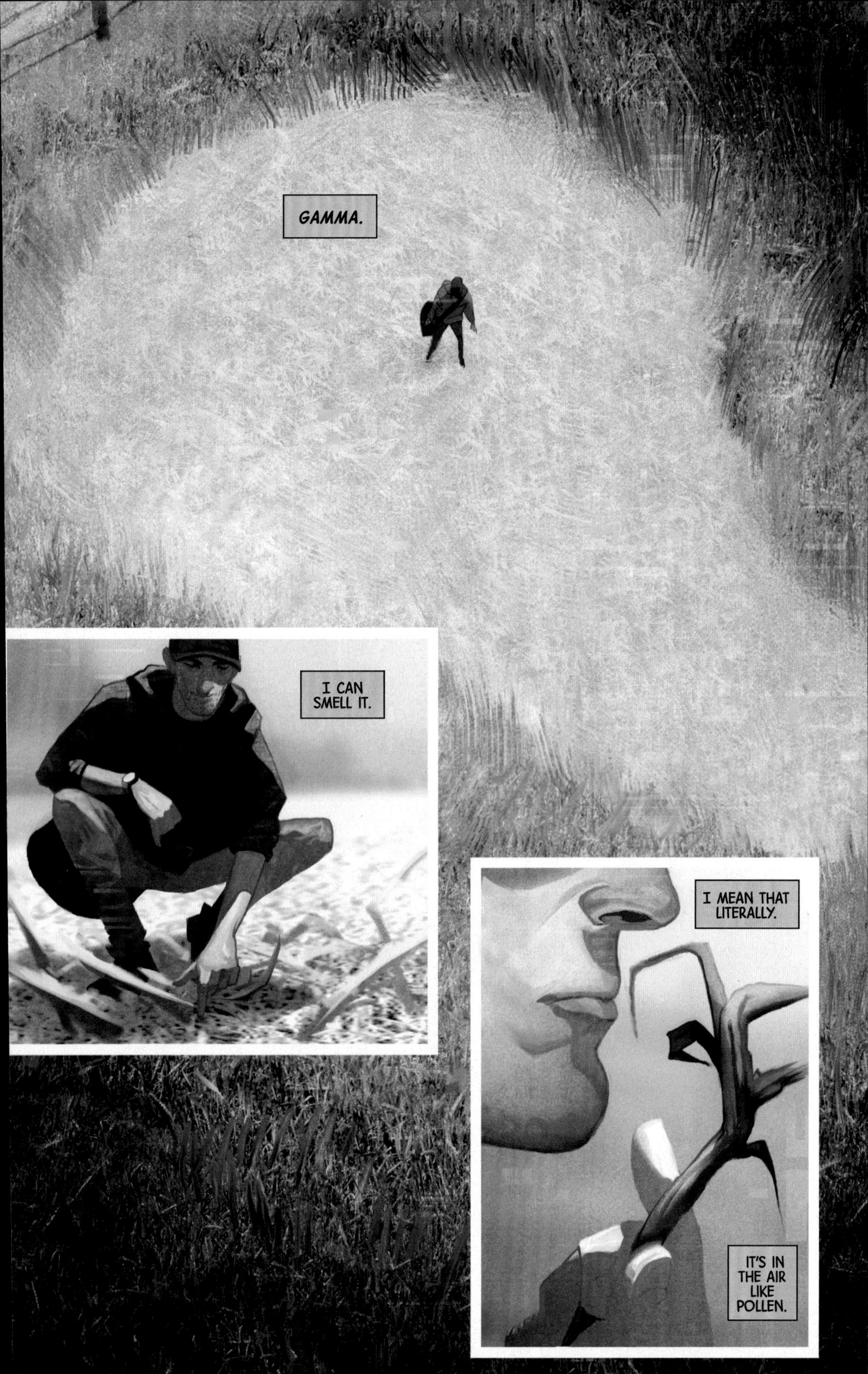
GAMMA.
I CAN SMELL IT.
I MEAN THAT LITERALLY.
IT'S IN THE AIR LIKE POLLEN.

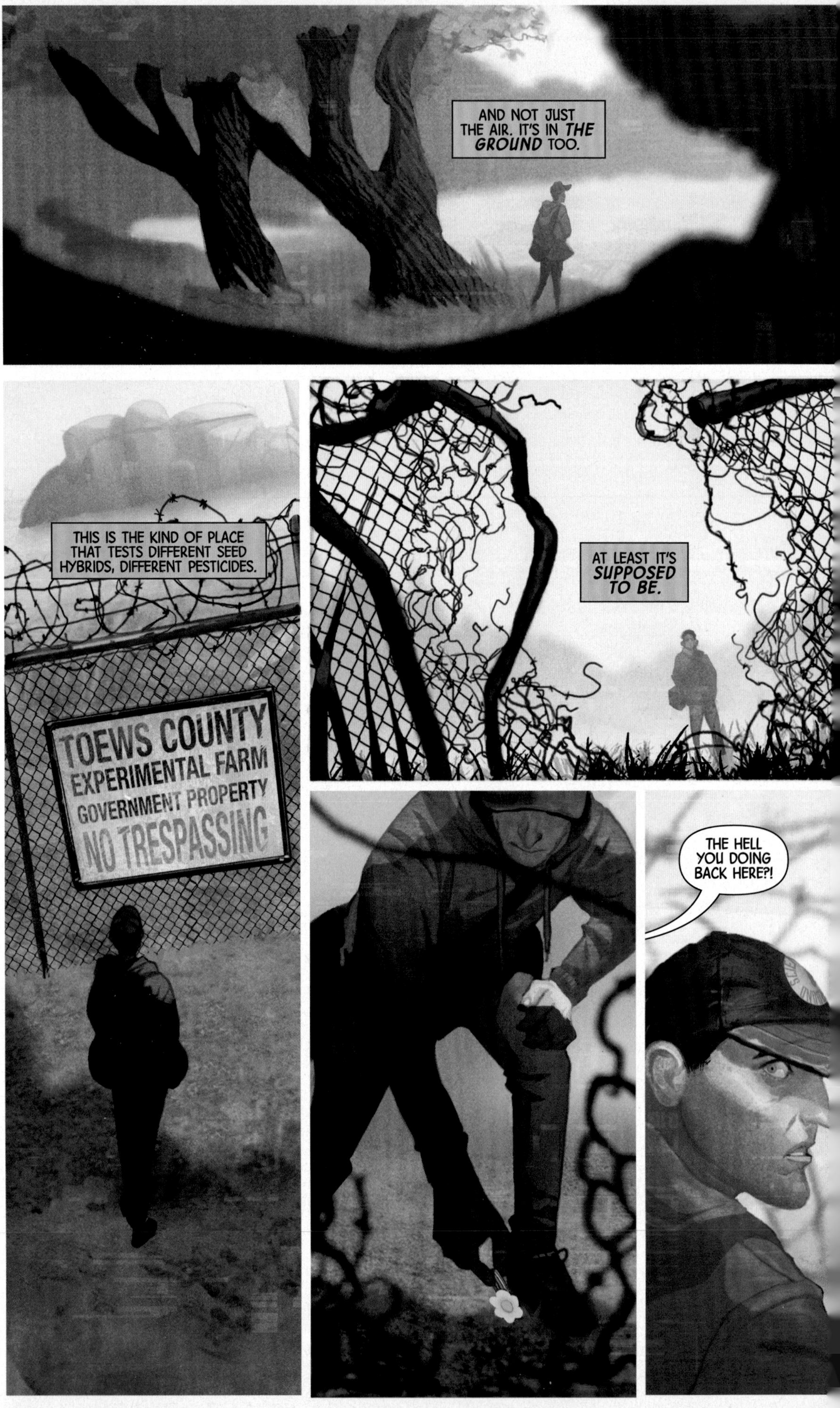
AND NOT JUST THE AIR. IT'S IN *THE GROUND* TOO.
THIS IS THE KIND OF PLACE THAT TESTS DIFFERENT SEED HYBRIDS, DIFFERENT PESTICIDES.
TOEWS COUNTY EXPERIMENTAL FARM GOVERNMENT PROPERTY NO TRESPASSING
AT LEAST IT'S *SUPPOSED TO BE.*
THE HELL YOU DOING BACK HERE?!

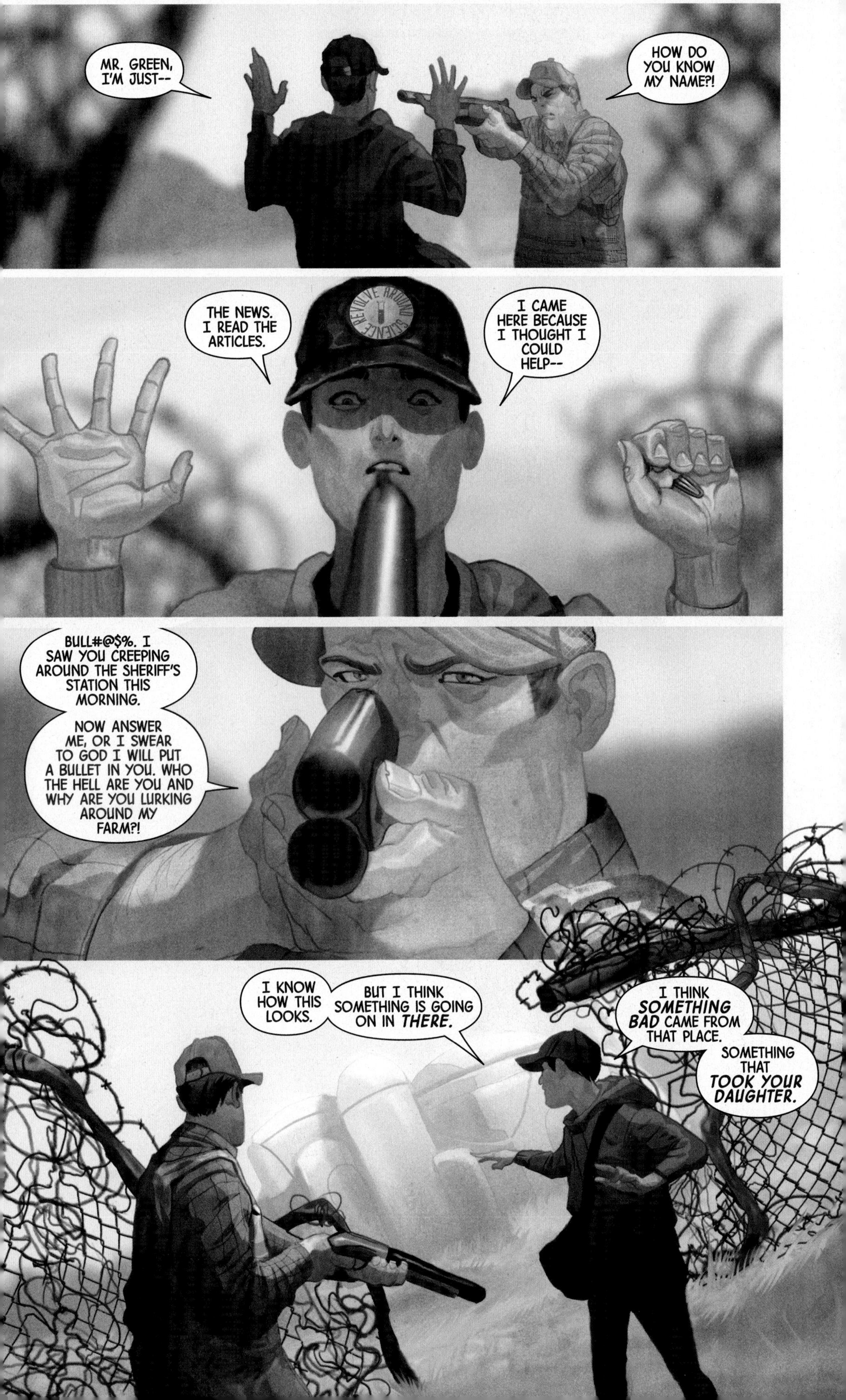
MR. GREEN, I'M JUST--
HOW DO YOU KNOW MY NAME?!
REVOLVE AROUND SCIENCE
THE NEWS. I READ THE ARTICLES.
I CAME HERE BECAUSE I THOUGHT I COULD HELP--
BULL#@$%. I SAW YOU CREEPING AROUND THE SHERIFF'S STATION THIS MORNING.
NOW ANSWER ME, OR I SWEAR TO GOD I WILL PUT A BULLET IN YOU. WHO THE HELL ARE YOU AND WHY ARE YOU LURKING AROUND MY FARM?!
I KNOW HOW THIS LOOKS.
BUT I THINK SOMETHING IS GOING ON IN *THERE.*
I THINK ***SOMETHING BAD*** CAME FROM THAT PLACE.
SOMETHING THAT ***TOOK YOUR DAUGHTER.***

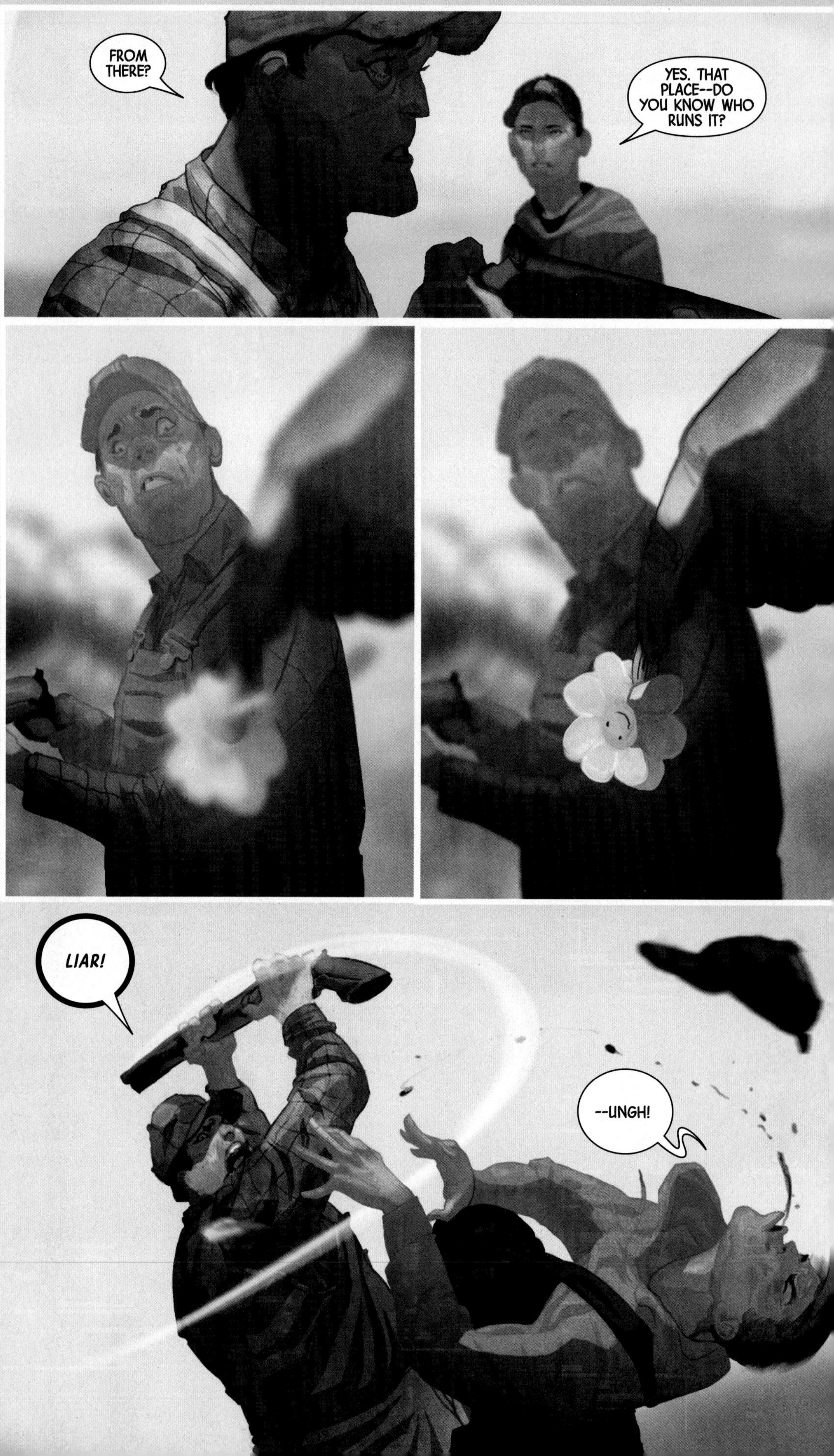
FROM THERE?
YES. THAT PLACE--DO YOU KNOW WHO RUNS IT?
LIAR!
--UNGH!

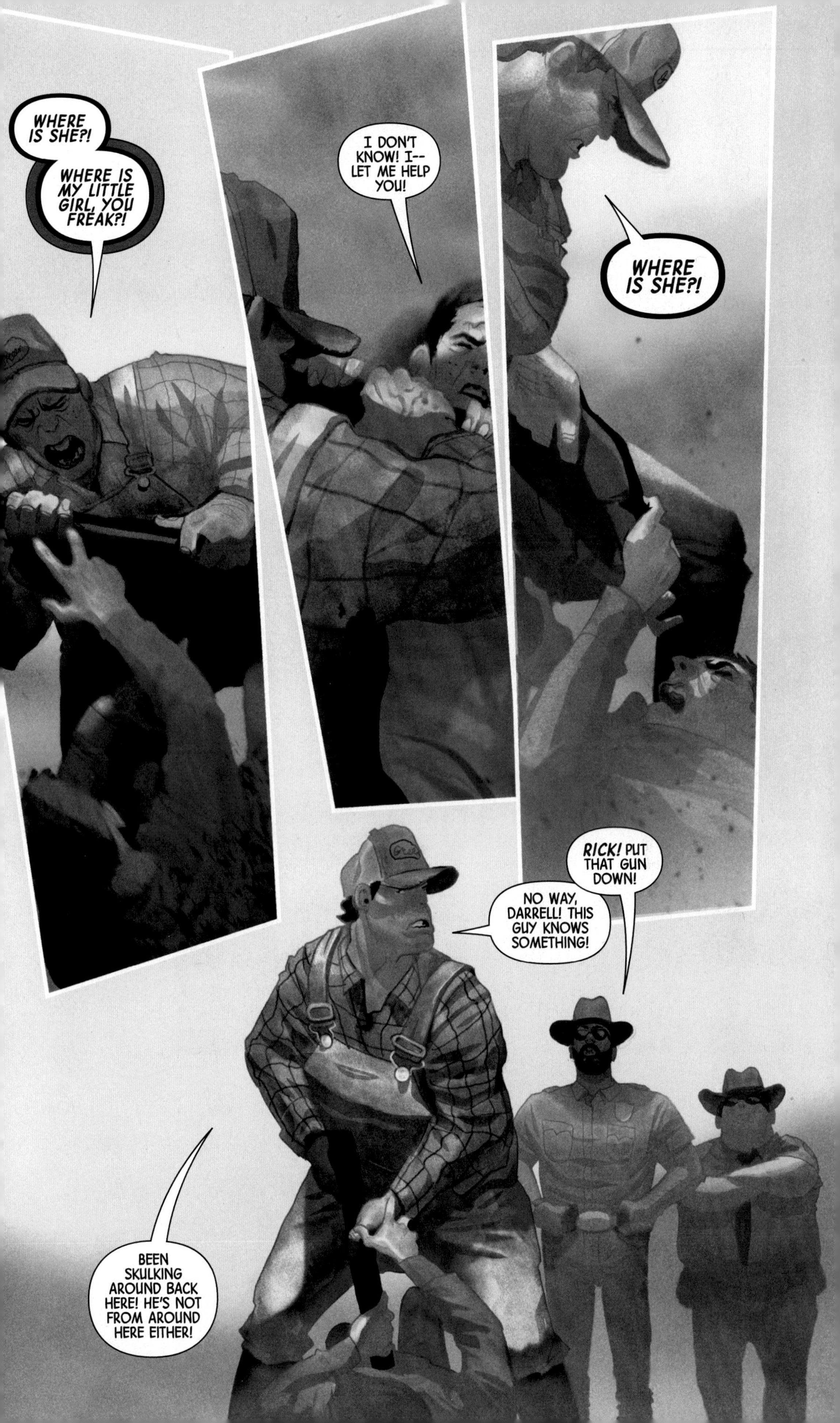
WHERE IS SHE?!
WHERE IS MY LITTLE GIRL, YOU FREAK?!
I DON'T KNOW! I-- LET ME HELP YOU!
WHERE IS SHE?!
RICK! PUT THAT GUN DOWN!
NO WAY, DARRELL! THIS GUY KNOWS SOMETHING!
BEEN SKULKING AROUND BACK HERE! HE'S NOT FROM AROUND HERE EITHER!

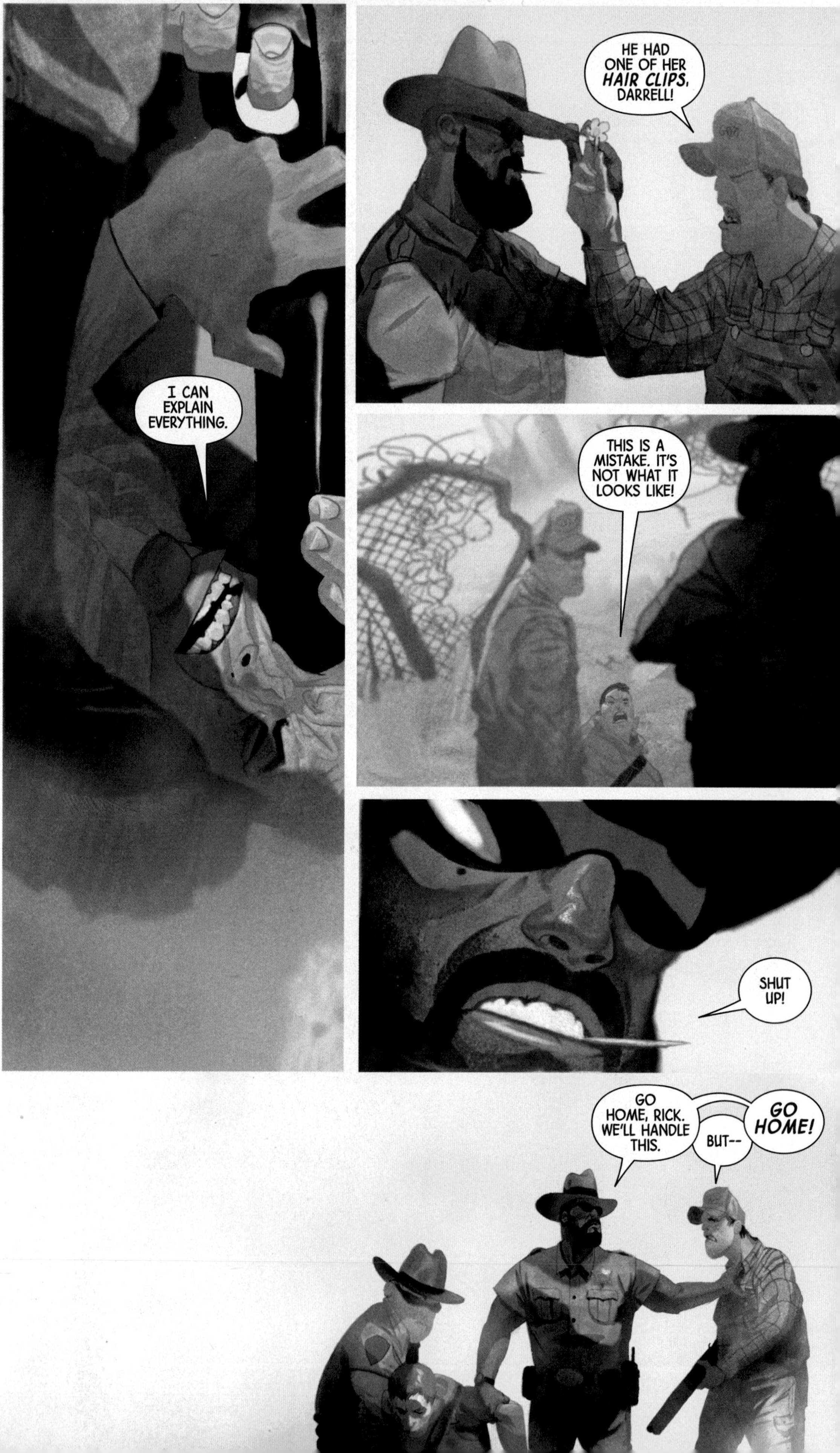
I CAN EXPLAIN EVERYTHING.
HE HAD ONE OF HER HAIR CLIPS, DARRELL!
THIS IS A MISTAKE. IT'S NOT WHAT IT LOOKS LIKE!
SHUT UP!
GO HOME, RICK. WE'LL HANDLE THIS.
BUT--
GO HOME!

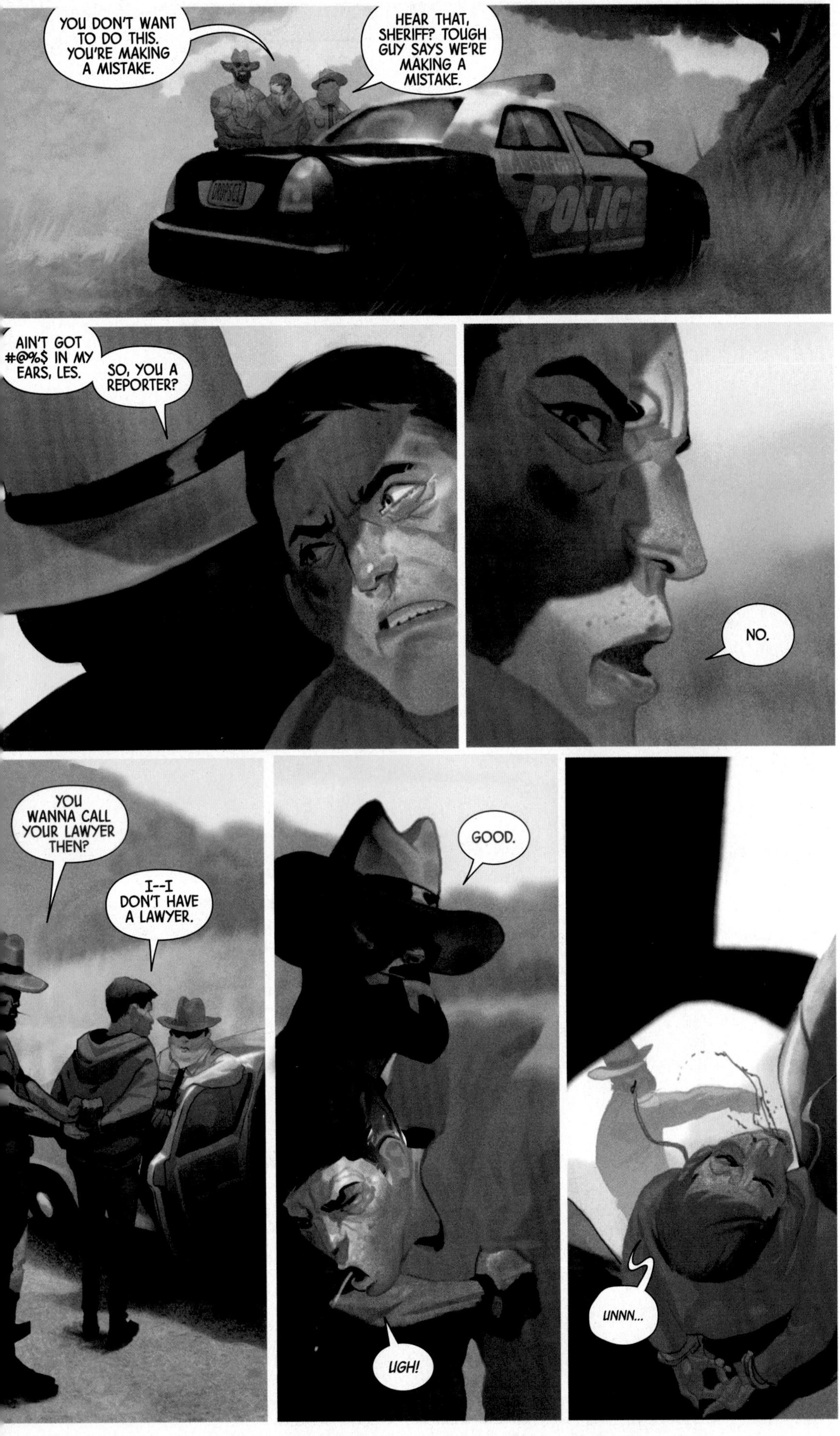
YOU DON'T WANT TO DO THIS. YOU'RE MAKING A MISTAKE.
HEAR THAT, SHERIFF? TOUGH GUY SAYS WE'RE MAKING A MISTAKE.
POLICE
AIN'T GOT #@%$ IN MY EARS, LES.
SO, YOU A REPORTER?
NO.
YOU WANNA CALL YOUR LAWYER THEN?
I--I DON'T HAVE A LAWYER.
GOOD.
UGH!
UNNN...

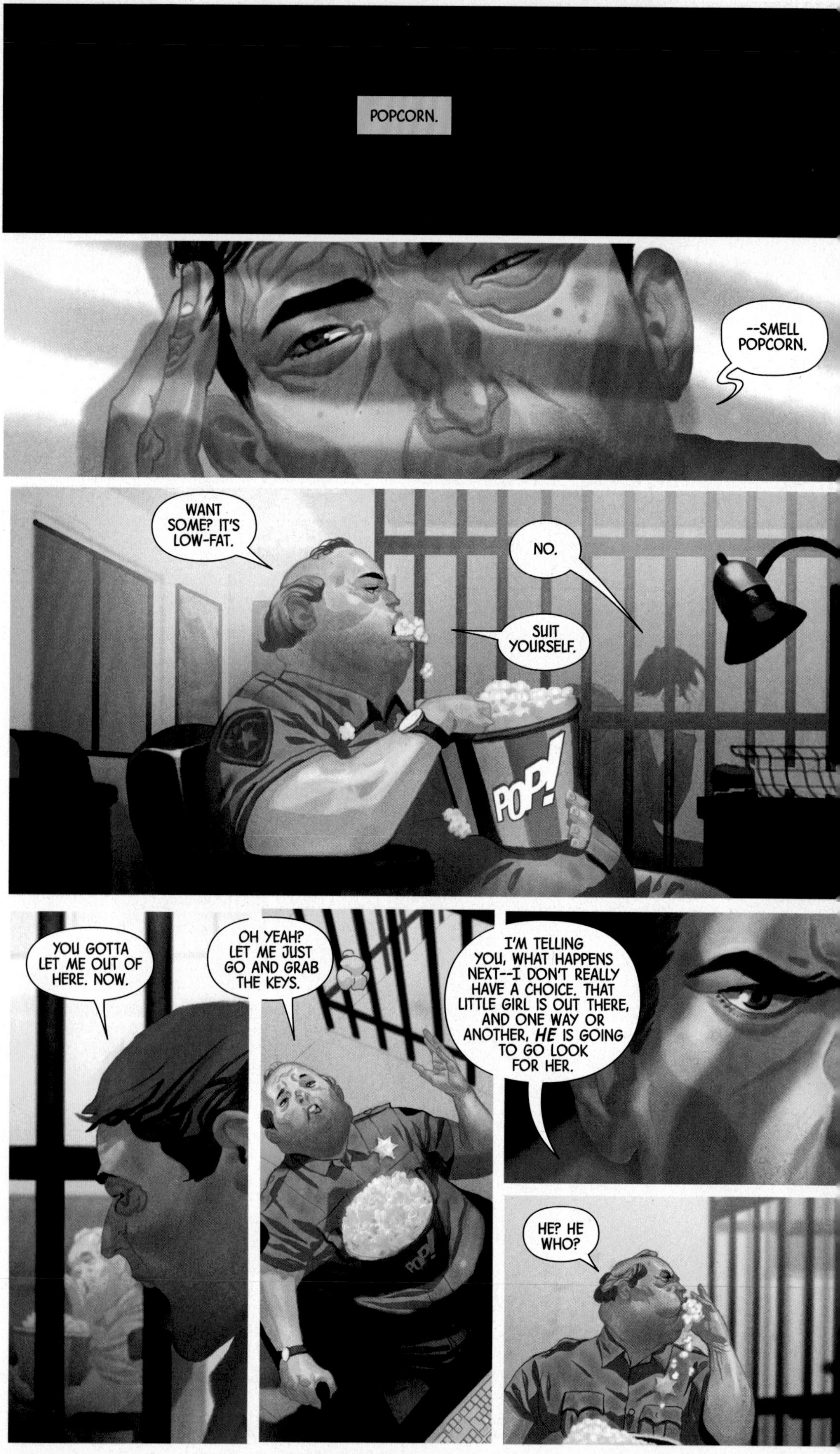
POPCORN.
--SMELL POPCORN.
WANT SOME? IT'S LOW-FAT.
NO.
SUIT YOURSELF.
POP!
YOU GOTTA LET ME OUT OF HERE. NOW.
OH YEAH? LET ME JUST GO AND GRAB THE KEYS.
I'M TELLING YOU, WHAT HAPPENS NEXT--I DON'T REALLY HAVE A CHOICE. THAT LITTLE GIRL IS OUT THERE, AND ONE WAY OR ANOTHER, *HE* IS GOING TO GO LOOK FOR HER.
HE? HE WHO?

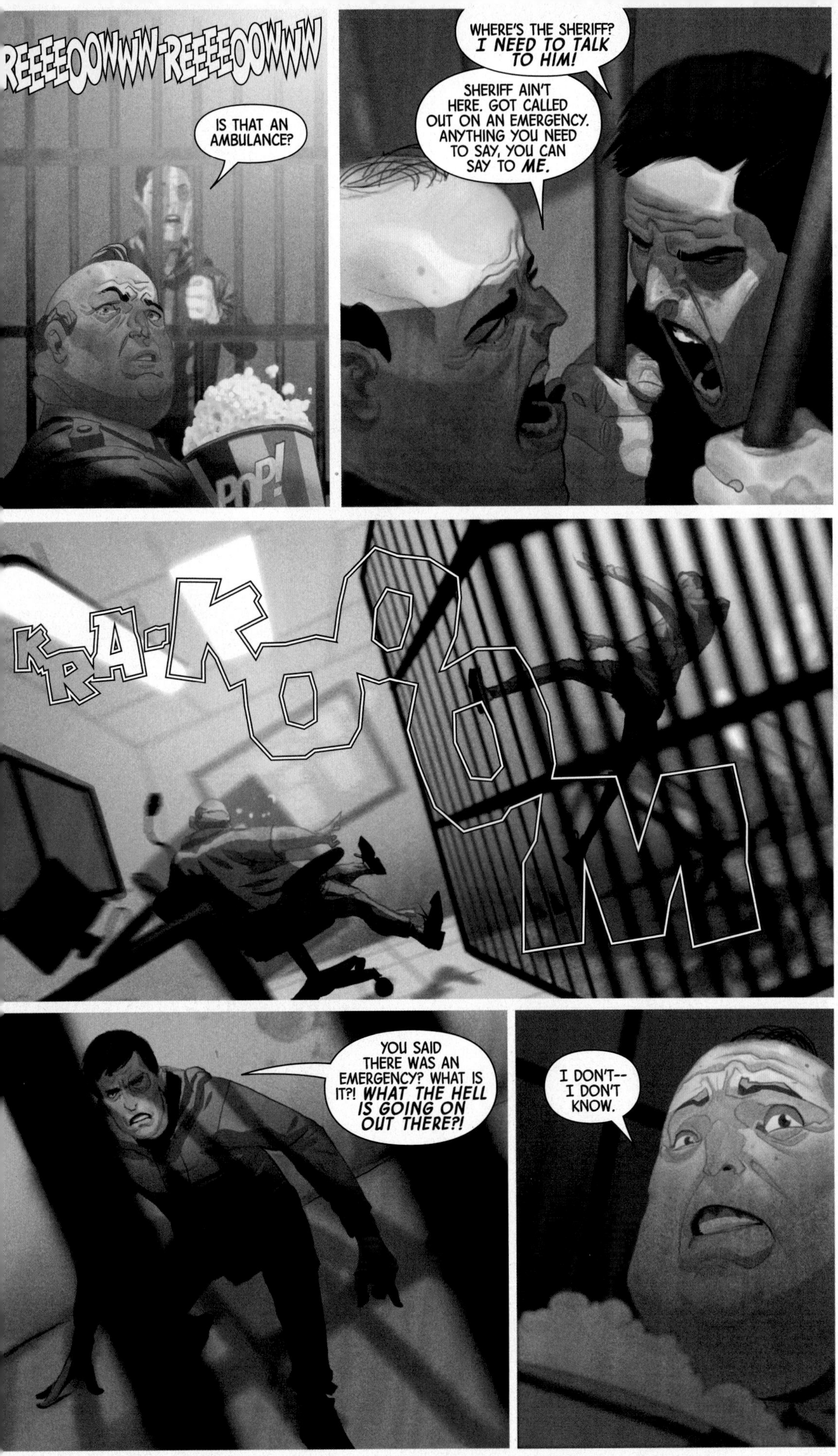
REEEEOOWWW-REEEEOOWWW
IS THAT AN AMBULANCE?
POP!
WHERE'S THE SHERIFF? *I NEED TO TALK TO HIM!*
SHERIFF AIN'T HERE. GOT CALLED OUT ON AN EMERGENCY. ANYTHING YOU NEED TO SAY, YOU CAN SAY TO *ME.*
KRA-KOOOOM
YOU SAID THERE WAS AN EMERGENCY? WHAT IS IT?! *WHAT THE HELL IS GOING ON OUT THERE?!*
I DON'T-- I DON'T KNOW.

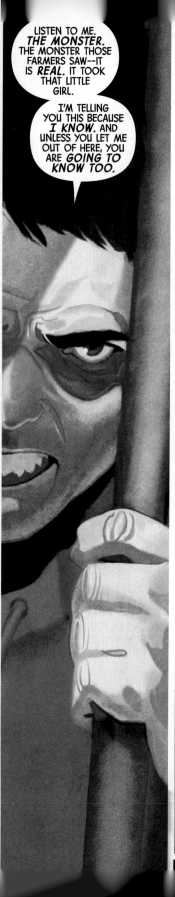

LISTEN TO ME. *THE MONSTER.* THE MONSTER THOSE FARMERS SAW--IT IS *REAL.* IT TOOK THAT LITTLE GIRL.

I'M TELLING YOU THIS BECAUSE *I KNOW.* AND UNLESS YOU LET ME OUT OF HERE, YOU ARE *GOING TO KNOW TOO.*

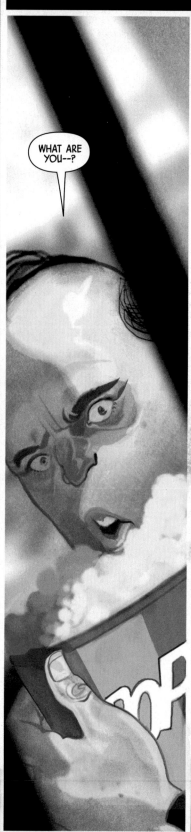

WHAT ARE YOU--?

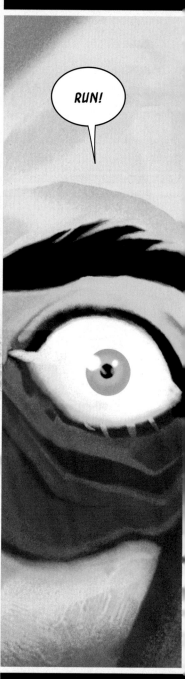

RUN!

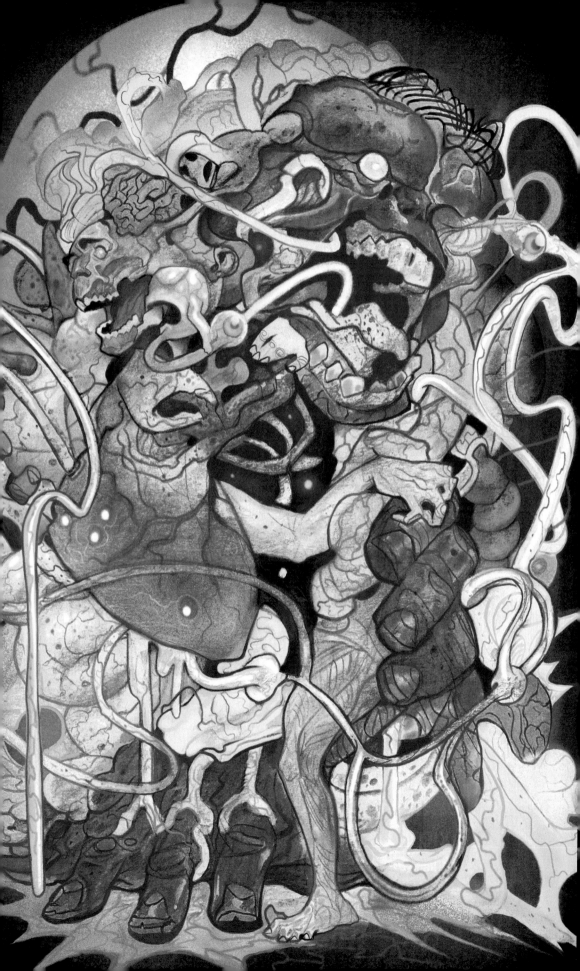

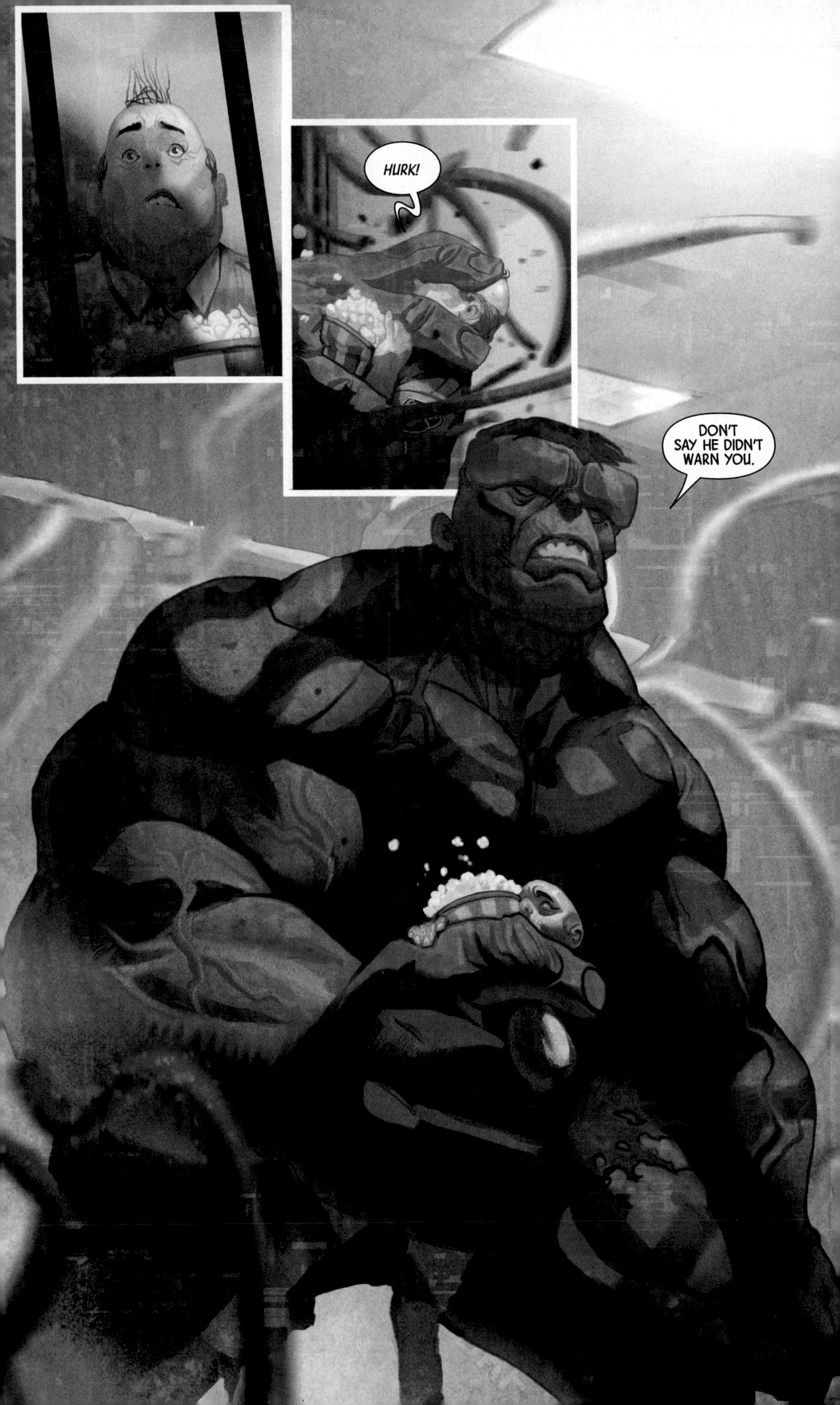
HURK!
DON'T SAY HE DIDN'T WARN YOU.

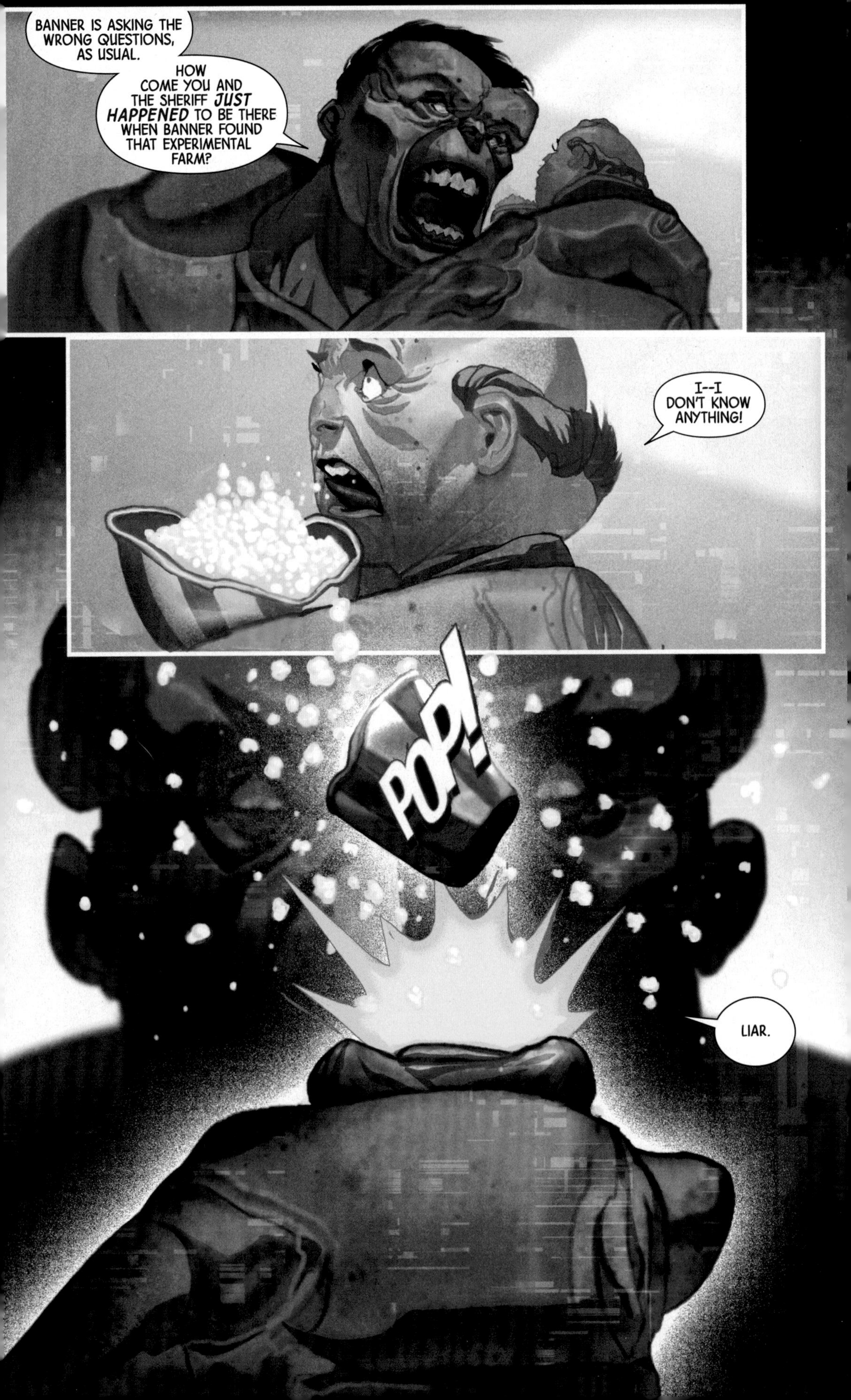
BANNER IS ASKING THE WRONG QUESTIONS, AS USUAL.
HOW COME YOU AND THE SHERIFF *JUST HAPPENED* TO BE THERE WHEN BANNER FOUND THAT EXPERIMENTAL FARM?
I--I DON'T KNOW ANYTHING!
POP!
LIAR.

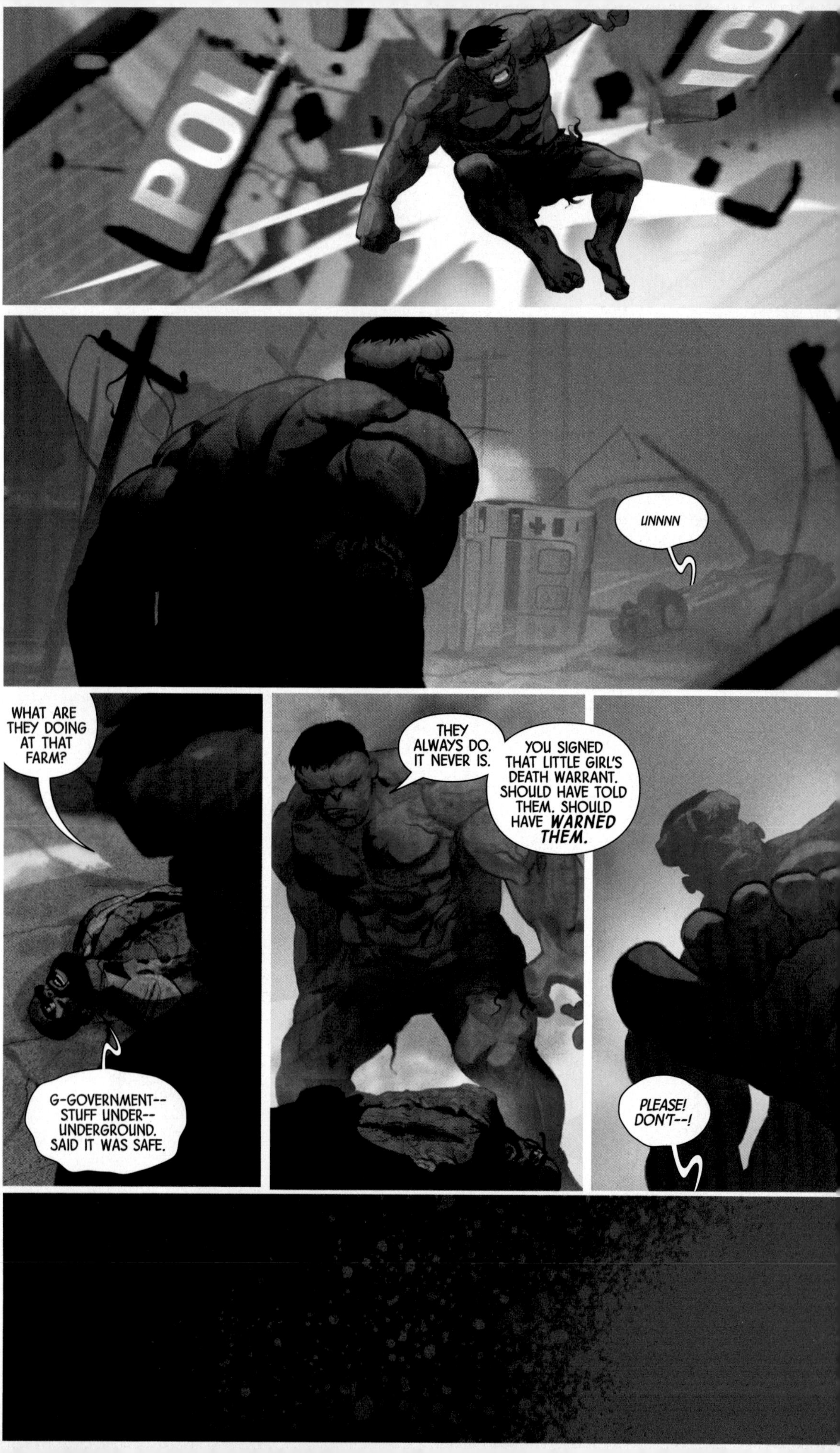
UNNNN
WHAT ARE THEY DOING AT THAT FARM?
G-GOVERNMENT-- STUFF UNDER-- UNDERGROUND. SAID IT WAS SAFE.
THEY ALWAYS DO. IT NEVER IS.
YOU SIGNED THAT LITTLE GIRL'S DEATH WARRANT. SHOULD HAVE TOLD THEM. SHOULD HAVE WARNED THEM.
PLEASE! DON'T--!

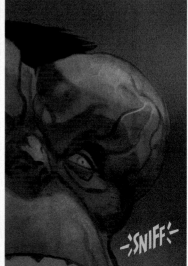

-SNIFF-

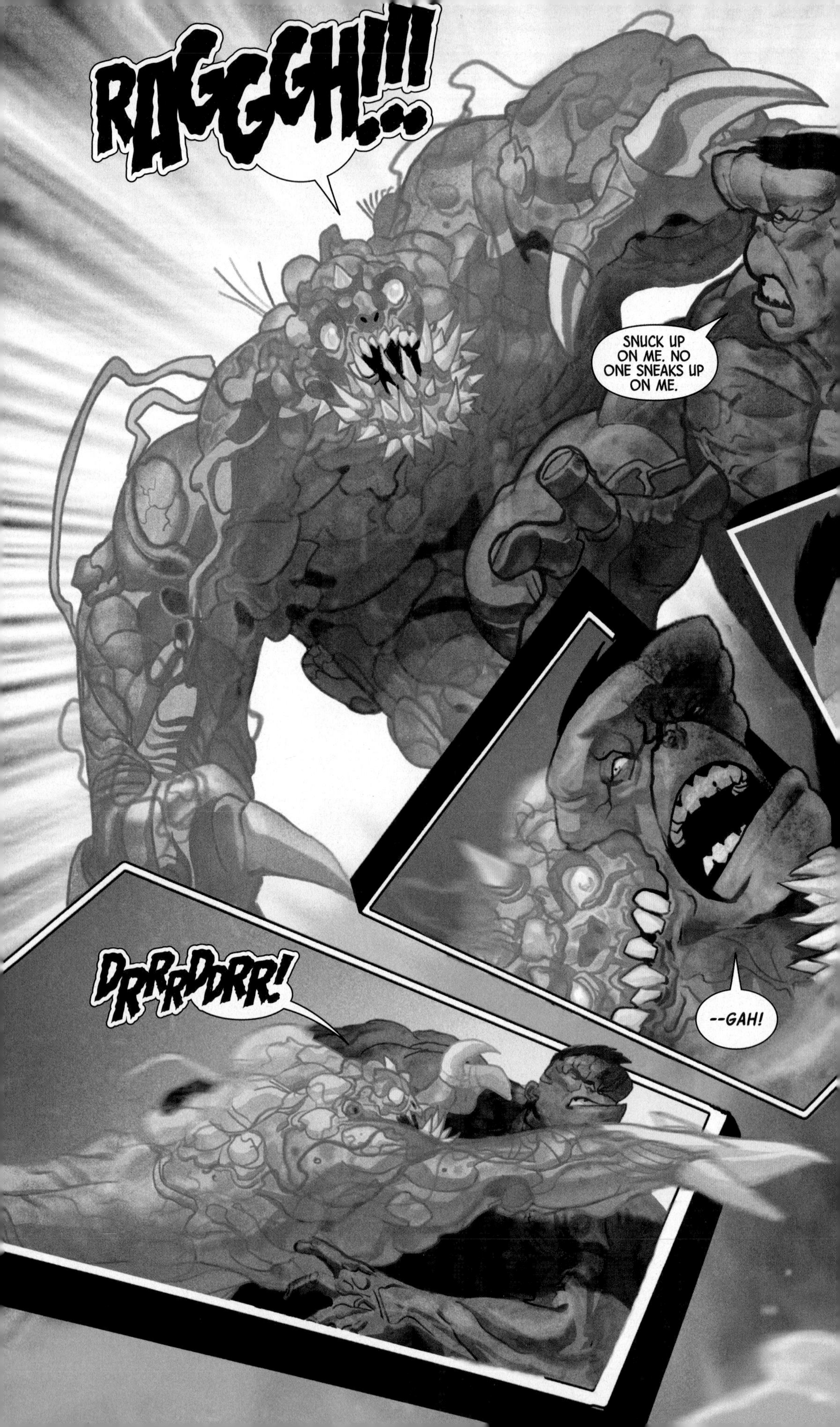
RAGGGH!!!...
SNUCK UP ON ME. NO ONE SNEAKS UP ON ME.
--GAH!
DRRRDDRR!

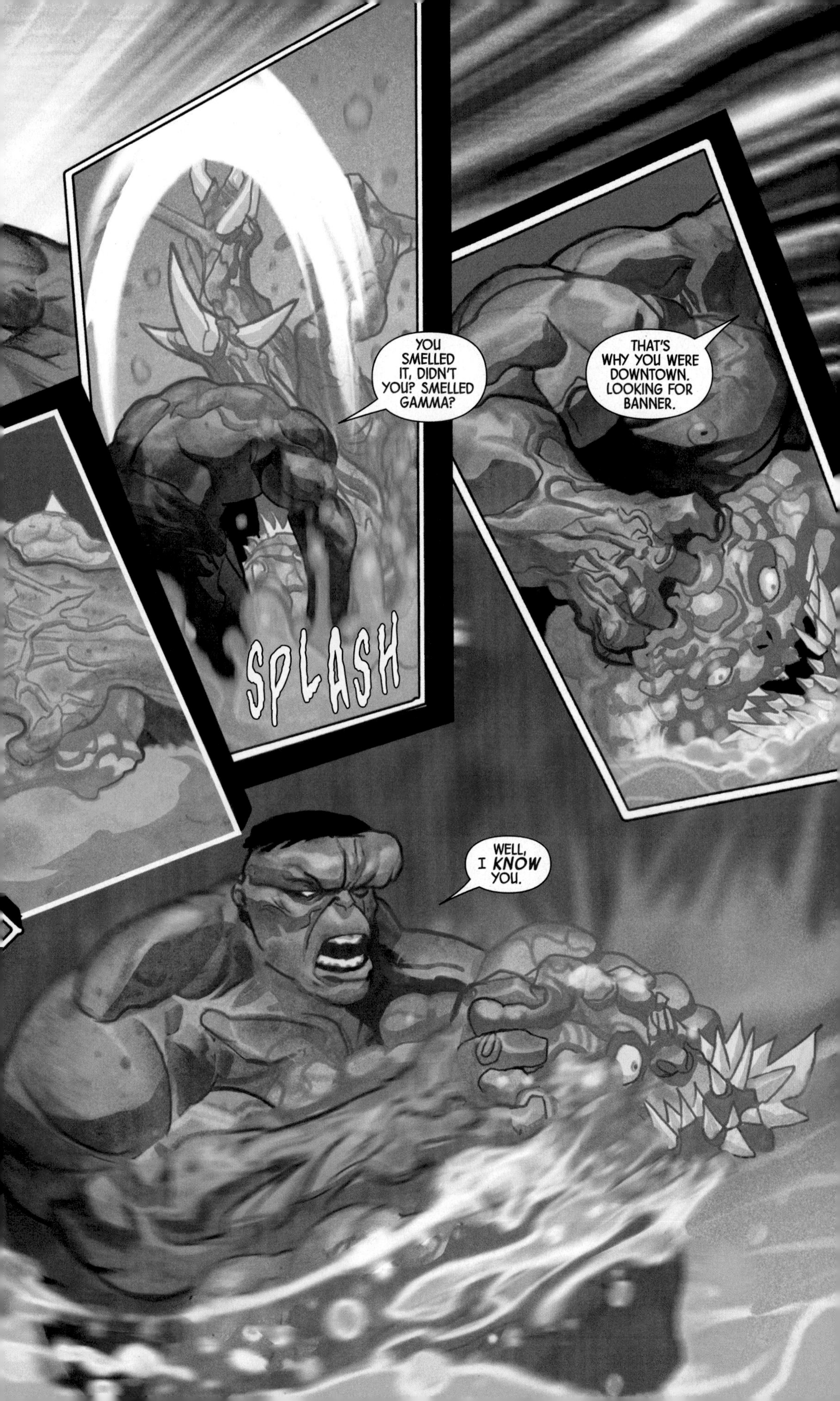
YOU SMELLED IT, DIDN'T YOU? SMELLED GAMMA?
SPLASH
THAT'S WHY YOU WERE DOWNTOWN. LOOKING FOR BANNER.
WELL, I KNOW YOU.

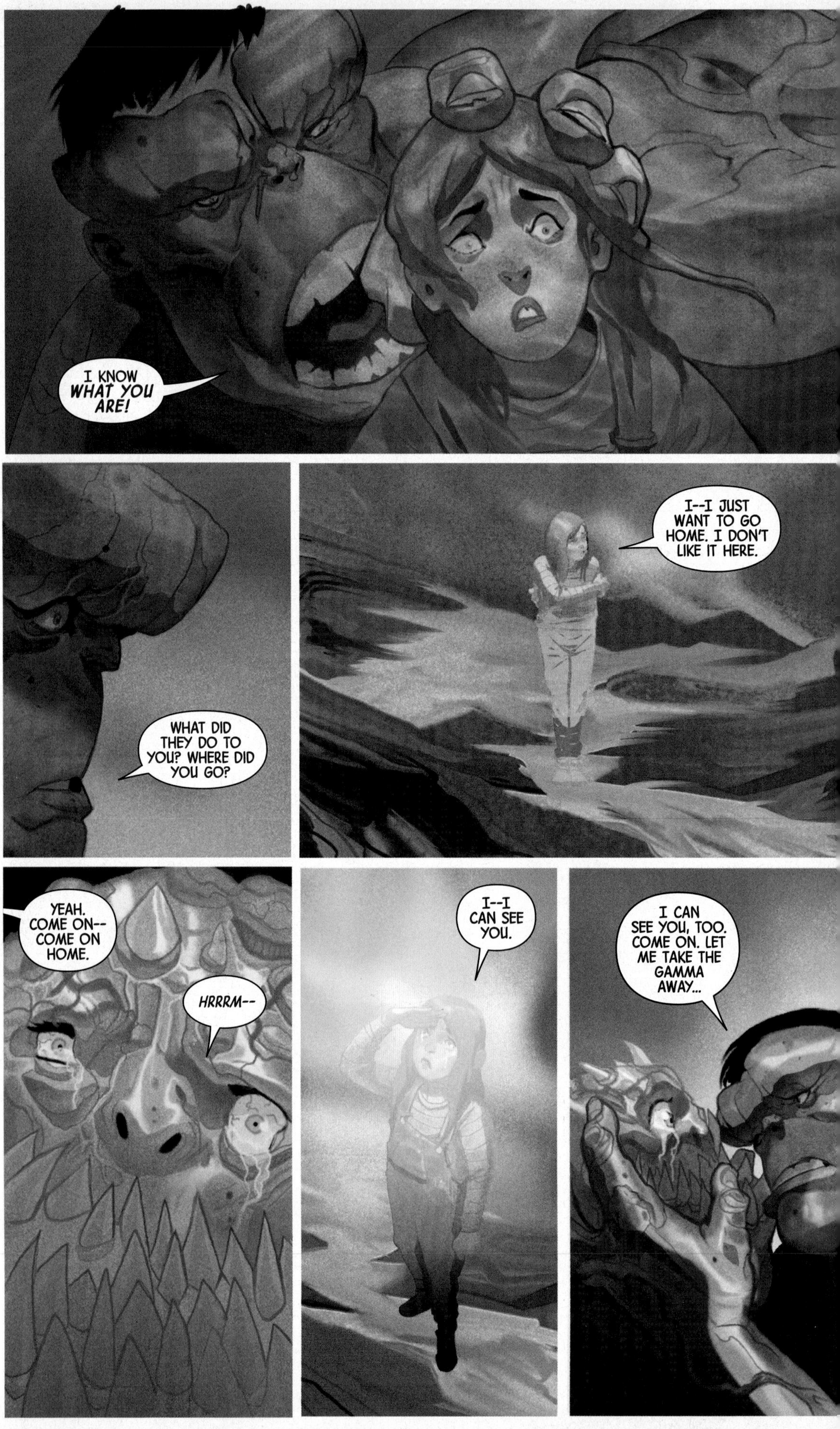
I KNOW WHAT YOU ARE!
WHAT DID THEY DO TO YOU? WHERE DID YOU GO?
I--I JUST WANT TO GO HOME. I DON'T LIKE IT HERE.
YEAH. COME ON-- COME ON HOME.
HRRRM--
I--I CAN SEE YOU.
I CAN SEE YOU, TOO. COME ON. LET ME TAKE THE GAMMA AWAY...

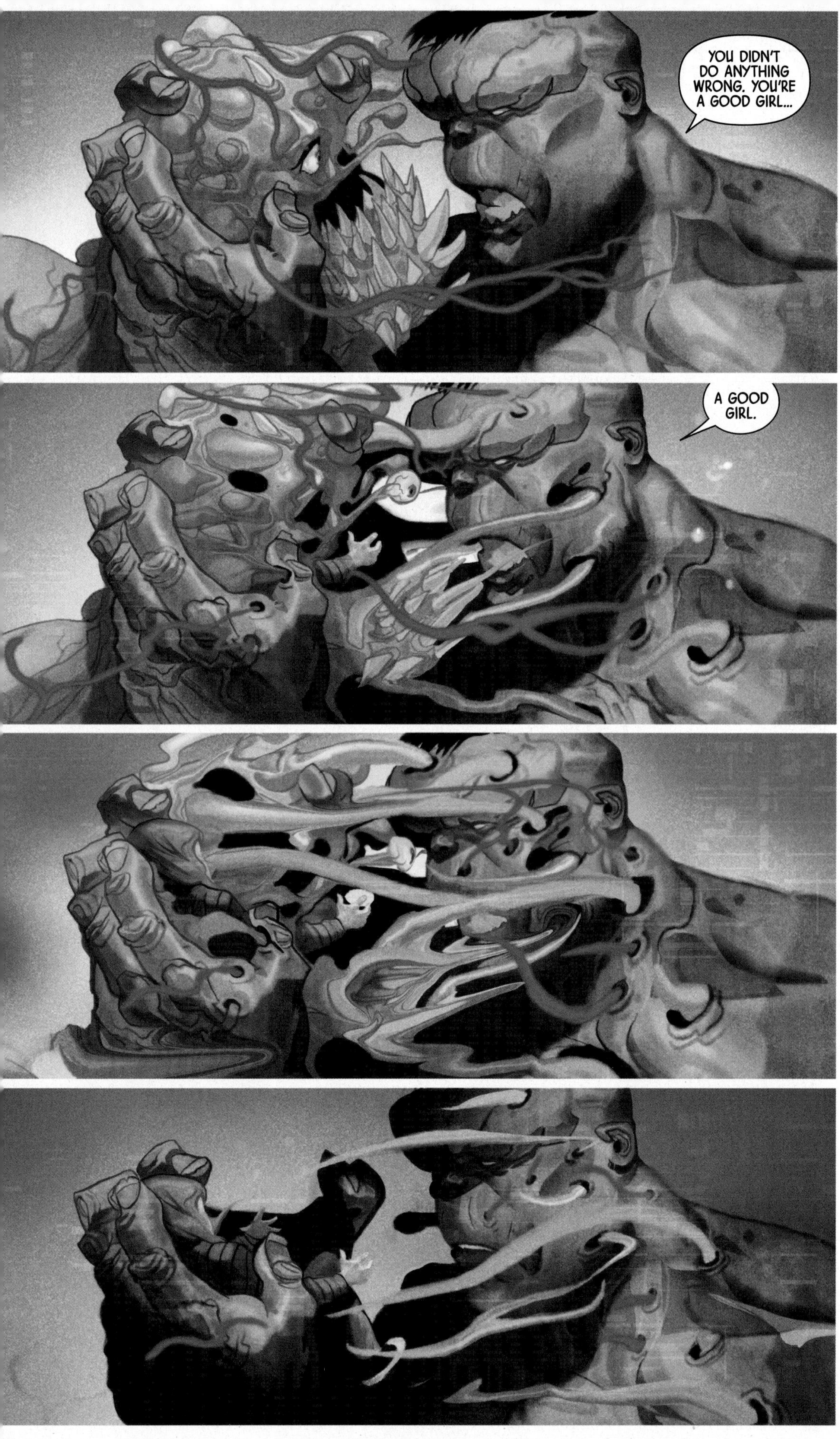
YOU DIDN'T DO ANYTHING WRONG. YOU'RE A GOOD GIRL...
A GOOD GIRL.

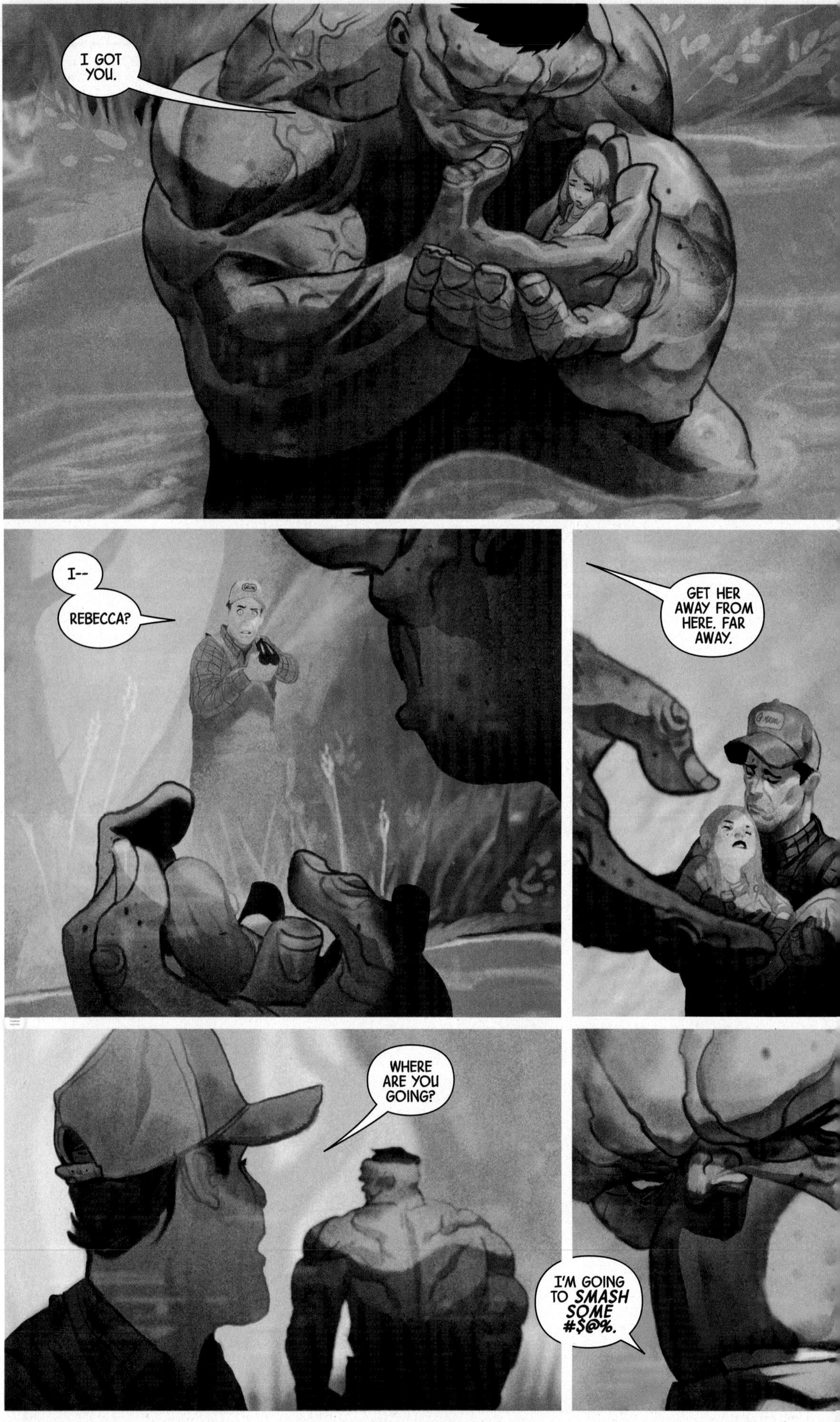

I GOT YOU.
I--
REBECCA?
GET HER AWAY FROM HERE. FAR AWAY.
WHERE ARE YOU GOING?
I'M GOING TO *SMASH SOME* #$@%.

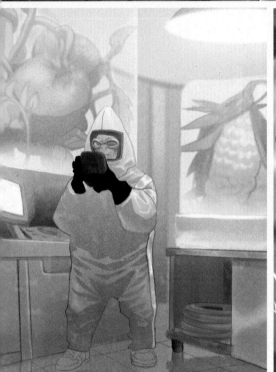

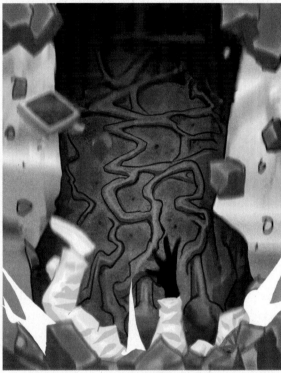

WELL, LOOK AT ALL THIS. AREN'T YOU ALL *SO CLEVER.*

GAMMA TO GROW SUPER-CROPS. BET YOU THOUGHT YOU WERE DOING GOOD, HUH? GOING TO HELP THE FARMERS? GOING TO FEED THE WORLD?

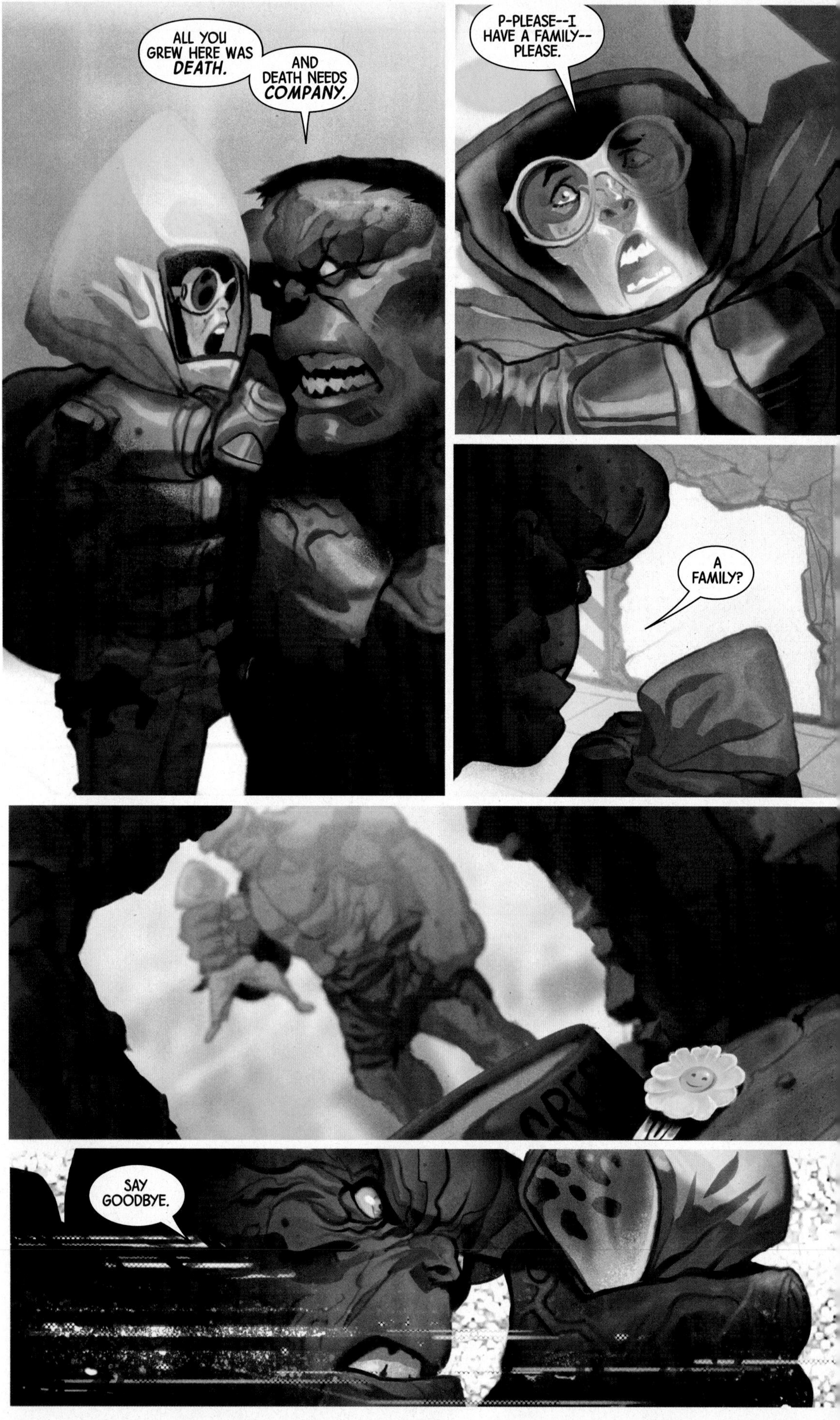
ALL YOU GREW HERE WAS *DEATH.*
AND DEATH NEEDS *COMPANY.*
P-PLEASE--I HAVE A FAMILY-- PLEASE.
A FAMILY?
SAY GOODBYE.

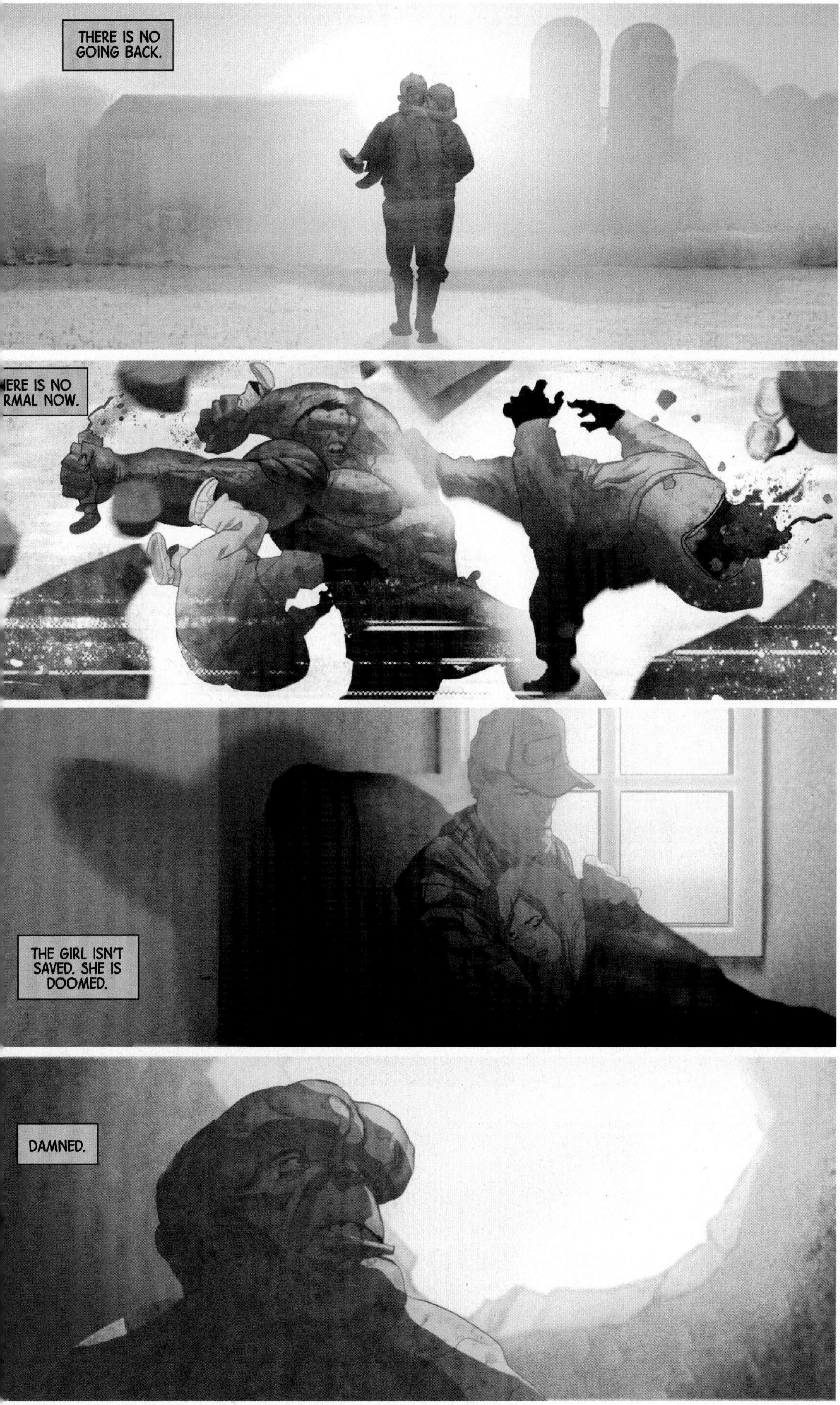
THERE IS NO GOING BACK.
ERE IS NO RMAL NOW.
THE GIRL ISN'T SAVED. SHE IS DOOMED.
DAMNED.

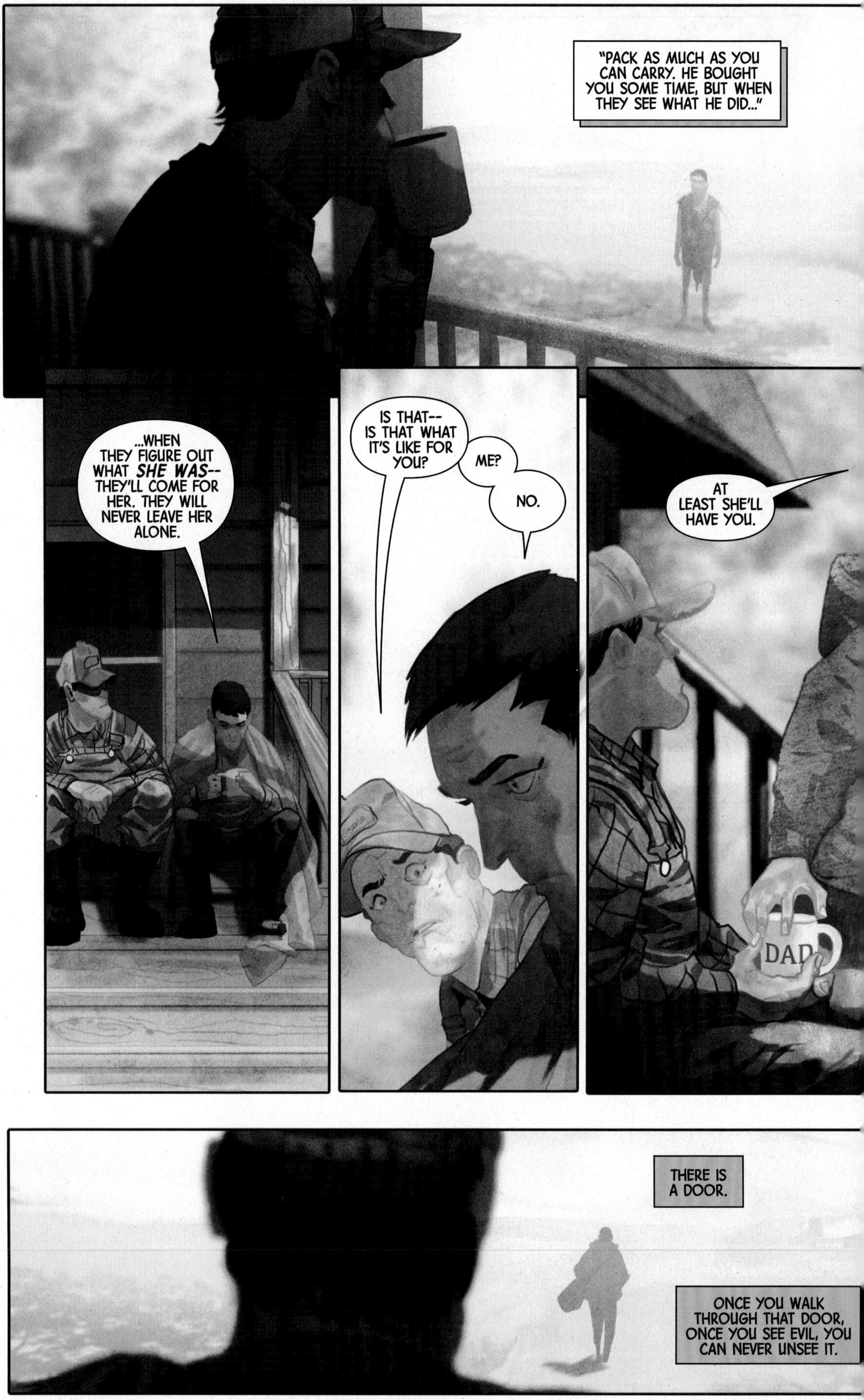

"PACK AS MUCH AS YOU CAN CARRY. HE BOUGHT YOU SOME TIME, BUT WHEN THEY SEE WHAT HE DID..."
...WHEN THEY FIGURE OUT WHAT *SHE WAS*-- THEY'LL COME FOR HER. THEY WILL NEVER LEAVE HER ALONE.
IS THAT-- IS THAT WHAT IT'S LIKE FOR YOU?
ME?
NO.
AT LEAST SHE'LL HAVE YOU.
DAD
THERE IS A DOOR.
ONCE YOU WALK THROUGH THAT DOOR, ONCE YOU SEE EVIL, YOU CAN NEVER UNSEE IT.

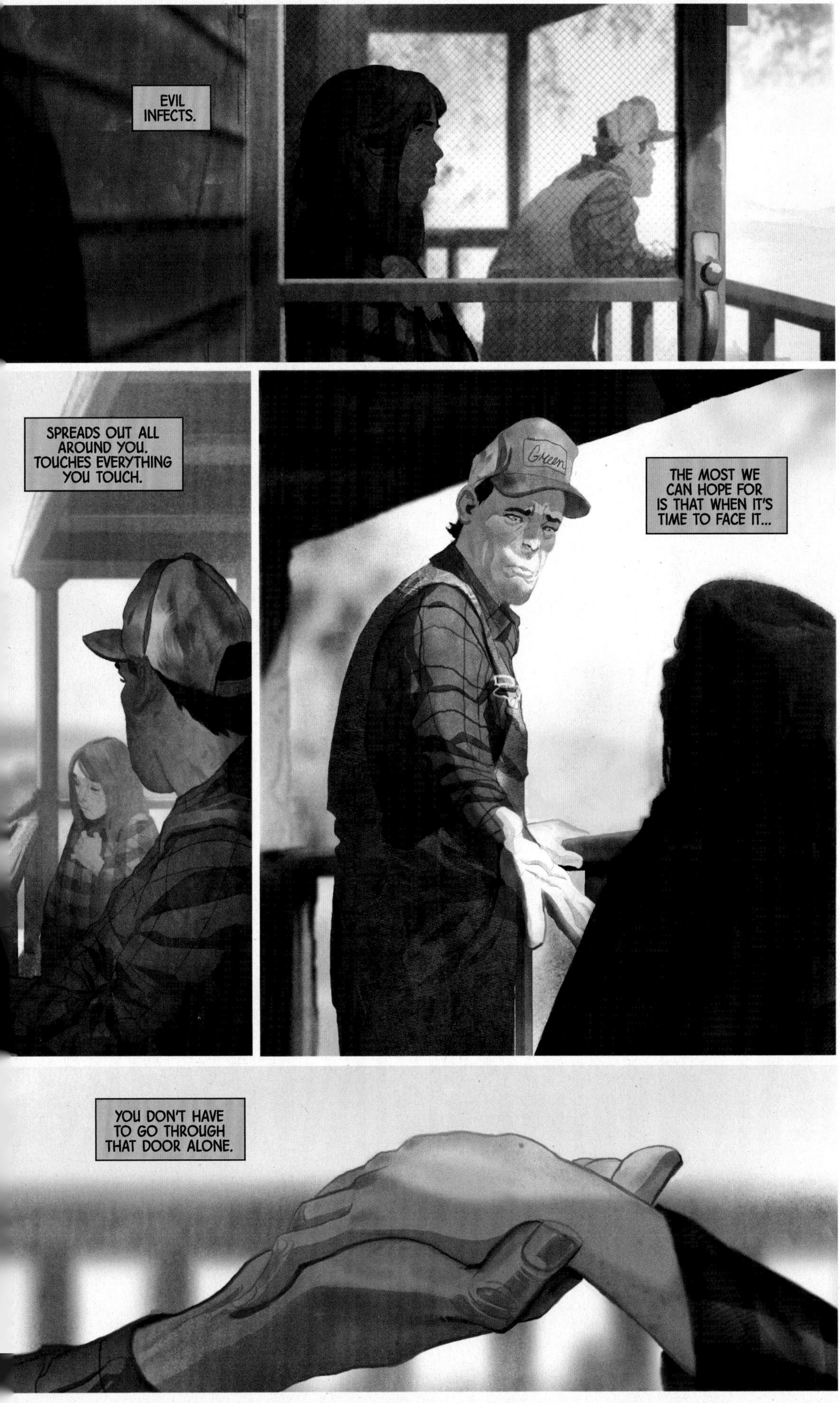
EVIL INFECTS.
SPREADS OUT ALL AROUND YOU. TOUCHES EVERYTHING YOU TOUCH.
Green
THE MOST WE CAN HOPE FOR IS THAT WHEN IT'S TIME TO FACE IT...
YOU DON'T HAVE TO GO THROUGH THAT DOOR ALONE.

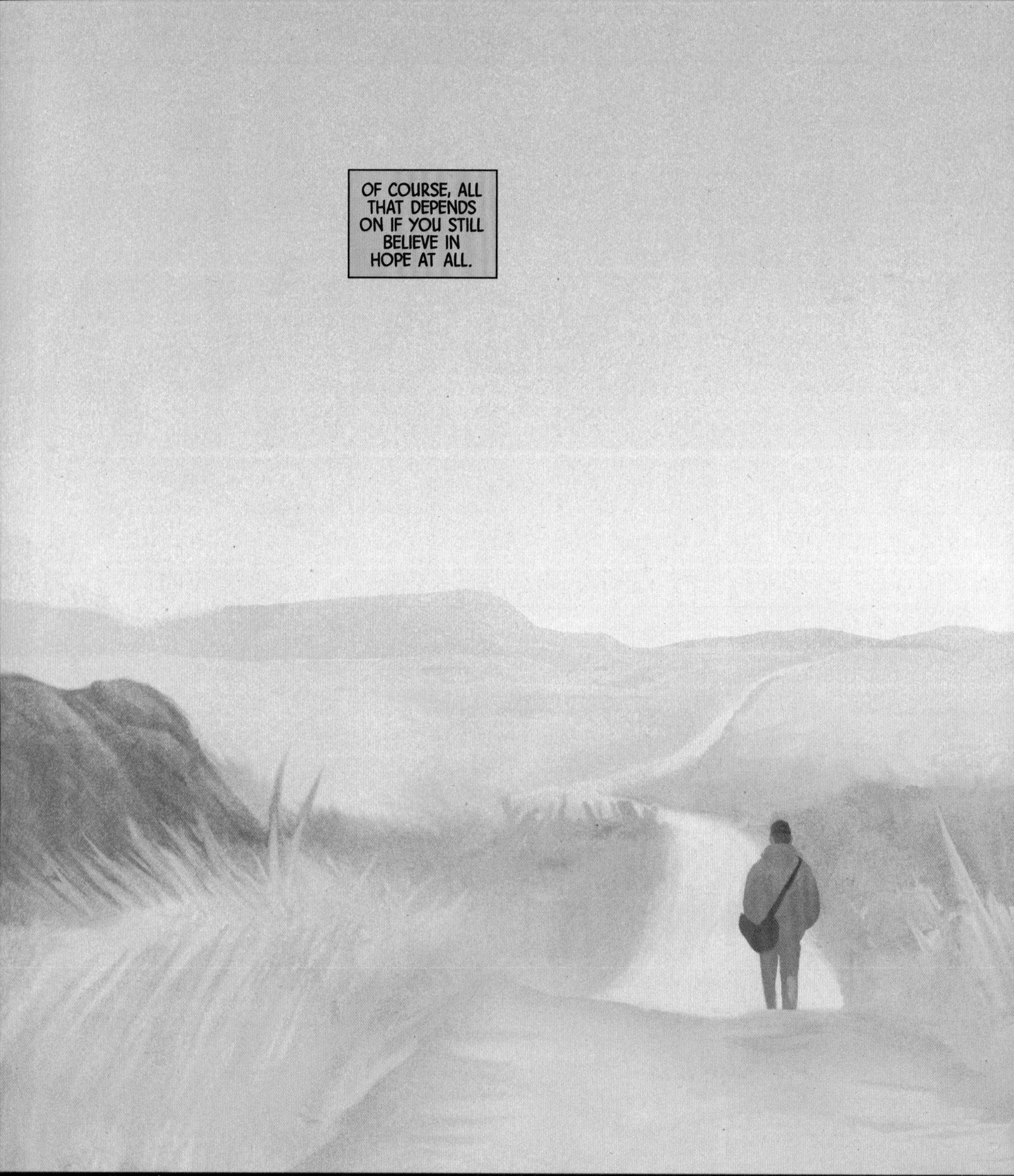
OF COURSE, ALL THAT DEPENDS ON IF YOU STILL BELIEVE IN HOPE AT ALL.

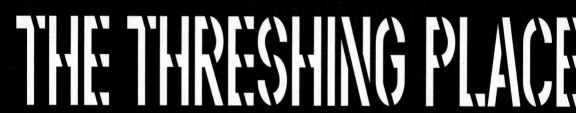

THE THRESHING PLACE

JEFF LEMIRE WRITER MIKE DEL MUNDO ARTIST MIKE DEL MUNDO & MARCO D'ALFONSO COLOR ARTIST

VC'S CORY PETIT LETTERER MIKE DEL MUNDO COVER

JOE BENNETT, RUY JOSÉ & PAUL MOUNTS VARIANT COVER ARTISTS

SARAH BRUNSTAD ASSOCIATE EDITOR WIL MOSS EDITOR TOM BREVOORT EXECUTIVE EDITOR C.B. CEBULSKI EDITOR IN CHIEF

HULK CREATED BY STAN LEE & JACK KIRBY

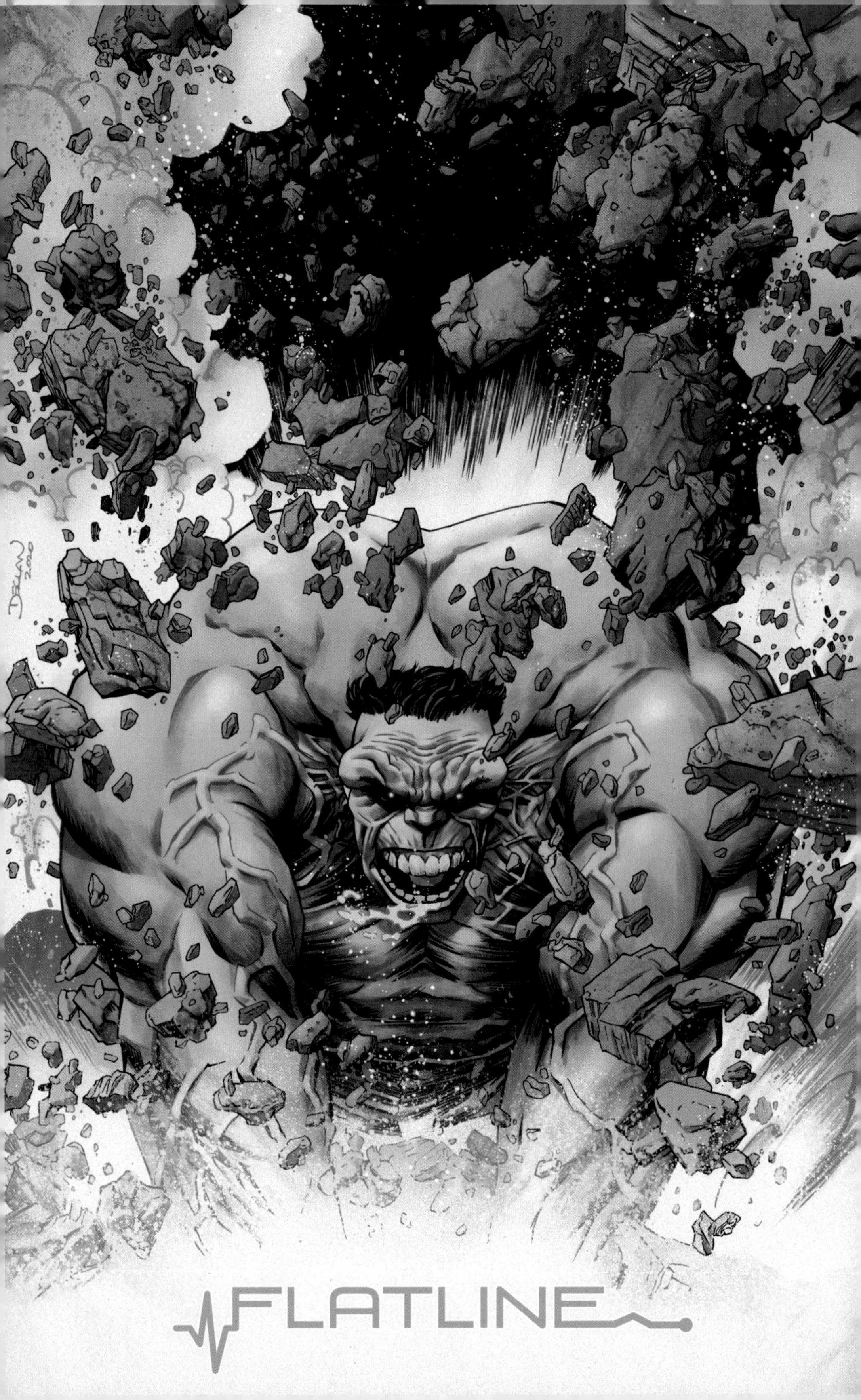
FLATLINE

"MANY TIMES HE DIED, MANY TIMES ROSE AGAIN."

— WILLIAM BUTLER YEATS, "DEATH"

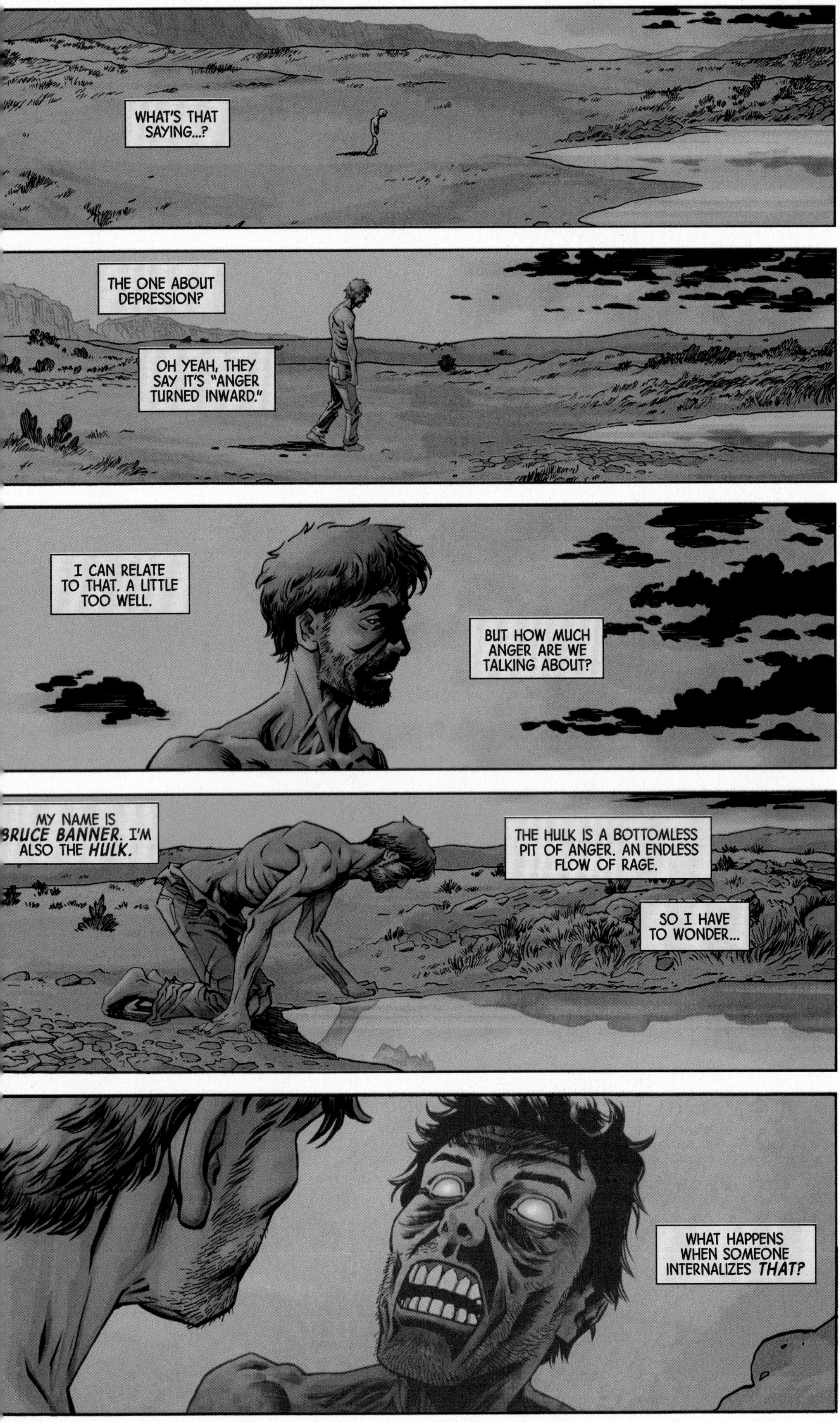
WHAT'S THAT SAYING...?
THE ONE ABOUT DEPRESSION?
OH YEAH, THEY SAY IT'S "ANGER TURNED INWARD."
I CAN RELATE TO THAT. A LITTLE TOO WELL.
BUT HOW MUCH ANGER ARE WE TALKING ABOUT?
MY NAME IS BRUCE BANNER. I'M ALSO THE HULK.
THE HULK IS A BOTTOMLESS PIT OF ANGER. AN ENDLESS FLOW OF RAGE.
SO I HAVE TO WONDER...
WHAT HAPPENS WHEN SOMEONE INTERNALIZES THAT?

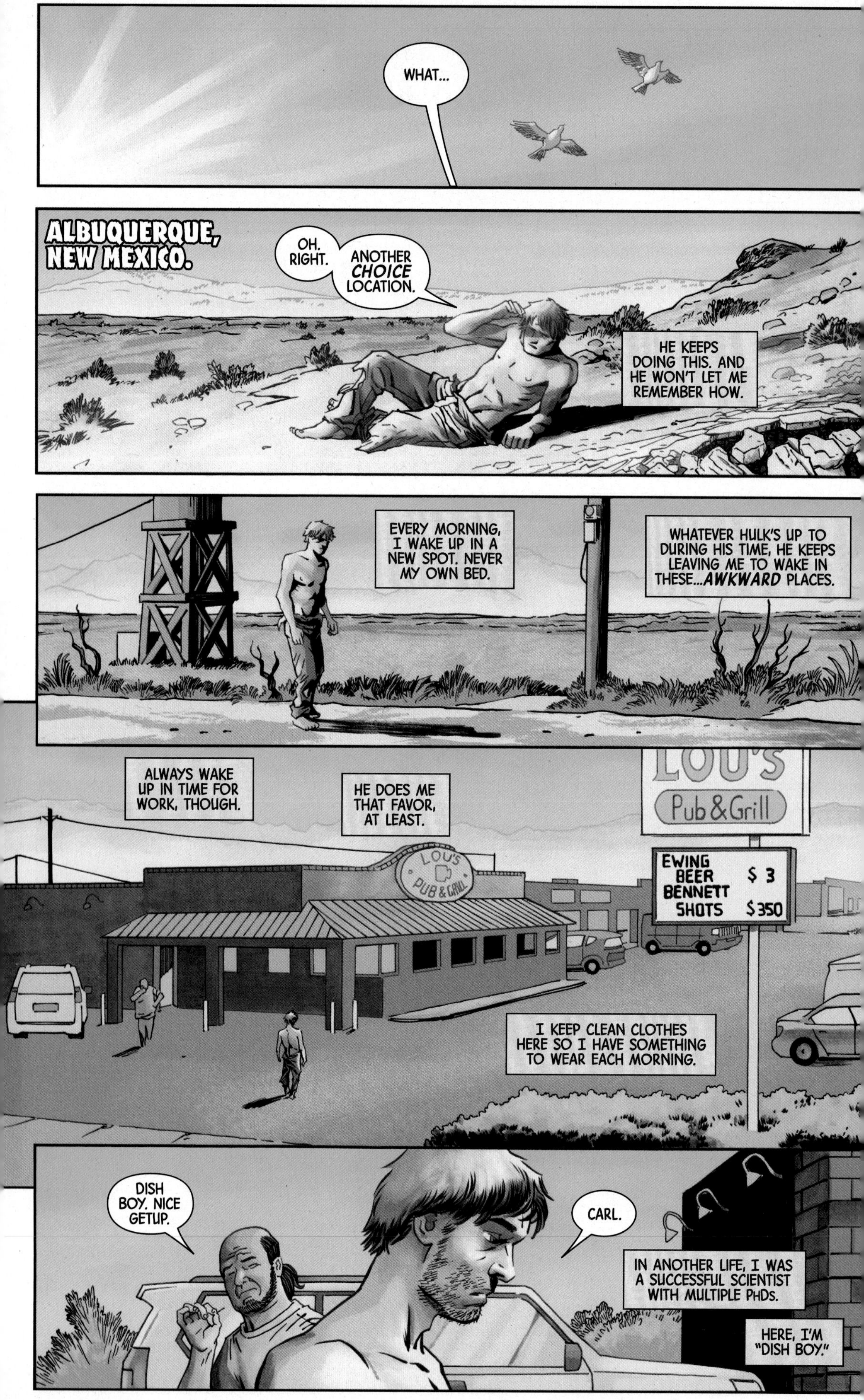
WHAT...
ALBUQUERQUE, NEW MEXICO.
OH. RIGHT.
ANOTHER CHOICE LOCATION.
HE KEEPS DOING THIS. AND HE WON'T LET ME REMEMBER HOW.
EVERY MORNING, I WAKE UP IN A NEW SPOT. NEVER MY OWN BED.
WHATEVER HULK'S UP TO DURING HIS TIME, HE KEEPS LEAVING ME TO WAKE IN THESE...AWKWARD PLACES.
ALWAYS WAKE UP IN TIME FOR WORK, THOUGH.
HE DOES ME THAT FAVOR, AT LEAST.
LOU'S
Pub & Grill
EWING BEER $3
BENNETT SHOTS $350
I KEEP CLEAN CLOTHES HERE SO I HAVE SOMETHING TO WEAR EACH MORNING.
DISH BOY. NICE GETUP.
CARL.
IN ANOTHER LIFE, I WAS A SUCCESSFUL SCIENTIST WITH MULTIPLE PhDs.
HERE, I'M "DISH BOY."

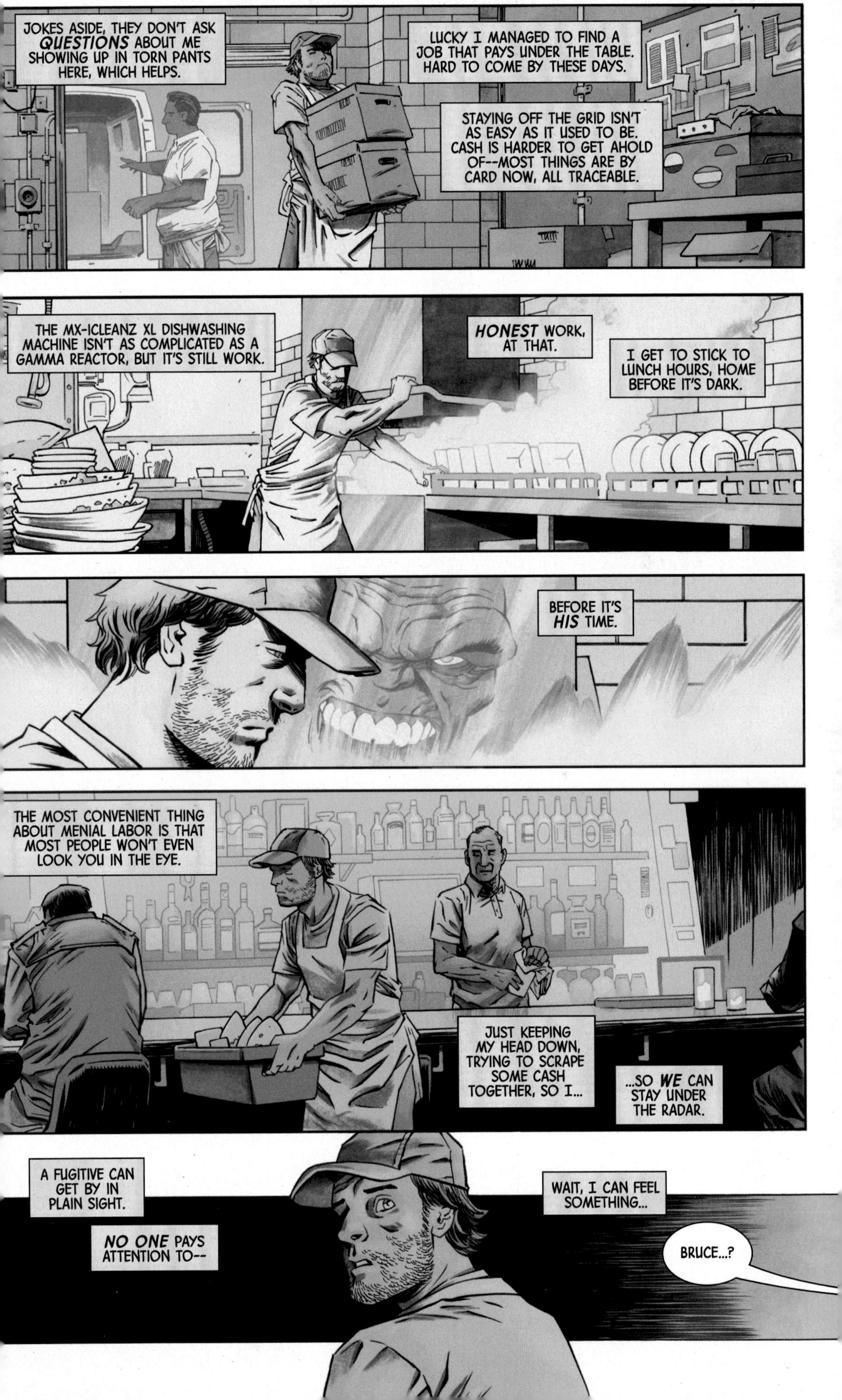
JOKES ASIDE, THEY DON'T ASK *QUESTIONS* ABOUT ME SHOWING UP IN TORN PANTS HERE, WHICH HELPS.
LUCKY I MANAGED TO FIND A JOB THAT PAYS UNDER THE TABLE. HARD TO COME BY THESE DAYS.
STAYING OFF THE GRID ISN'T AS EASY AS IT USED TO BE. CASH IS HARDER TO GET AHOLD OF--MOST THINGS ARE BY CARD NOW, ALL TRACEABLE.
THE MX-ICLEANZ XL DISHWASHING MACHINE ISN'T AS COMPLICATED AS A GAMMA REACTOR, BUT IT'S STILL WORK.
HONEST WORK, AT THAT.
I GET TO STICK TO LUNCH HOURS, HOME BEFORE IT'S DARK.
BEFORE IT'S *HIS* TIME.
THE MOST CONVENIENT THING ABOUT MENIAL LABOR IS THAT MOST PEOPLE WON'T EVEN LOOK YOU IN THE EYE.
JUST KEEPING MY HEAD DOWN, TRYING TO SCRAPE SOME CASH TOGETHER, SO I...
...SO *WE* CAN STAY UNDER THE RADAR.
A FUGITIVE CAN GET BY IN PLAIN SIGHT.
NO ONE PAYS ATTENTION TO--
WAIT, I CAN FEEL SOMETHING...
BRUCE...?

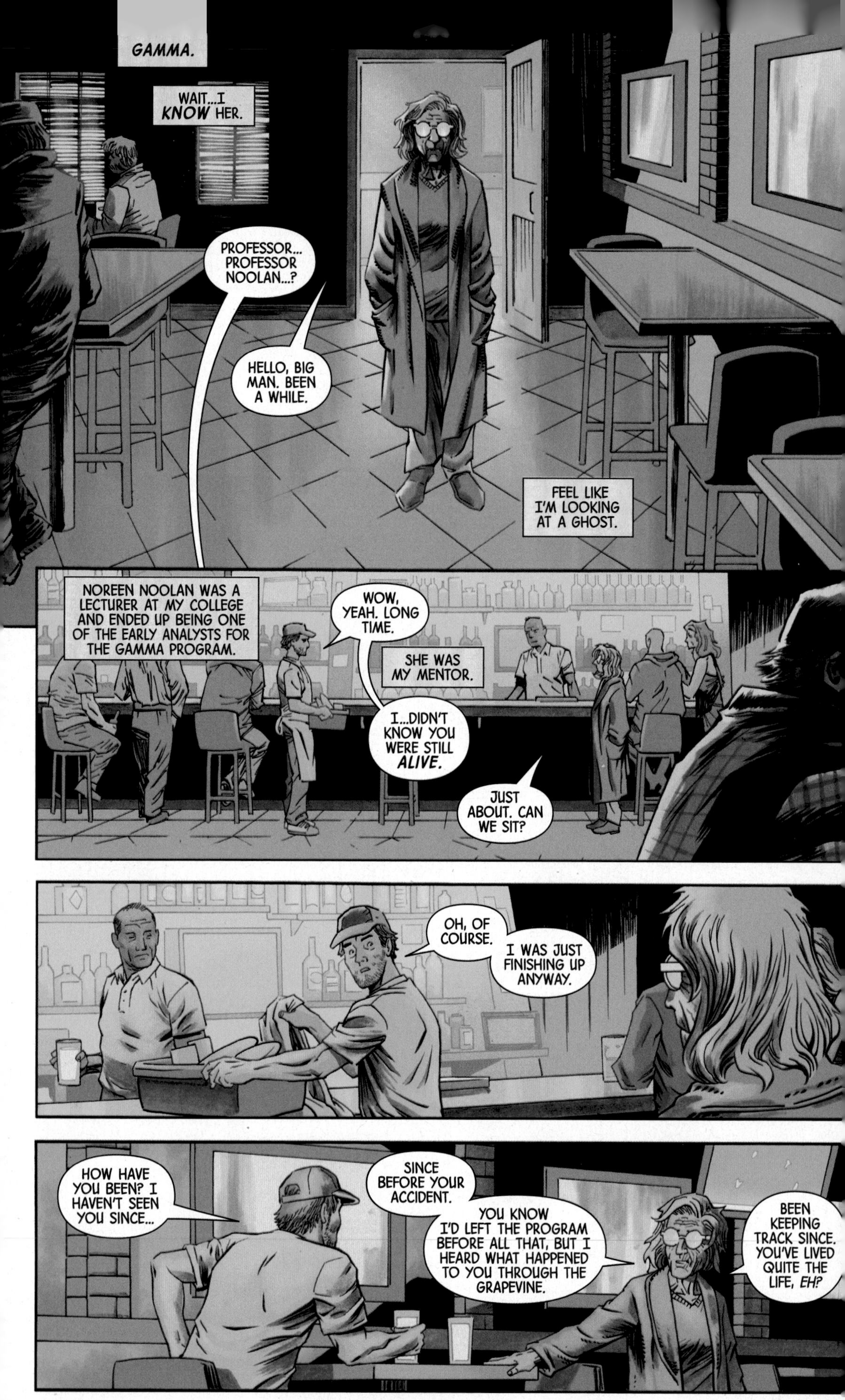
GAMMA.
WAIT...I KNOW HER.
PROFESSOR... PROFESSOR NOOLAN...?
HELLO, BIG MAN. BEEN A WHILE.
FEEL LIKE I'M LOOKING AT A GHOST.
NOREEN NOOLAN WAS A LECTURER AT MY COLLEGE AND ENDED UP BEING ONE OF THE EARLY ANALYSTS FOR THE GAMMA PROGRAM.
WOW, YEAH. LONG TIME.
SHE WAS MY MENTOR.
I...DIDN'T KNOW YOU WERE STILL ALIVE.
JUST ABOUT. CAN WE SIT?
OH, OF COURSE.
I WAS JUST FINISHING UP ANYWAY.
HOW HAVE YOU BEEN? I HAVEN'T SEEN YOU SINCE...
SINCE BEFORE YOUR ACCIDENT.
YOU KNOW I'D LEFT THE PROGRAM BEFORE ALL THAT, BUT I HEARD WHAT HAPPENED TO YOU THROUGH THE GRAPEVINE.
BEEN KEEPING TRACK SINCE. YOU'VE LIVED QUITE THE LIFE, EH?

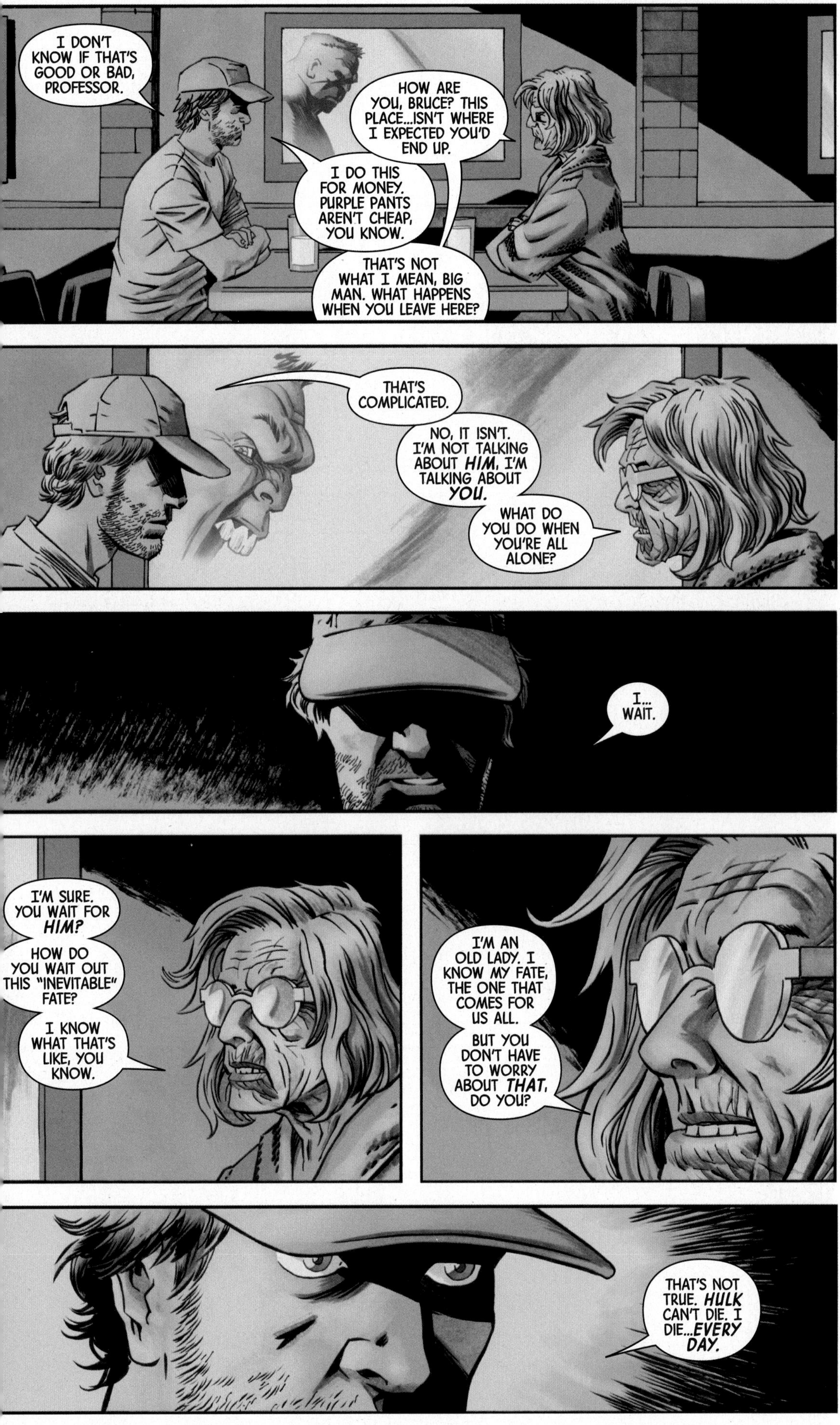
I DON'T KNOW IF THAT'S GOOD OR BAD, PROFESSOR.
HOW ARE YOU, BRUCE? THIS PLACE...ISN'T WHERE I EXPECTED YOU'D END UP.
I DO THIS FOR MONEY. PURPLE PANTS AREN'T CHEAP, YOU KNOW.
THAT'S NOT WHAT I MEAN, BIG MAN. WHAT HAPPENS WHEN YOU LEAVE HERE?
THAT'S COMPLICATED.
NO, IT ISN'T. I'M NOT TALKING ABOUT HIM, I'M TALKING ABOUT YOU.
WHAT DO YOU DO WHEN YOU'RE ALL ALONE?
I... WAIT.
I'M SURE. YOU WAIT FOR HIM?
HOW DO YOU WAIT OUT THIS "INEVITABLE" FATE?
I KNOW WHAT THAT'S LIKE, YOU KNOW.
I'M AN OLD LADY. I KNOW MY FATE, THE ONE THAT COMES FOR US ALL.
BUT YOU DON'T HAVE TO WORRY ABOUT THAT, DO YOU?
THAT'S NOT TRUE. HULK CAN'T DIE. I DIE...EVERY DAY.

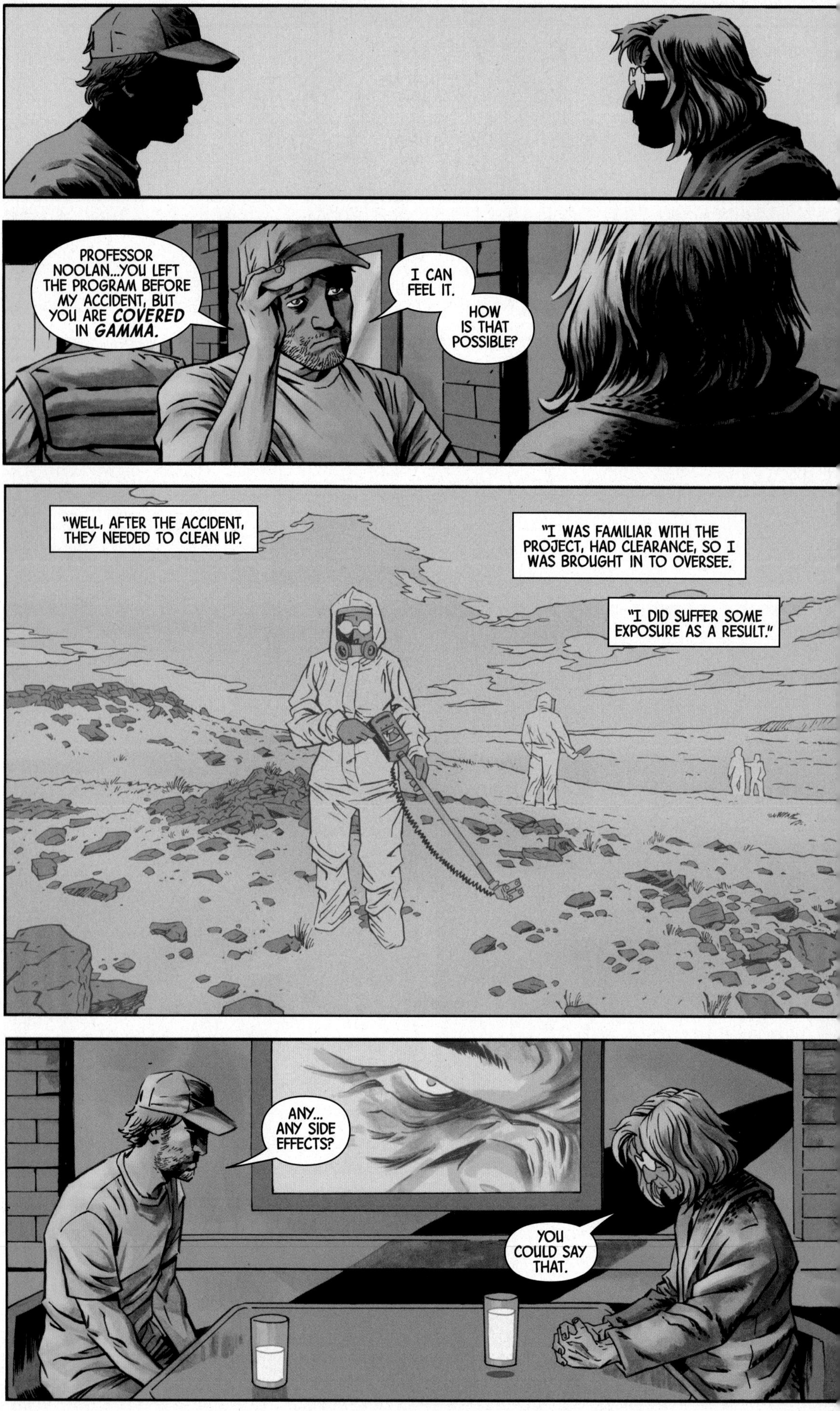
PROFESSOR NOOLAN...YOU LEFT THE PROGRAM BEFORE MY ACCIDENT, BUT YOU ARE COVERED IN GAMMA.
I CAN FEEL IT.
HOW IS THAT POSSIBLE?
"WELL, AFTER THE ACCIDENT, THEY NEEDED TO CLEAN UP.
"I WAS FAMILIAR WITH THE PROJECT, HAD CLEARANCE, SO I WAS BROUGHT IN TO OVERSEE.
"I DID SUFFER SOME EXPOSURE AS A RESULT."
ANY... ANY SIDE EFFECTS?
YOU COULD SAY THAT.

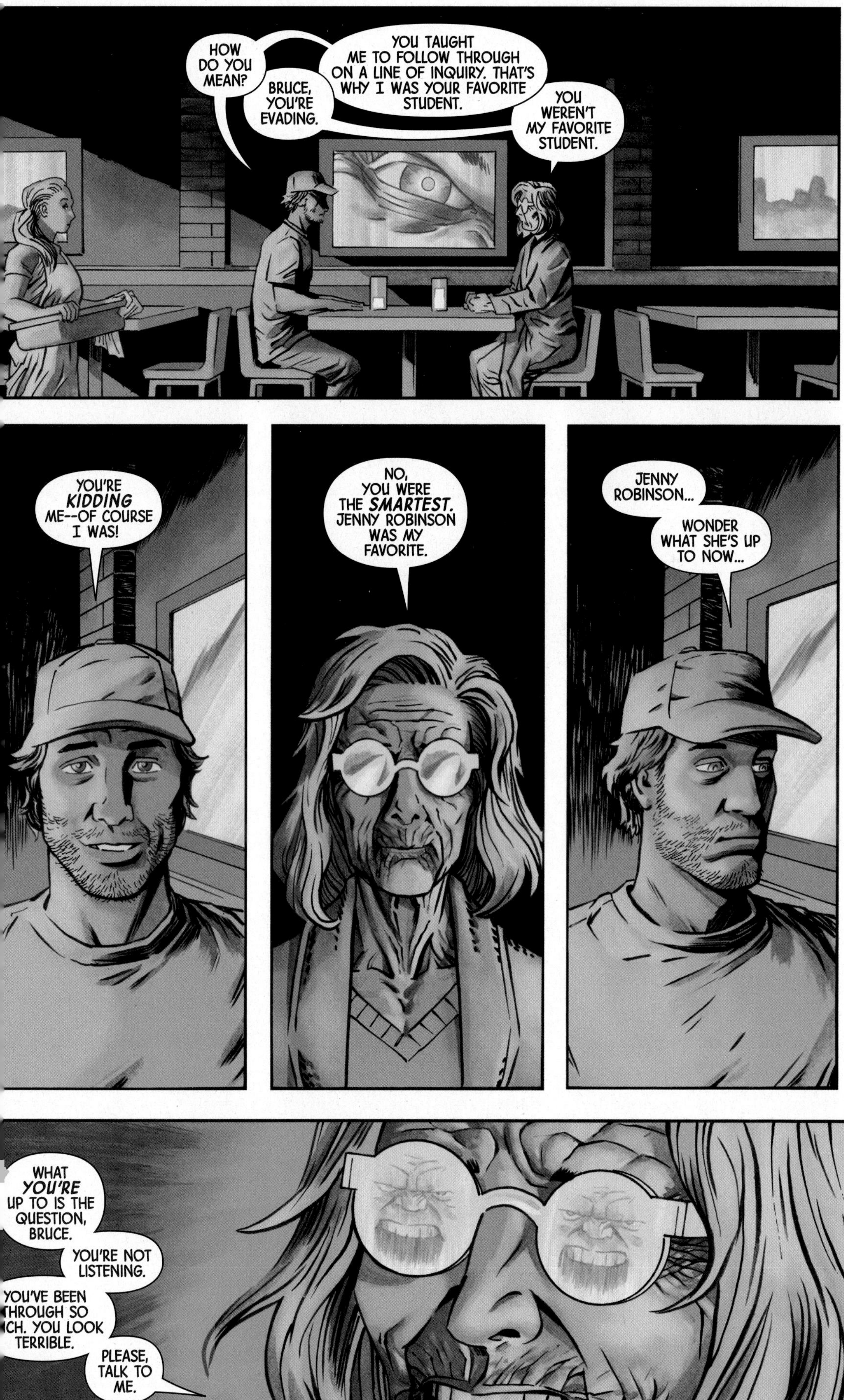
HOW DO YOU MEAN?
BRUCE, YOU'RE EVADING.
YOU TAUGHT ME TO FOLLOW THROUGH ON A LINE OF INQUIRY. THAT'S WHY I WAS YOUR FAVORITE STUDENT.
YOU WEREN'T MY FAVORITE STUDENT.
YOU'RE KIDDING ME--OF COURSE I WAS!
NO, YOU WERE THE SMARTEST. JENNY ROBINSON WAS MY FAVORITE.
JENNY ROBINSON...
WONDER WHAT SHE'S UP TO NOW...
WHAT YOU'RE UP TO IS THE QUESTION, BRUCE.
YOU'RE NOT LISTENING.
YOU'VE BEEN THROUGH SO CH. YOU LOOK TERRIBLE.
PLEASE, TALK TO ME.

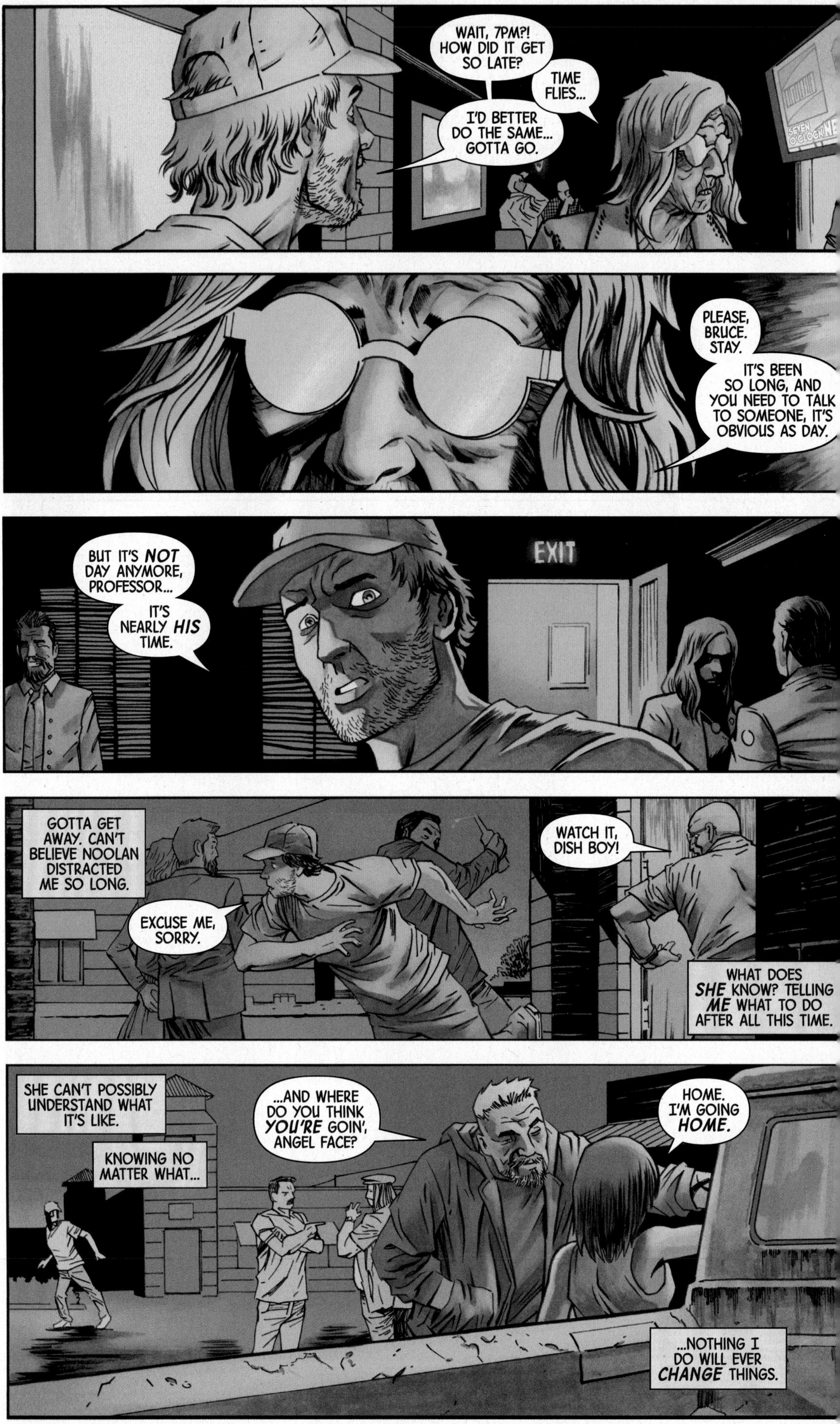
WAIT, 7PM?! HOW DID IT GET SO LATE?
TIME FLIES...
I'D BETTER DO THE SAME... GOTTA GO.
SEVEN O'CLOCK NE
PLEASE, BRUCE. STAY.
IT'S BEEN SO LONG, AND YOU NEED TO TALK TO SOMEONE, IT'S OBVIOUS AS DAY.
BUT IT'S NOT DAY ANYMORE, PROFESSOR...
IT'S NEARLY HIS TIME.
EXIT
GOTTA GET AWAY. CAN'T BELIEVE NOOLAN DISTRACTED ME SO LONG.
EXCUSE ME, SORRY.
WATCH IT, DISH BOY!
WHAT DOES SHE KNOW? TELLING ME WHAT TO DO AFTER ALL THIS TIME.
SHE CAN'T POSSIBLY UNDERSTAND WHAT IT'S LIKE.
KNOWING NO MATTER WHAT...
...AND WHERE DO YOU THINK YOU'RE GOIN', ANGEL FACE?
HOME. I'M GOING HOME.
...NOTHING I DO WILL EVER CHANGE THINGS.

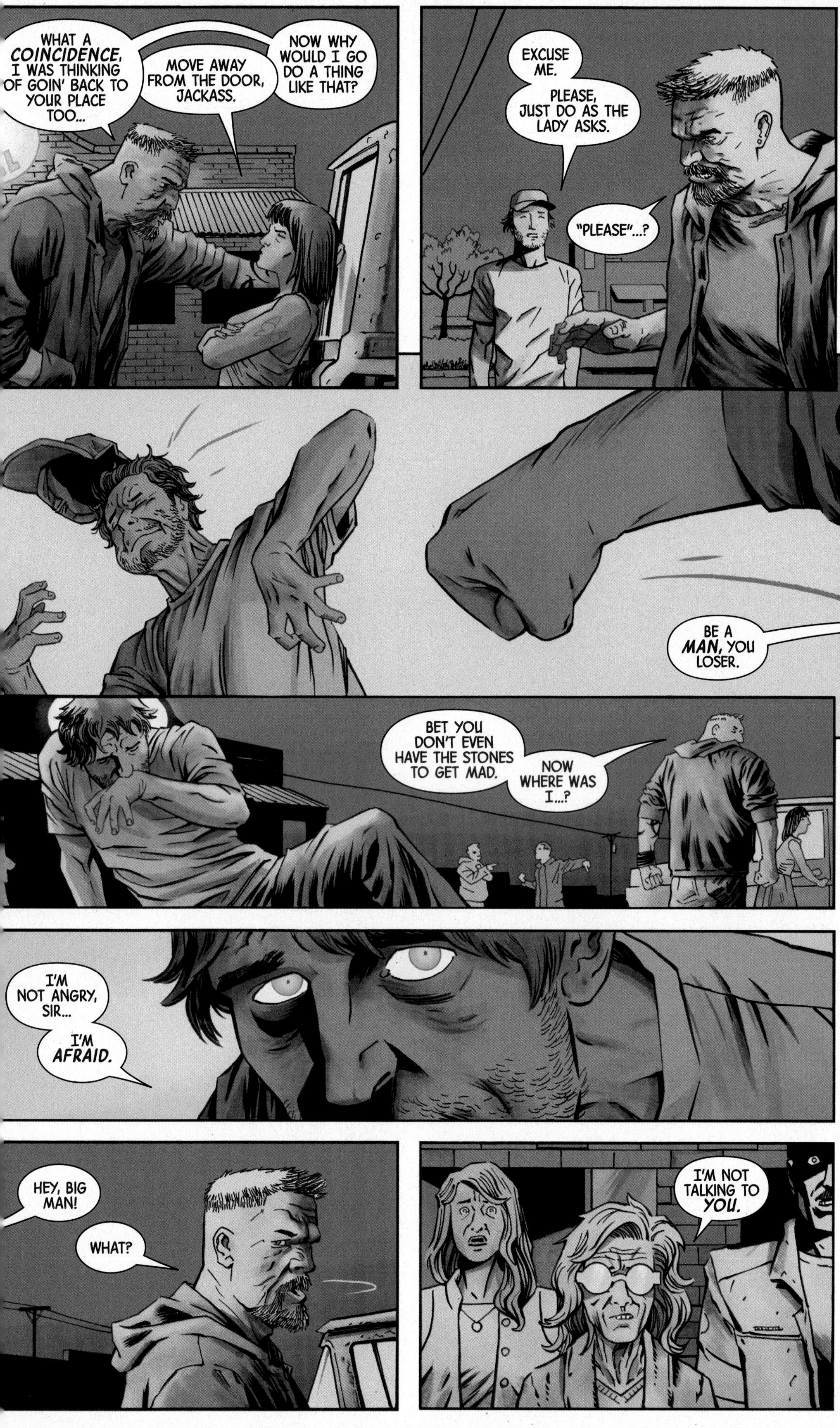
WHAT A COINCIDENCE, I WAS THINKING OF GOIN' BACK TO YOUR PLACE TOO...
MOVE AWAY FROM THE DOOR, JACKASS.
NOW WHY WOULD I GO DO A THING LIKE THAT?
EXCUSE ME.
PLEASE, JUST DO AS THE LADY ASKS.
"PLEASE"...?
BE A MAN, YOU LOSER.
BET YOU DON'T EVEN HAVE THE STONES TO GET MAD.
NOW WHERE WAS I...?
I'M NOT ANGRY, SIR...
I'M AFRAID.
HEY, BIG MAN!
WHAT?
I'M NOT TALKING TO YOU.

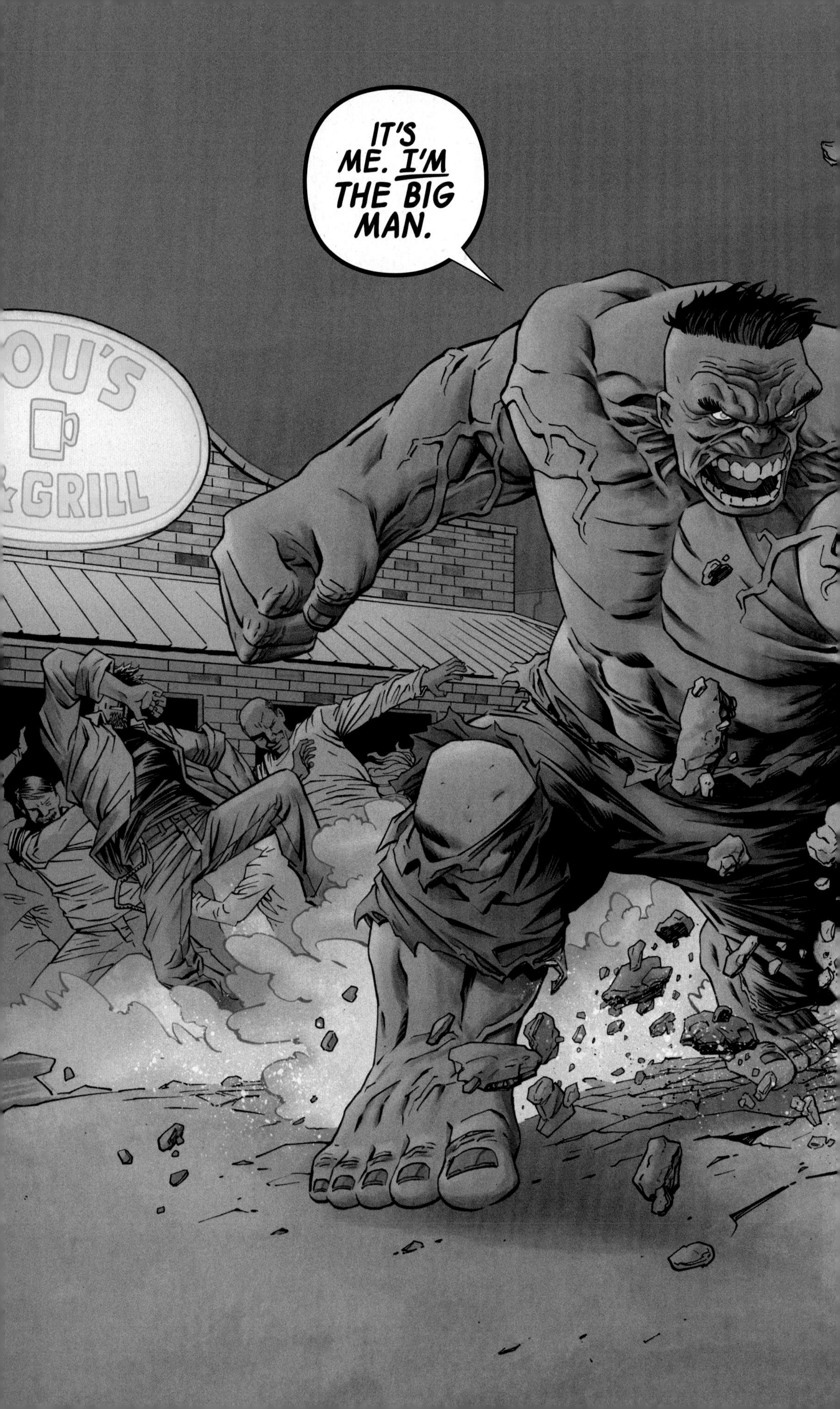
IT'S ME. I'M THE BIG MAN.
OU'S
&GRILL

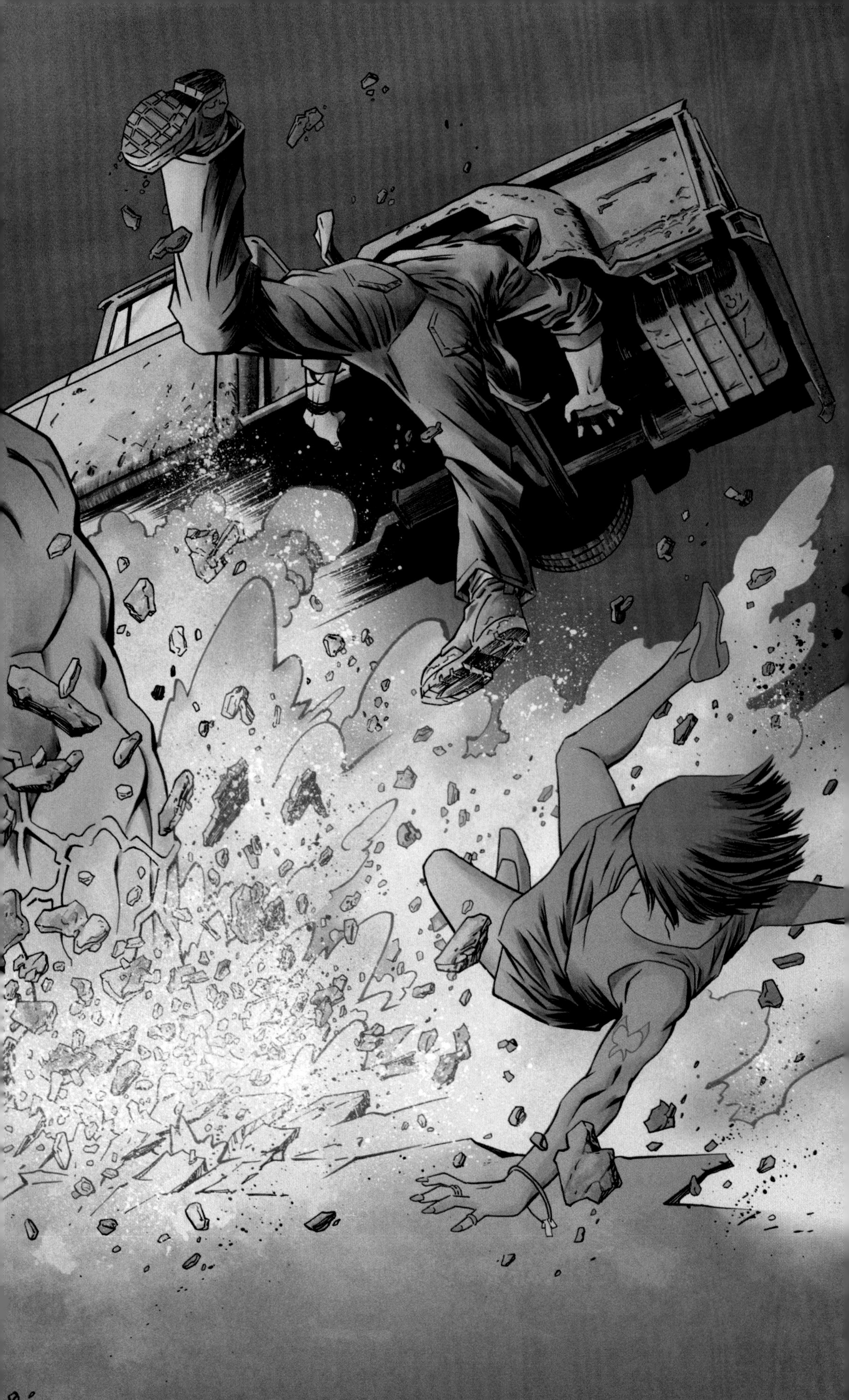

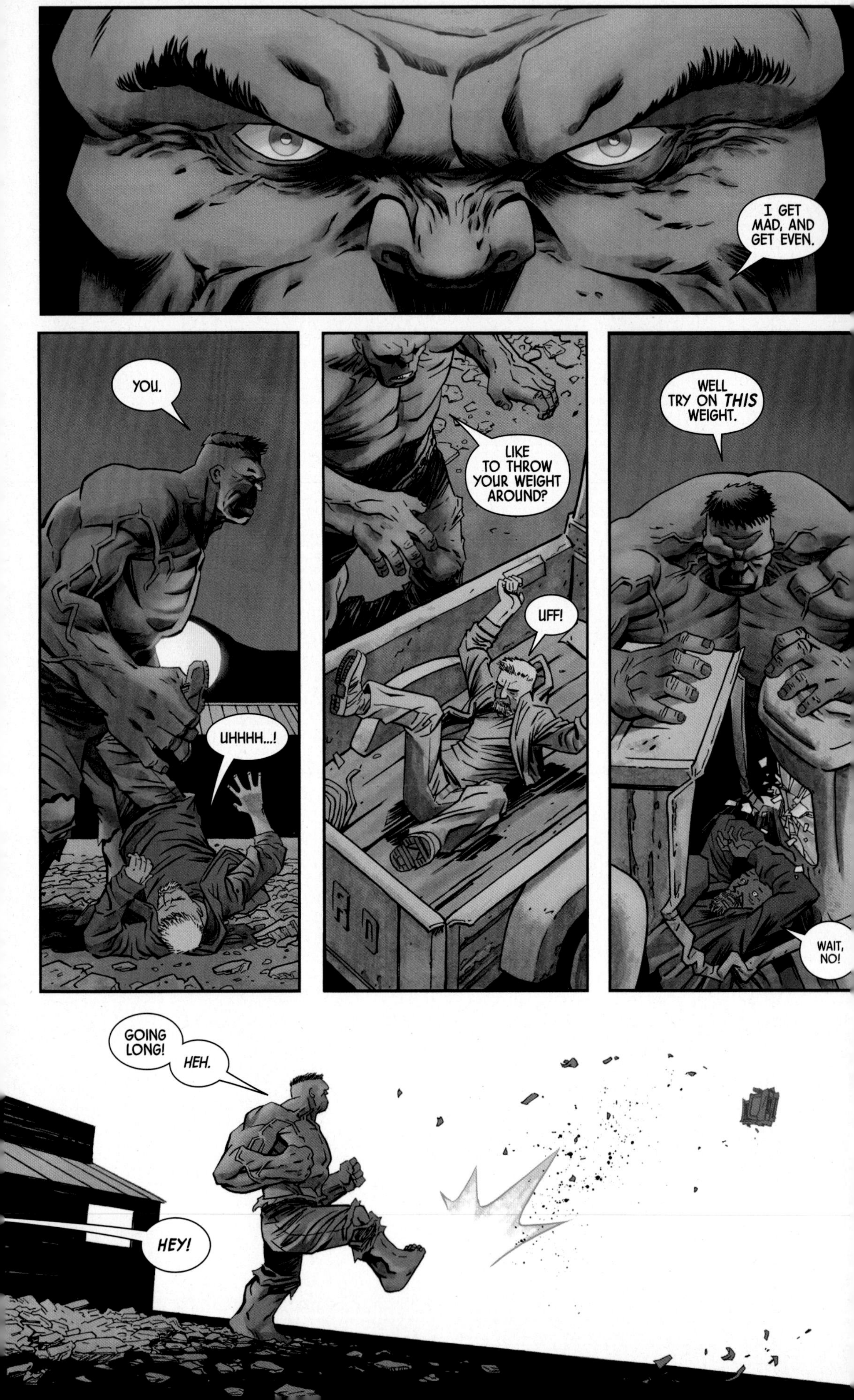
I GET MAD, AND GET EVEN.
YOU.
UHHHH...!
LIKE TO THROW YOUR WEIGHT AROUND?
UFF!
WELL TRY ON THIS WEIGHT.
WAIT, NO!
GOING LONG!
HEH.
HEY!

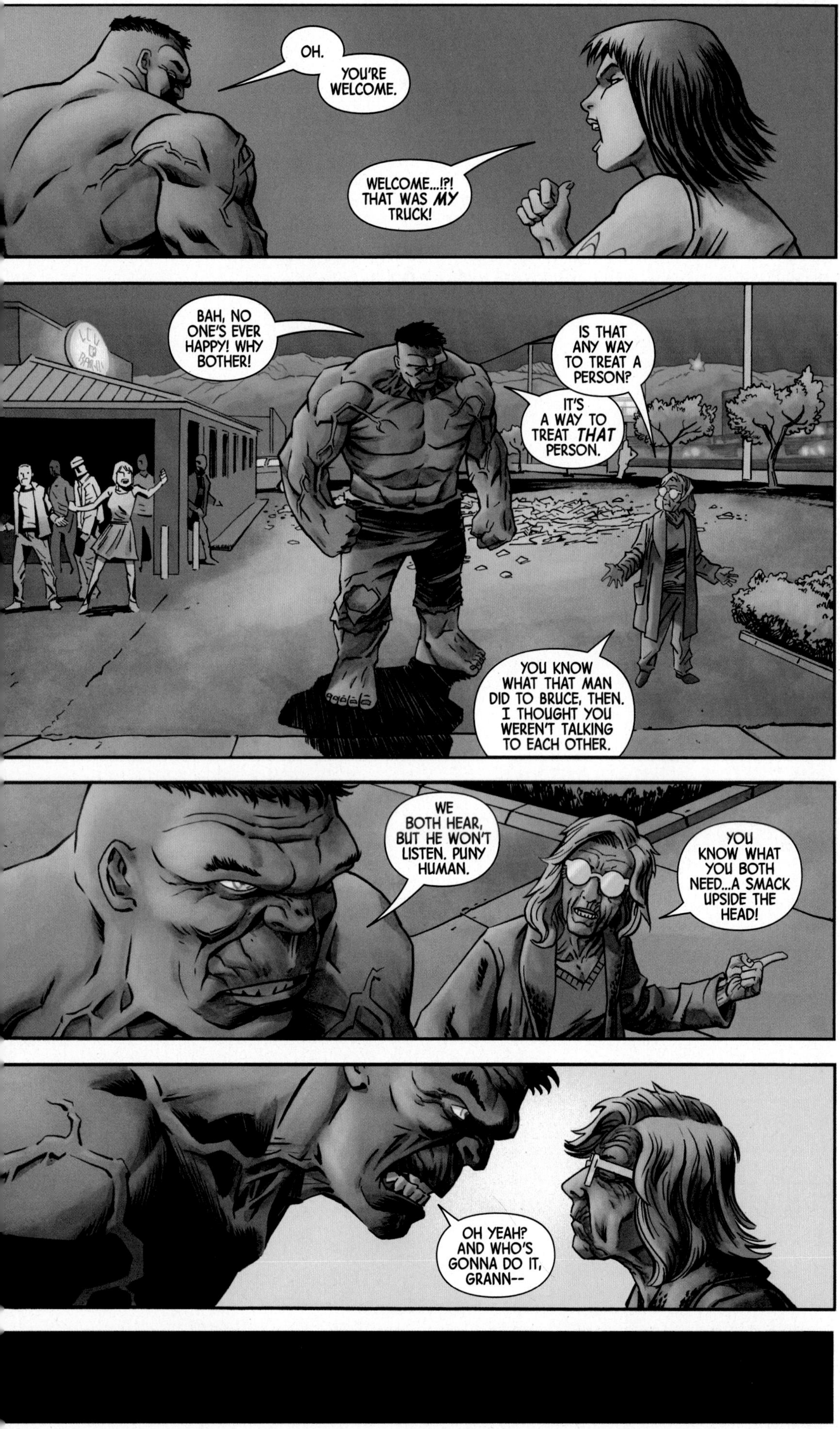
OH.
YOU'RE WELCOME.
WELCOME...!?! THAT WAS MY TRUCK!
BAH, NO ONE'S EVER HAPPY! WHY BOTHER!
IS THAT ANY WAY TO TREAT A PERSON?
IT'S A WAY TO TREAT THAT PERSON.
YOU KNOW WHAT THAT MAN DID TO BRUCE, THEN. I THOUGHT YOU WEREN'T TALKING TO EACH OTHER.
WE BOTH HEAR, BUT HE WON'T LISTEN. PUNY HUMAN.
YOU KNOW WHAT YOU BOTH NEED...A SMACK UPSIDE THE HEAD!
OH YEAH? AND WHO'S GONNA DO IT, GRANN--

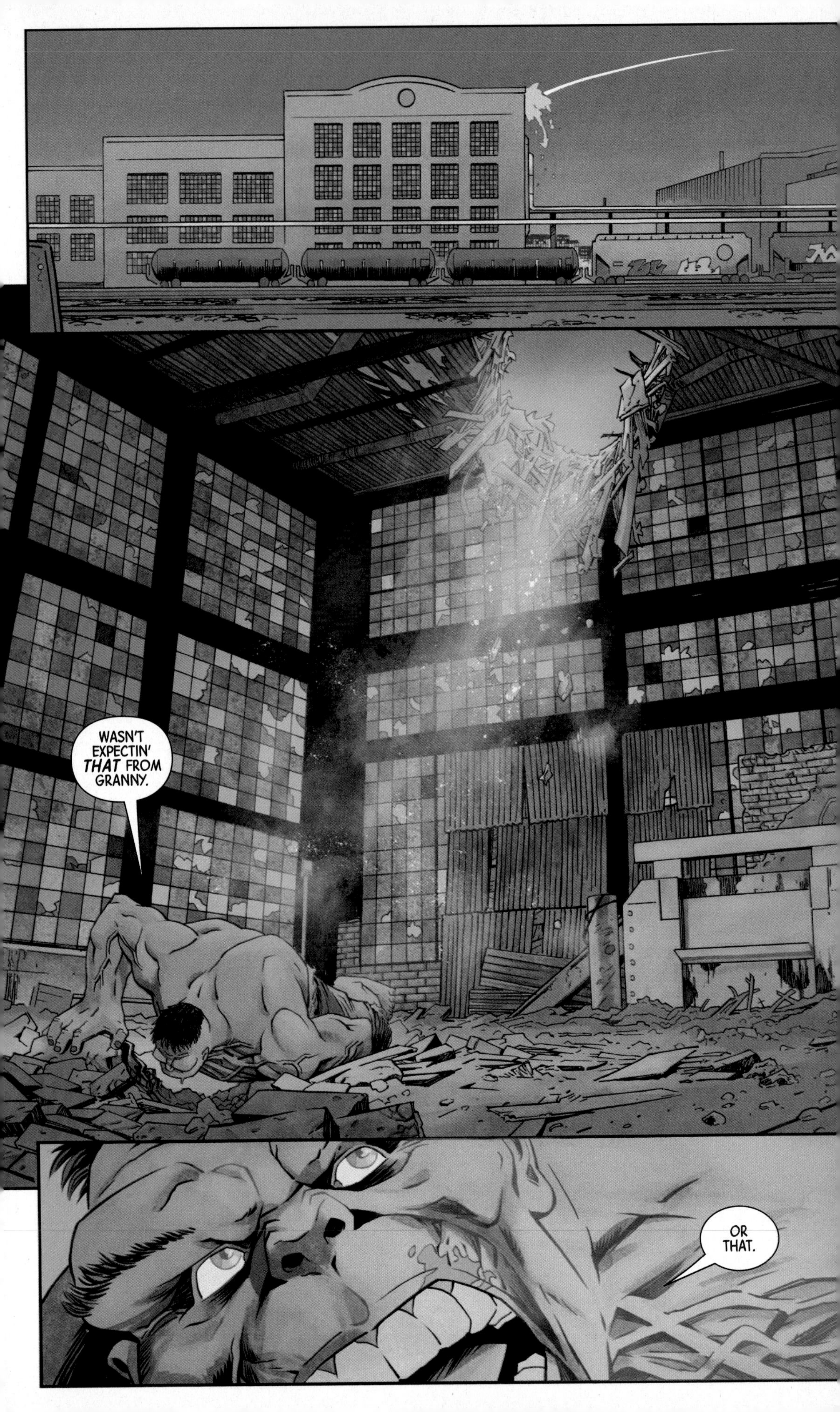
WASN'T EXPECTIN' *THAT* FROM GRANNY.
OR THAT.

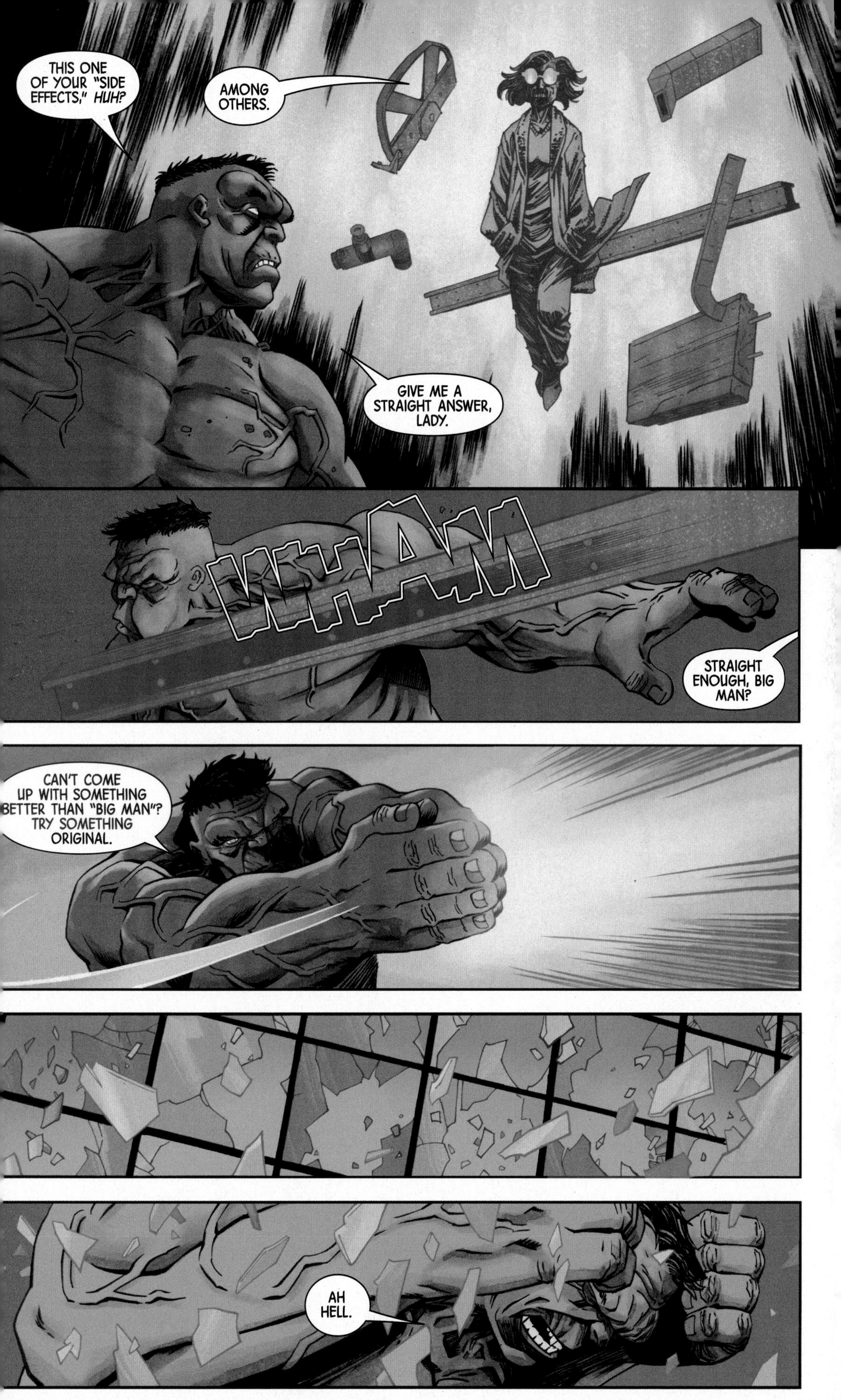

THIS ONE OF YOUR "SIDE EFFECTS," HUH?
AMONG OTHERS.
GIVE ME A STRAIGHT ANSWER, LADY.
WHAM
STRAIGHT ENOUGH, BIG MAN?
CAN'T COME UP WITH SOMETHING BETTER THAN "BIG MAN"? TRY SOMETHING ORIGINAL.
AH HELL.

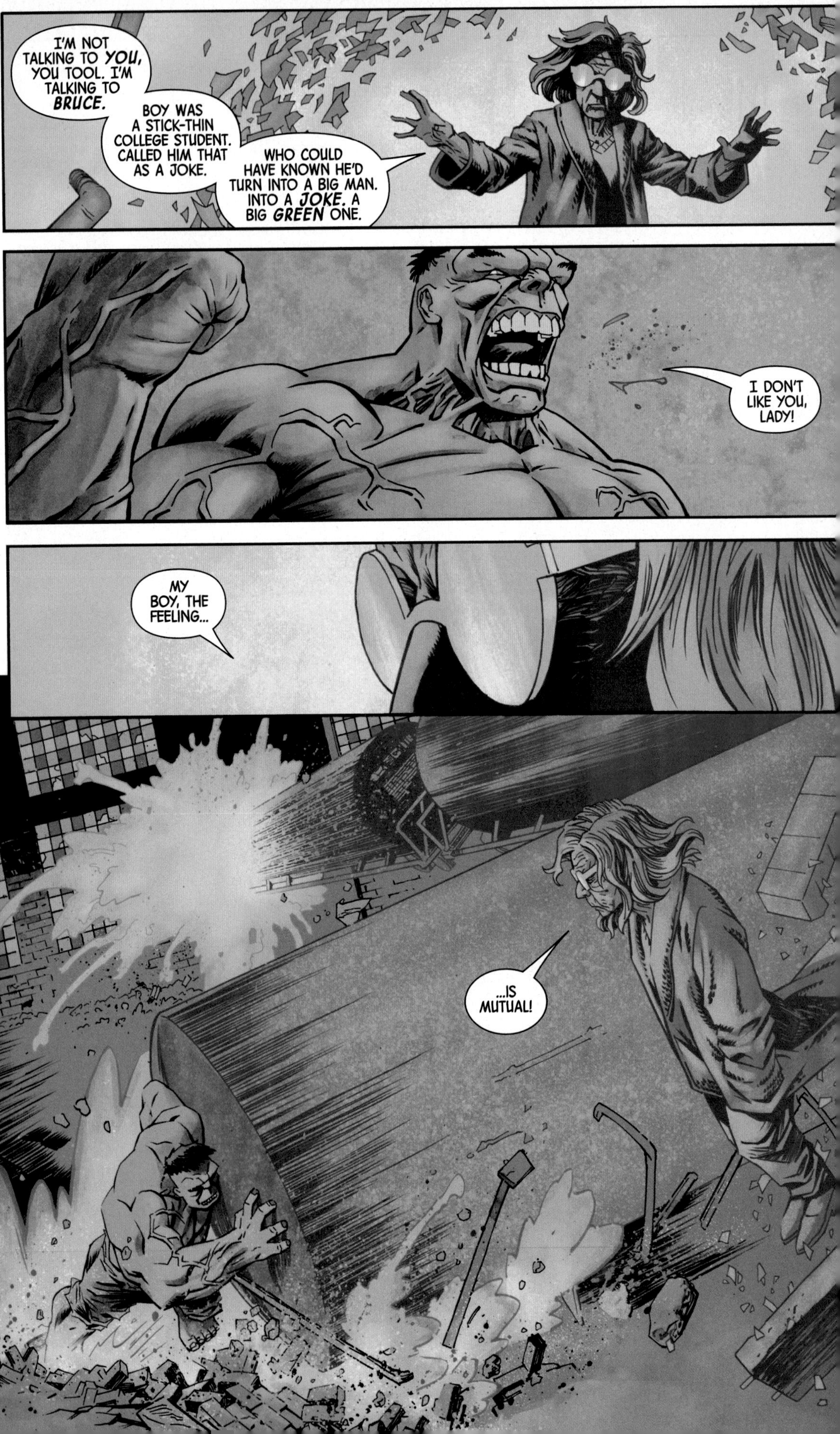
I'M NOT TALKING TO YOU, YOU TOOL. I'M TALKING TO BRUCE.
BOY WAS A STICK-THIN COLLEGE STUDENT. CALLED HIM THAT AS A JOKE.
WHO COULD HAVE KNOWN HE'D TURN INTO A BIG MAN. INTO A JOKE. A BIG GREEN ONE.
I DON'T LIKE YOU, LADY!
MY BOY, THE FEELING...
...IS MUTUAL!

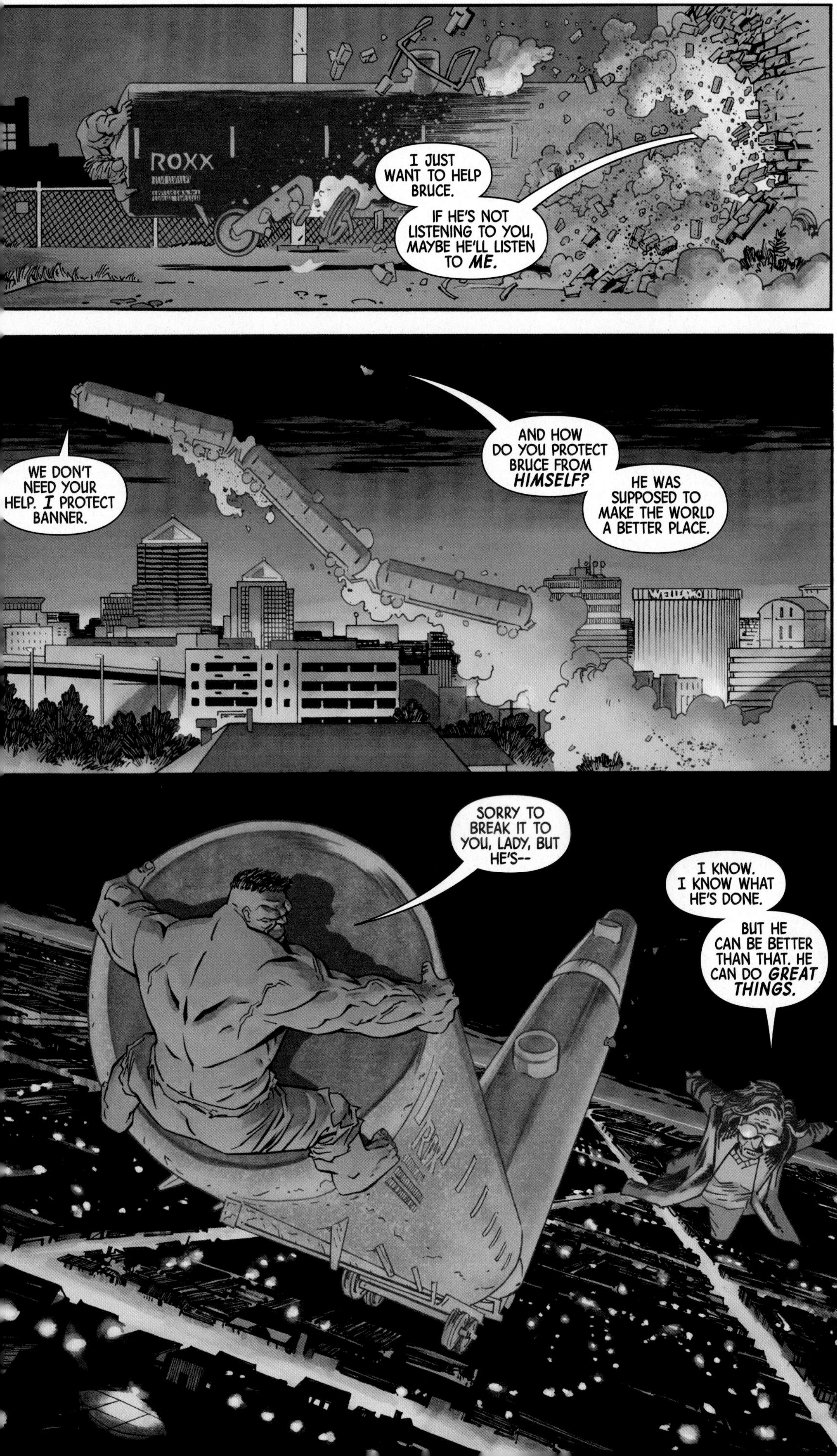

ROXX
I JUST WANT TO HELP BRUCE.
IF HE'S NOT LISTENING TO YOU, MAYBE HE'LL LISTEN TO *ME.*
WE DON'T NEED YOUR HELP. *I* PROTECT BANNER.
AND HOW DO YOU PROTECT BRUCE FROM *HIMSELF?*
HE WAS SUPPOSED TO MAKE THE WORLD A BETTER PLACE.
SORRY TO BREAK IT TO YOU, LADY, BUT HE'S--
I KNOW. I KNOW WHAT HE'S DONE.
BUT HE CAN BE BETTER THAN THAT. HE CAN DO *GREAT THINGS.*

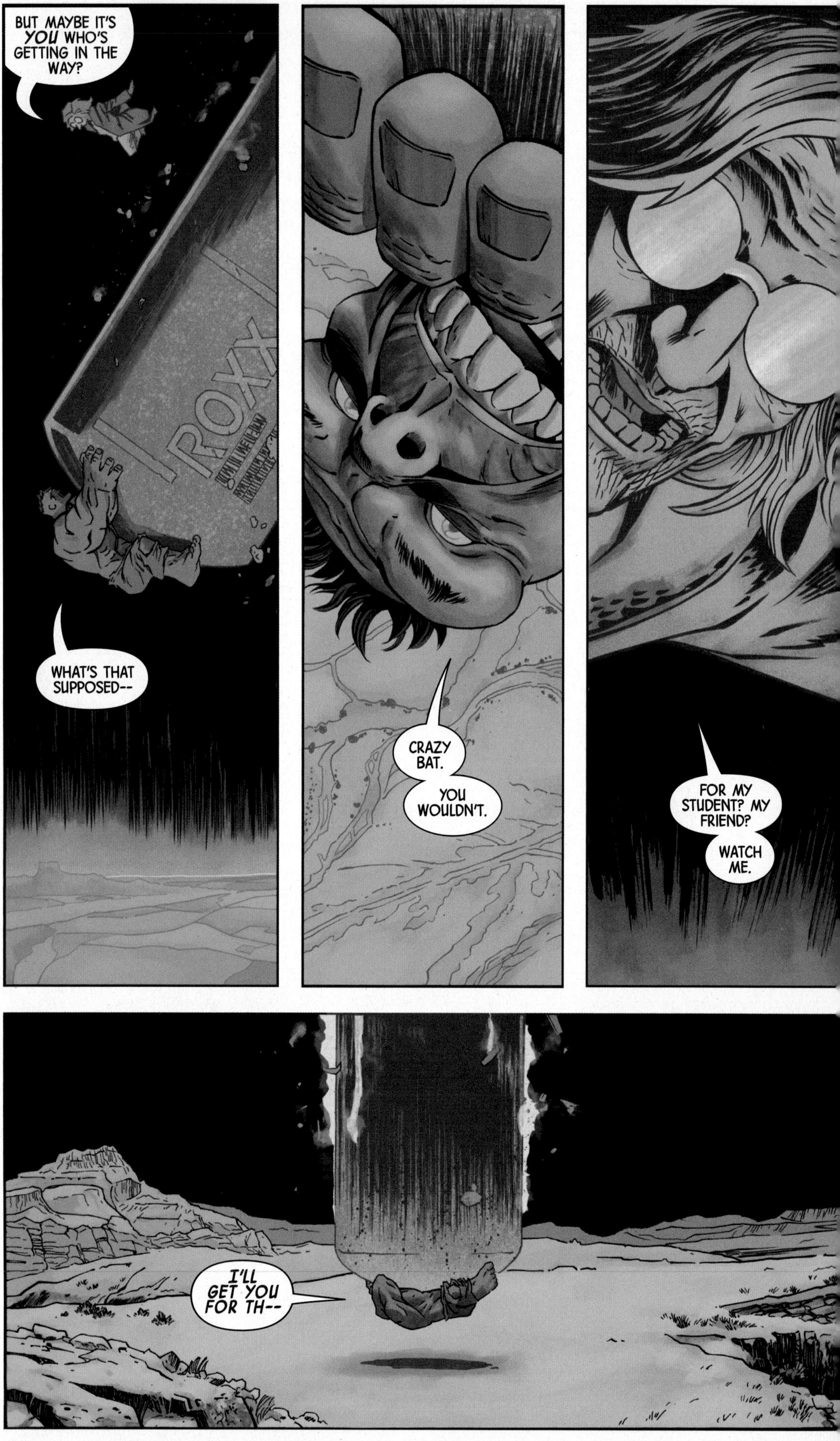
BUT MAYBE IT'S *YOU* WHO'S GETTING IN THE WAY?
WHAT'S THAT SUPPOSED--
CRAZY BAT.
YOU WOULDN'T.
FOR MY STUDENT? MY FRIEND?
WATCH ME.
I'LL GET YOU FOR TH--

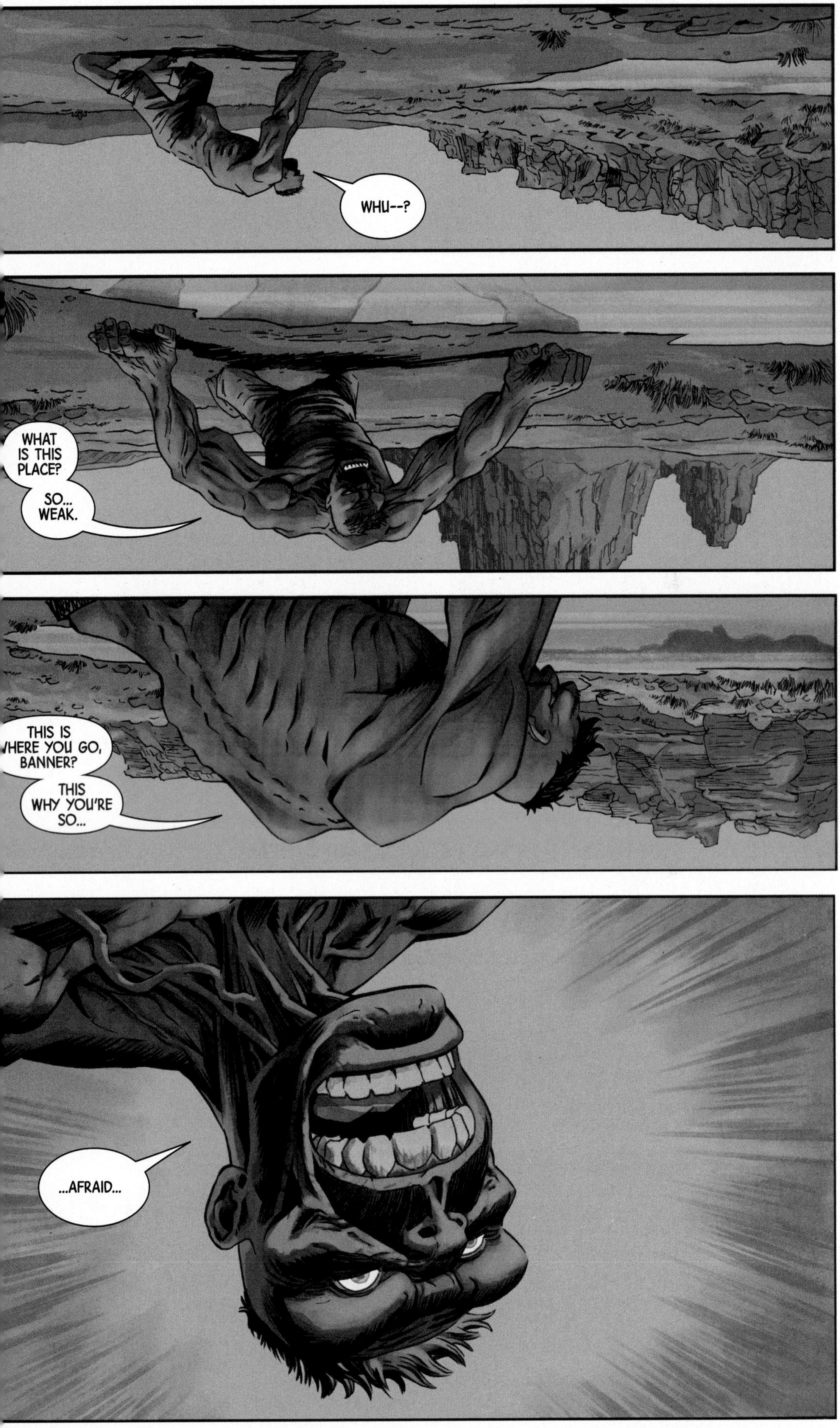
WHU--?
WHAT IS THIS PLACE?
SO... WEAK.
THIS IS WHERE YOU GO, BANNER?
THIS WHY YOU'RE SO...
...AFRAID...

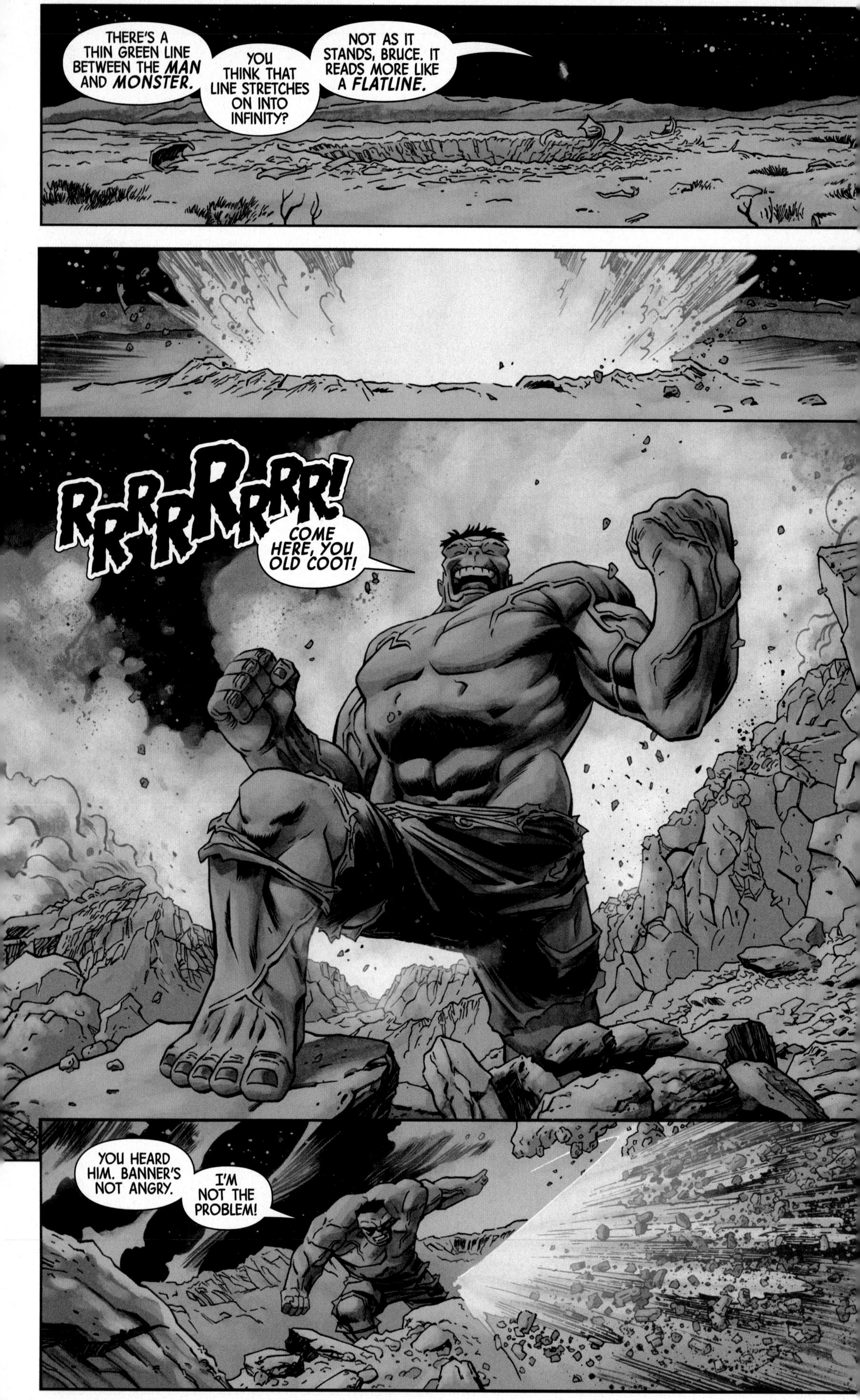
THERE'S A THIN GREEN LINE BETWEEN THE MAN AND MONSTER.
YOU THINK THAT LINE STRETCHES ON INTO INFINITY?
NOT AS IT STANDS, BRUCE. IT READS MORE LIKE A FLATLINE.
RRRRRRRR!
COME HERE, YOU OLD COOT!
YOU HEARD HIM. BANNER'S NOT ANGRY.
I'M NOT THE PROBLEM!

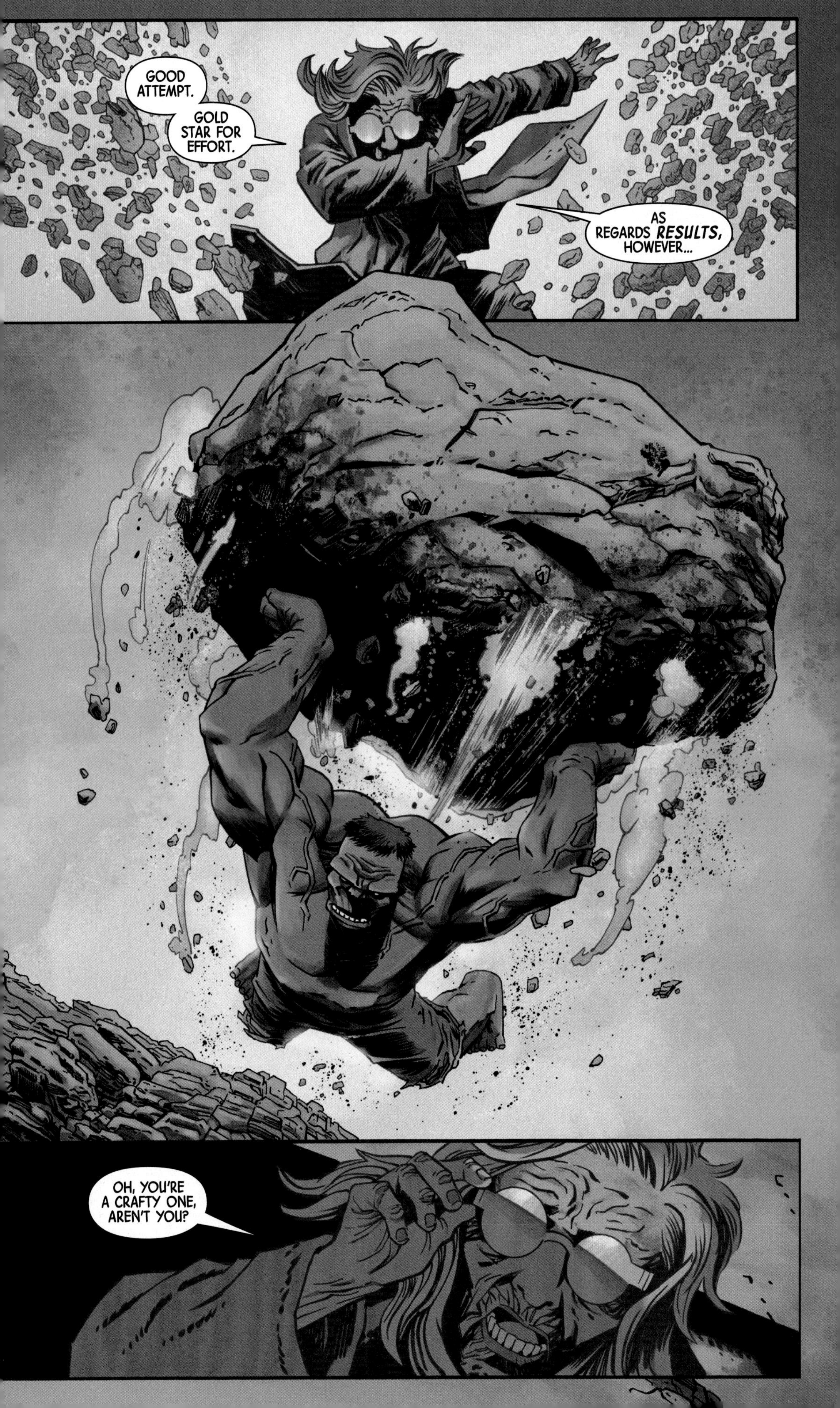
GOOD ATTEMPT.
GOLD STAR FOR EFFORT.
AS REGARDS RESULTS, HOWEVER...
OH, YOU'RE A CRAFTY ONE, AREN'T YOU?

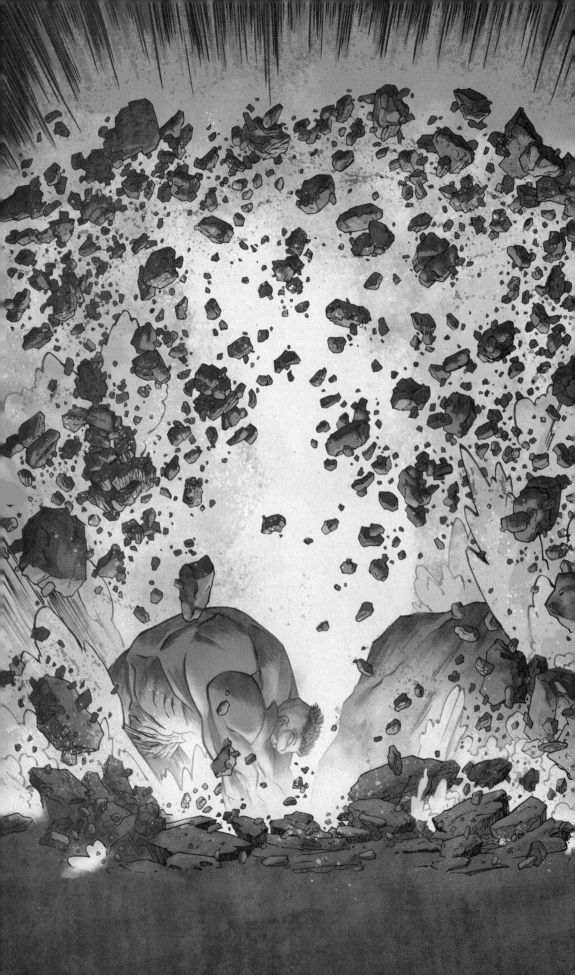

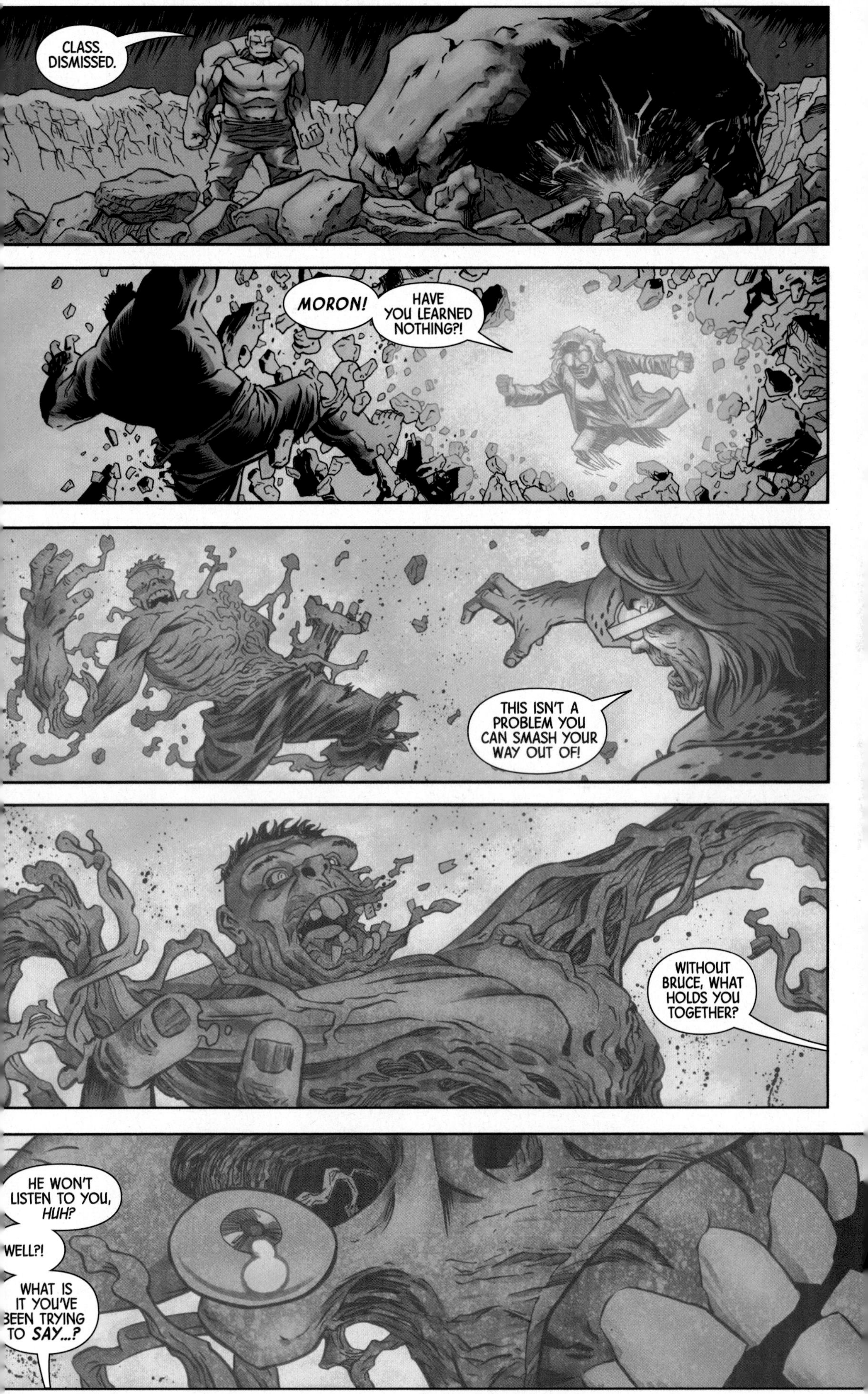
CLASS. DISMISSED.
MORON!
HAVE YOU LEARNED NOTHING?!
THIS ISN'T A PROBLEM YOU CAN SMASH YOUR WAY OUT OF!
WITHOUT BRUCE, WHAT HOLDS YOU TOGETHER?
HE WON'T LISTEN TO YOU, *HUH?*
WELL?!
WHAT IS IT YOU'VE BEEN TRYING TO *SAY...?*

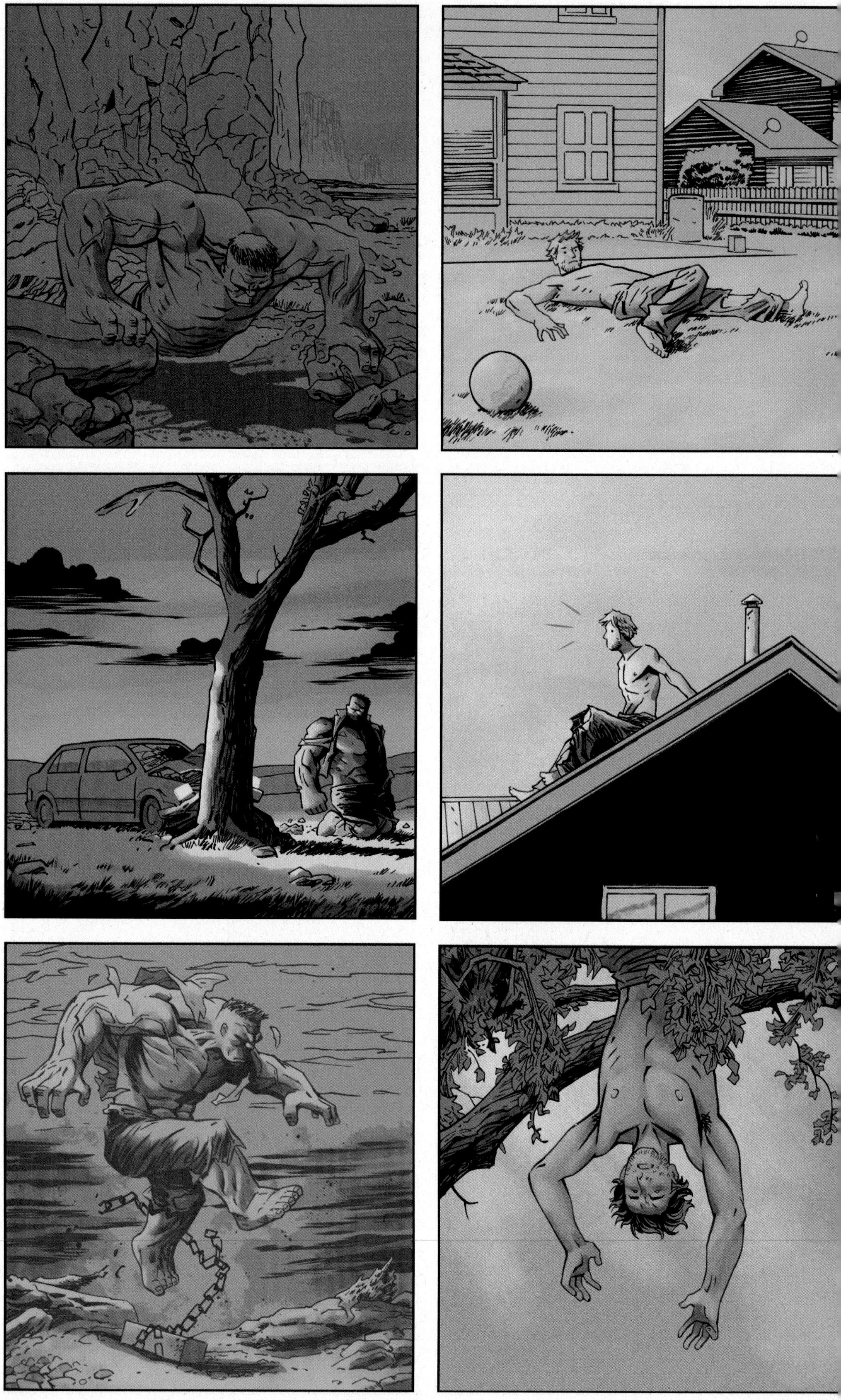

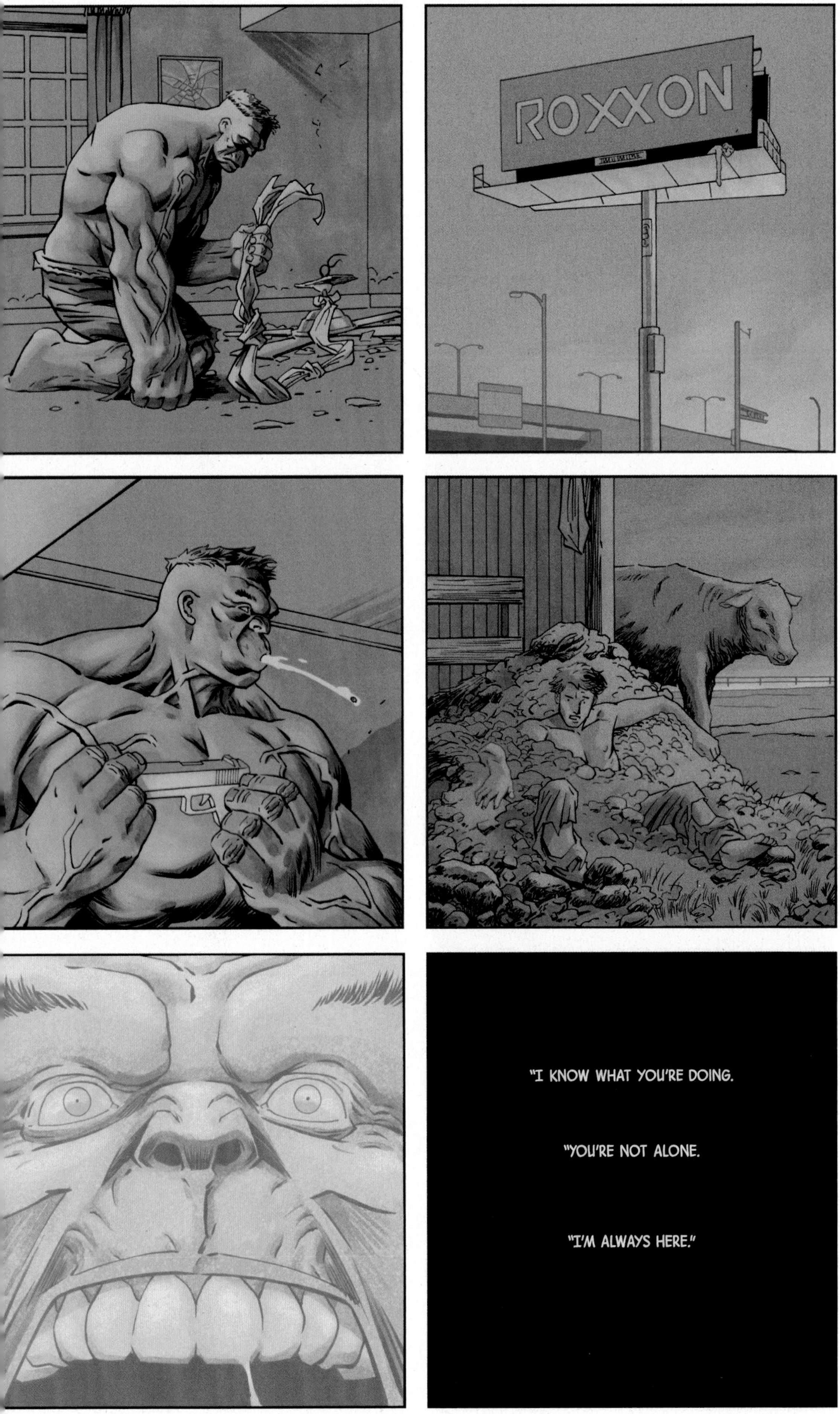
ROXXON
"I KNOW WHAT YOU'RE DOING.
"YOU'RE NOT ALONE.
"I'M ALWAYS HERE."

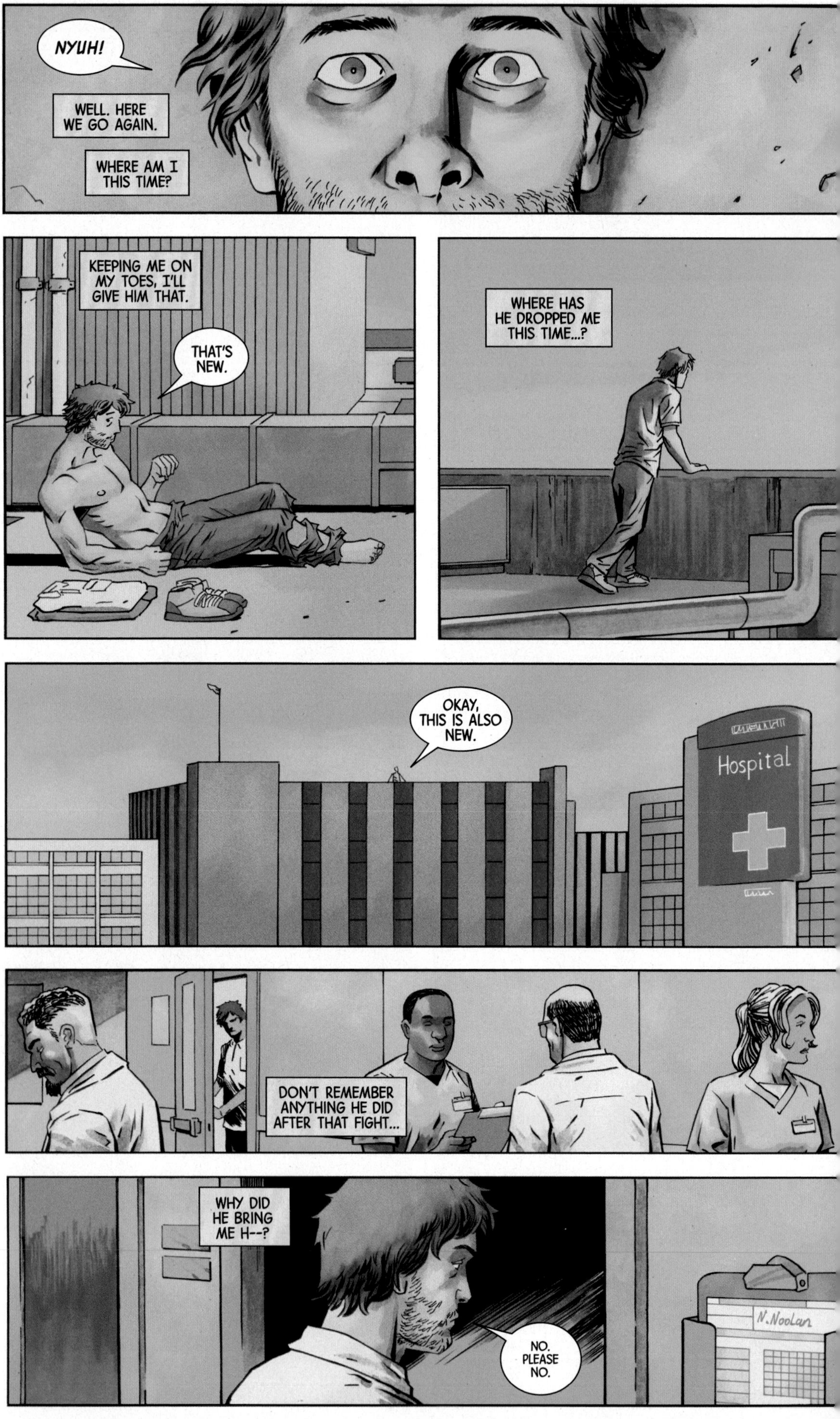
NYUH!
WELL. HERE WE GO AGAIN.
WHERE AM I THIS TIME?
KEEPING ME ON MY TOES, I'LL GIVE HIM THAT.
THAT'S NEW.
WHERE HAS HE DROPPED ME THIS TIME...?
OKAY, THIS IS ALSO NEW.
Hospital
DON'T REMEMBER ANYTHING HE DID AFTER THAT FIGHT...
WHY DID HE BRING ME H--?
N. Noolan
NO. PLEASE NO.

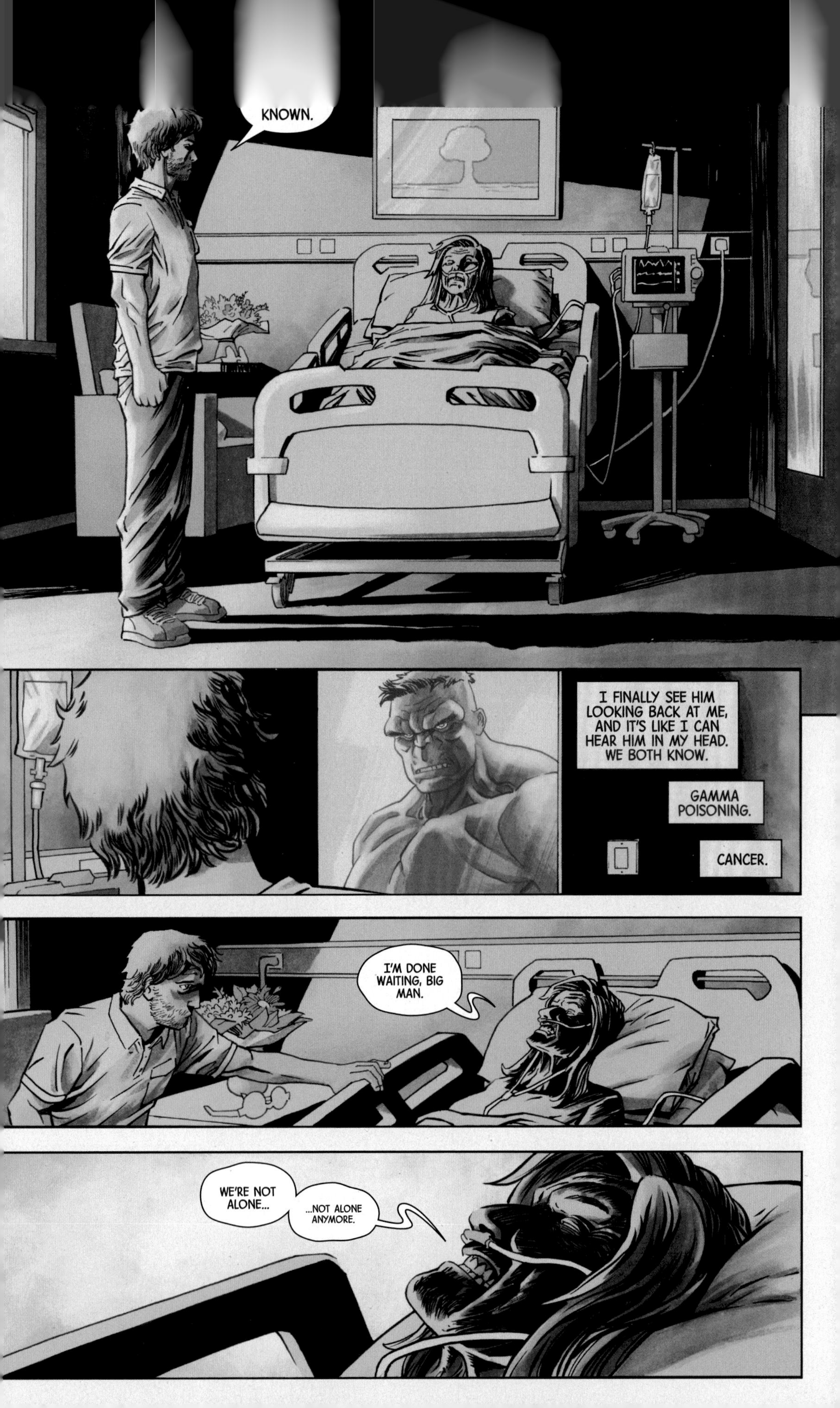
KNOWN.
I FINALLY SEE HIM LOOKING BACK AT ME, AND IT'S LIKE I CAN HEAR HIM IN MY HEAD. WE BOTH KNOW.
GAMMA POISONING.
CANCER.
I'M DONE WAITING, BIG MAN.
WE'RE NOT ALONE...
...NOT ALONE ANYMORE.

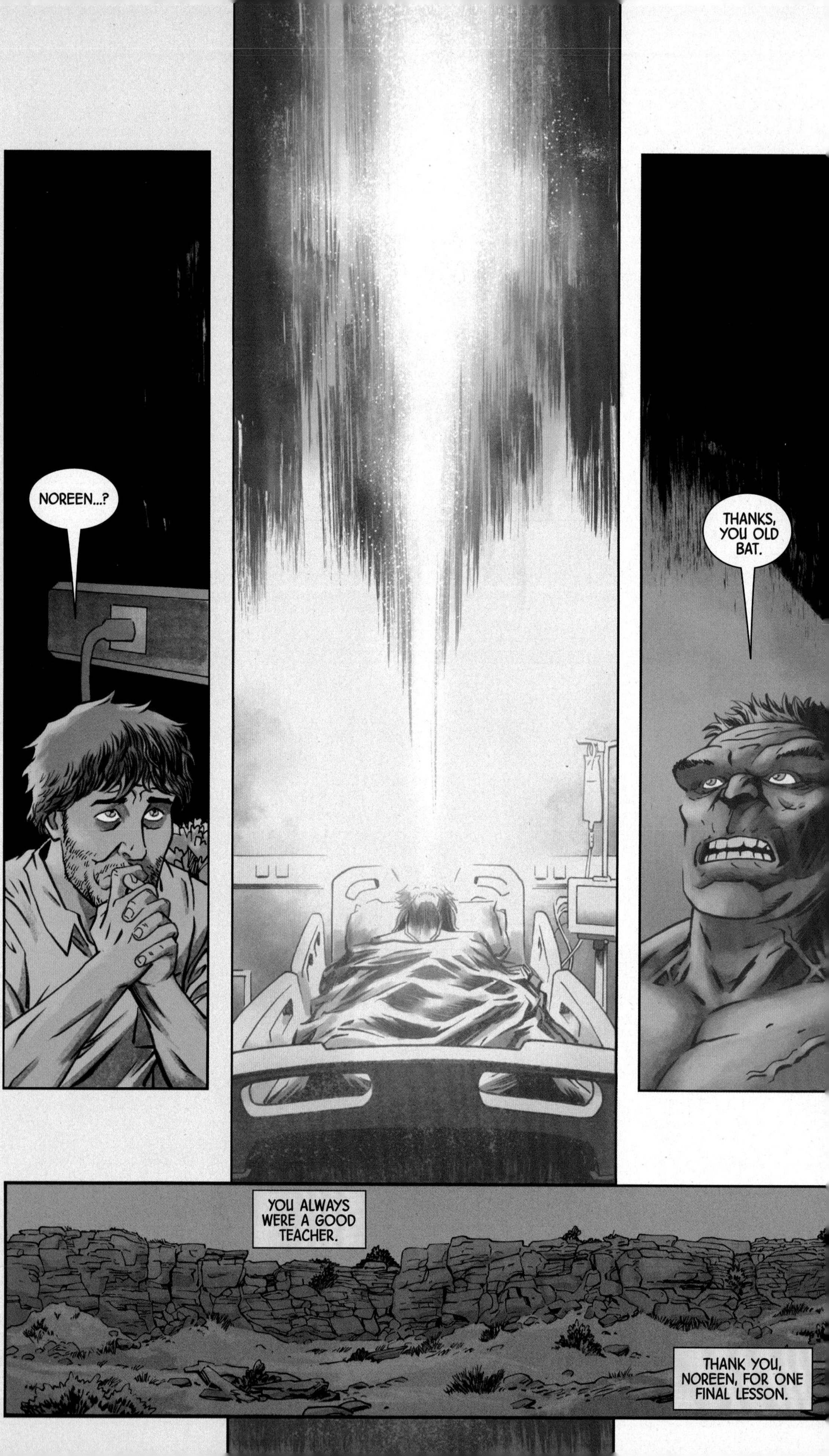
NOREEN...?
THANKS, YOU OLD BAT.
YOU ALWAYS WERE A GOOD TEACHER.
THANK YOU, NOREEN, FOR ONE FINAL LESSON.

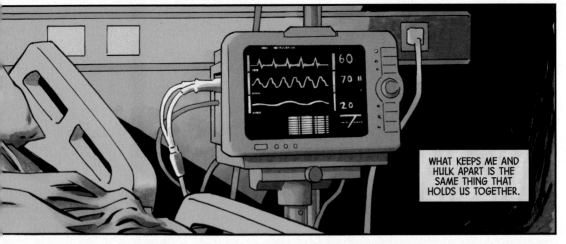

WHAT KEEPS ME AND HULK APART IS THE SAME THING THAT HOLDS US TOGETHER.

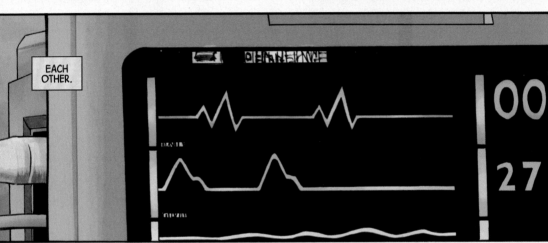

EACH OTHER.

THE GAMMA.

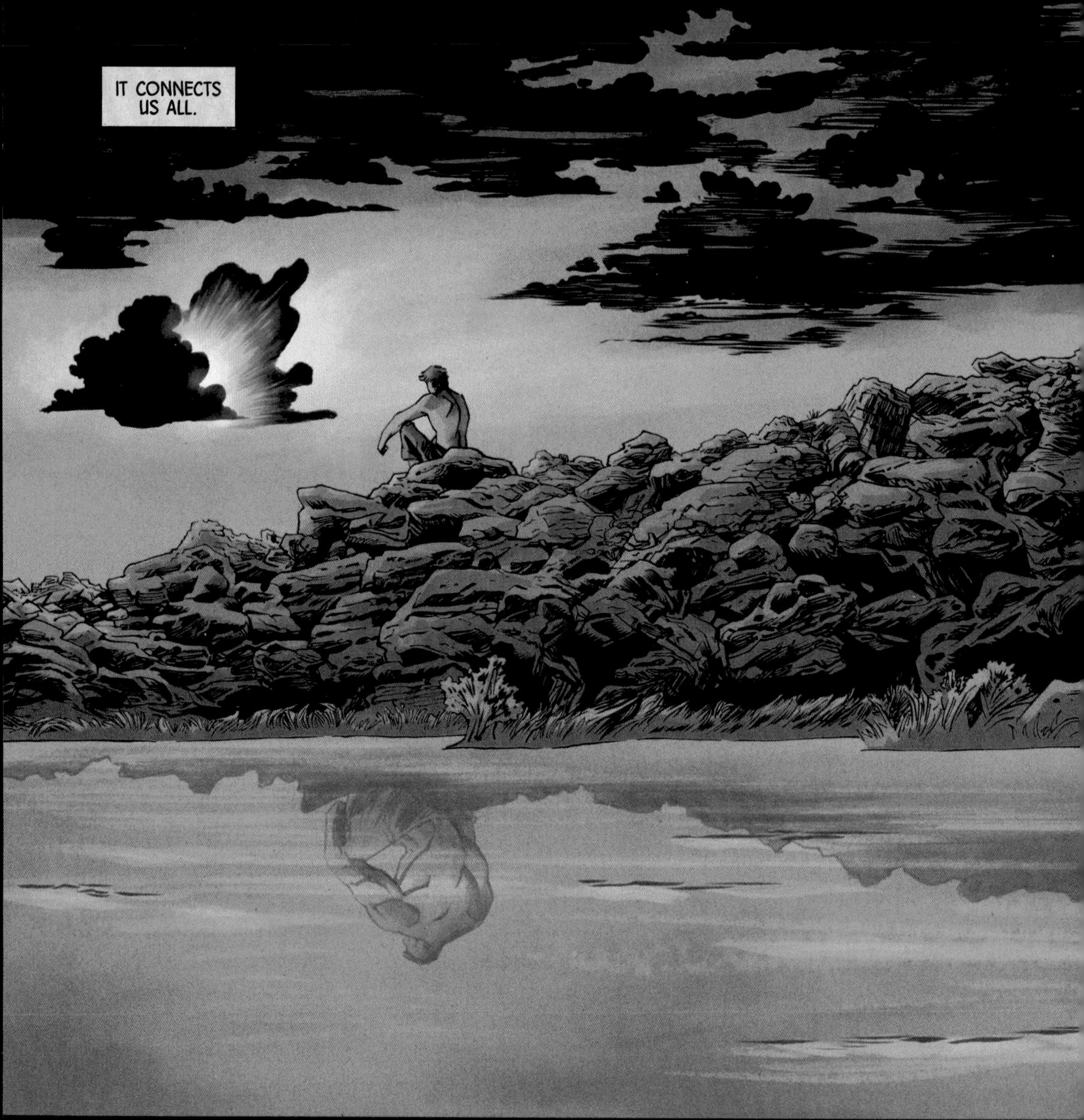
IT CONNECTS US ALL.

FLATLINE

DECLAN SHALVEY STORY, ART, COLORS & COVER

VC'S CORY PETIT LETTERER **KEVIN NOWLAN** VARIANT COVER

SARAH BRUNSTAD ASSOCIATE EDITOR WIL MOSS EDITOR TOM BREVOORT EXECUTIVE EDITOR C.B. CEBULSKI EDITOR IN CHI

HULK CREATED BY STAN LEE & JACK KIRBY

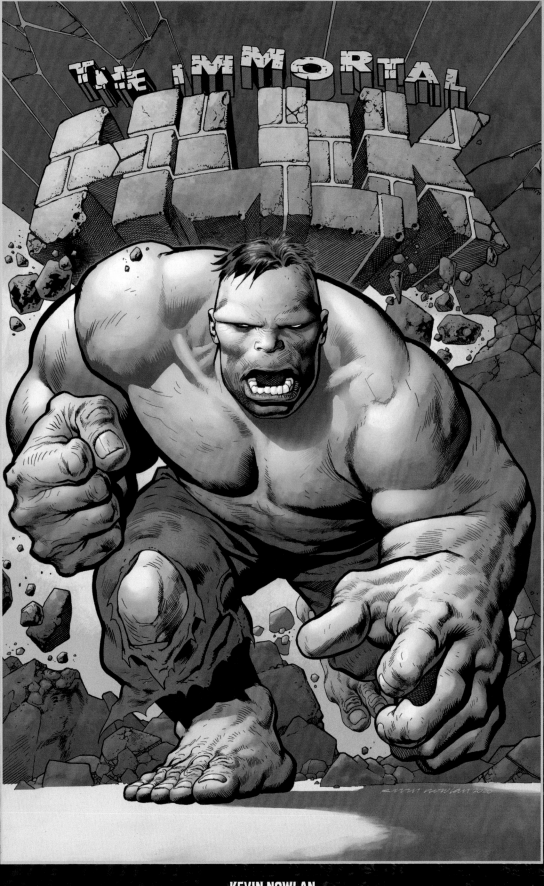

KEVIN NOWLAN
FLATLINE VARIANT

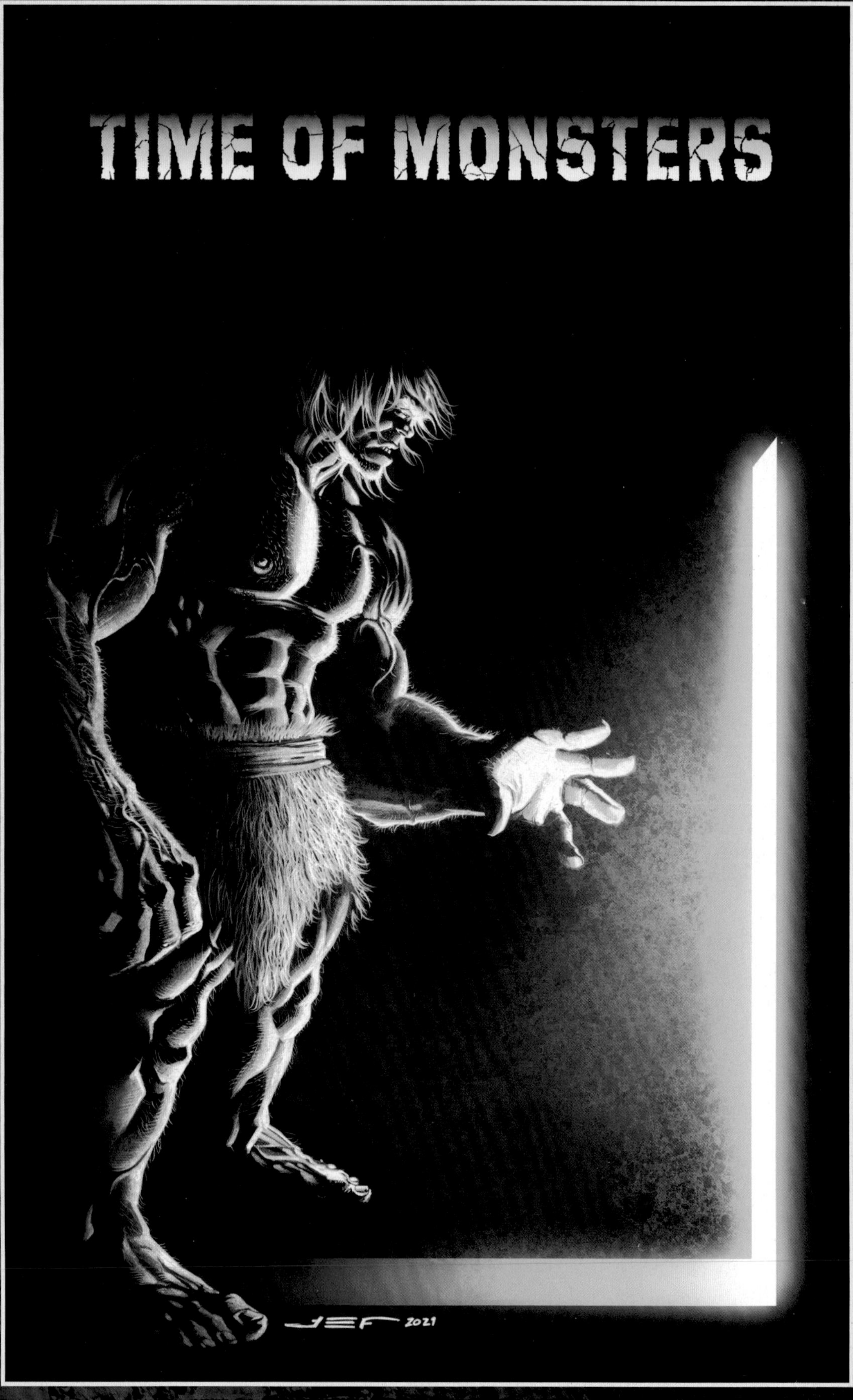
TIME OF MONSTERS
JEF 2021

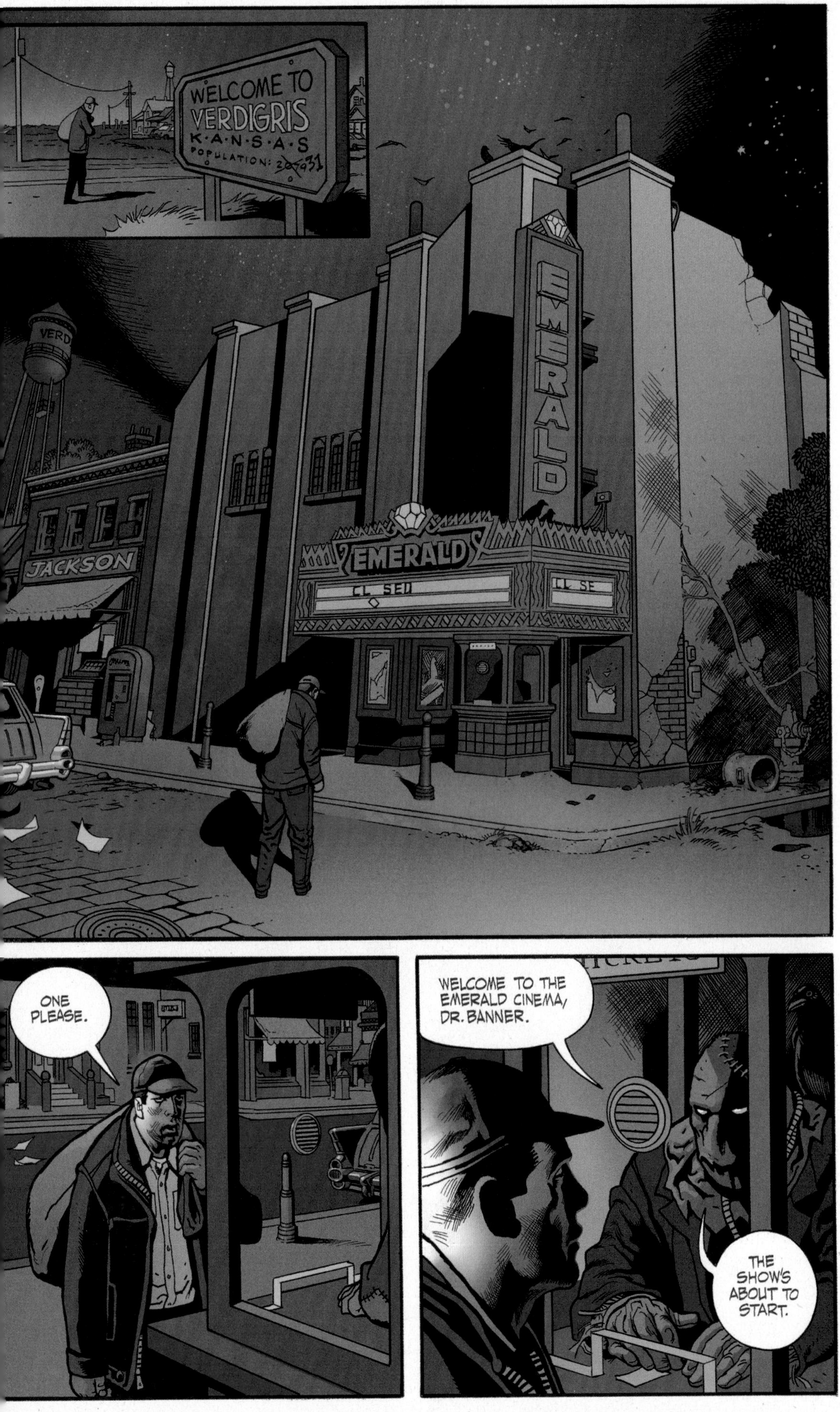

WELCOME TO
VERDIGRIS
K·A·N·S·A·S
POPULATION:
EMERALD
JACKSON
EMERALD
CL SED
CL SE
ONE PLEASE.
WELCOME TO THE EMERALD CINEMA, DR. BANNER.
THE SHOW'S ABOUT TO START.

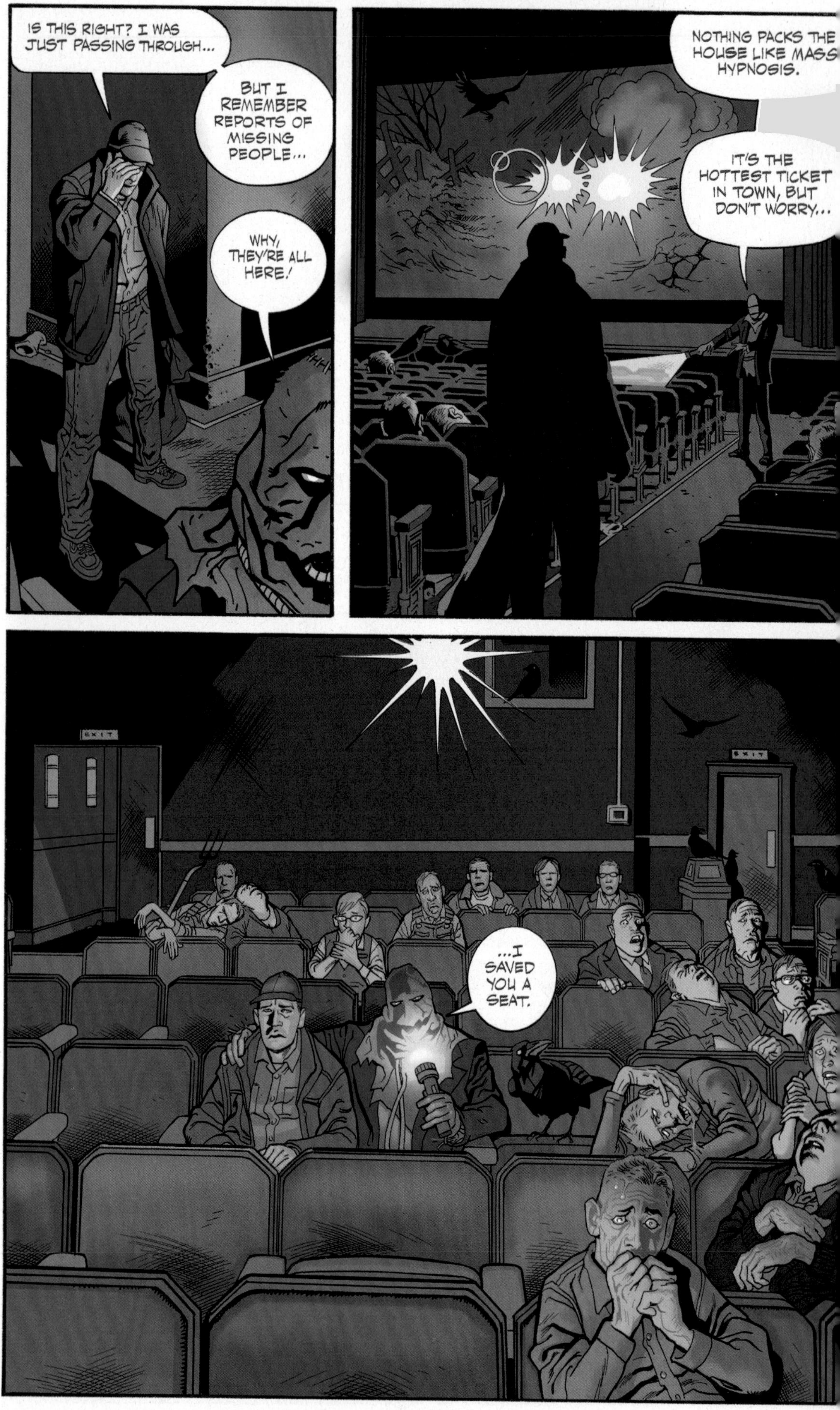

IS THIS RIGHT? I WAS JUST PASSING THROUGH...
BUT I REMEMBER REPORTS OF MISSING PEOPLE...
WHY, THEY'RE ALL HERE!
NOTHING PACKS THE HOUSE LIKE MASS HYPNOSIS.
IT'S THE HOTTEST TICKET IN TOWN, BUT DON'T WORRY...
EXIT
EXIT
...I SAVED YOU A SEAT.

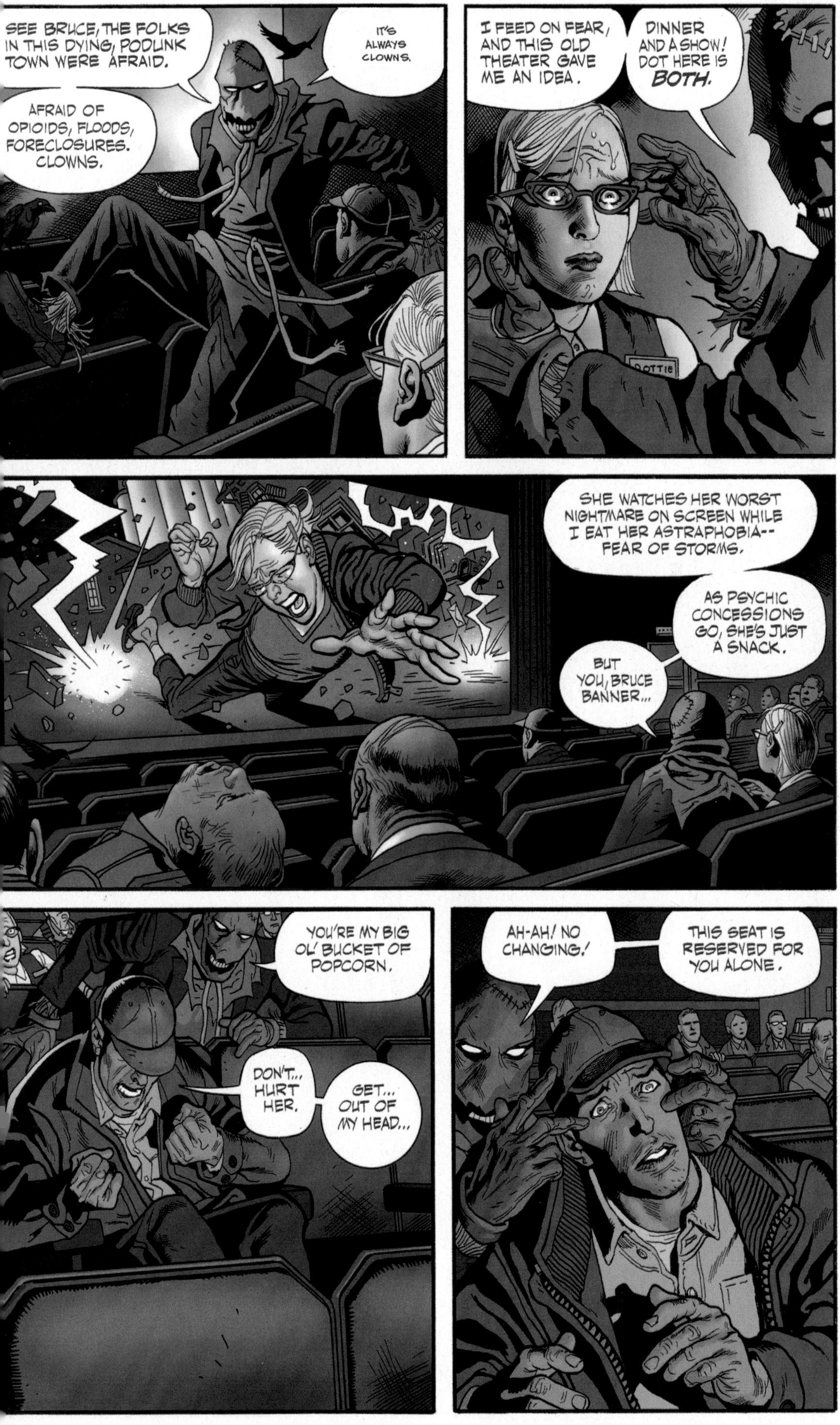

SEE BRUCE, THE FOLKS IN THIS DYING, PODUNK TOWN WERE AFRAID.
AFRAID OF OPIOIDS, FLOODS, FORECLOSURES. CLOWNS.
IT'S ALWAYS CLOWNS.
I FEED ON FEAR, AND THIS OLD THEATER GAVE ME AN IDEA.
DINNER AND A SHOW! DOT HERE IS BOTH.
DOTTIE
SHE WATCHES HER WORST NIGHTMARE ON SCREEN WHILE I EAT HER ASTRAPHOBIA-- FEAR OF STORMS.
AS PSYCHIC CONCESSIONS GO, SHE'S JUST A SNACK.
BUT YOU, BRUCE BANNER...
YOU'RE MY BIG OL' BUCKET OF POPCORN.
DON'T... HURT HER.
GET... OUT OF MY HEAD...
AH-AH! NO CHANGING!
THIS SEAT IS RESERVED FOR YOU ALONE.

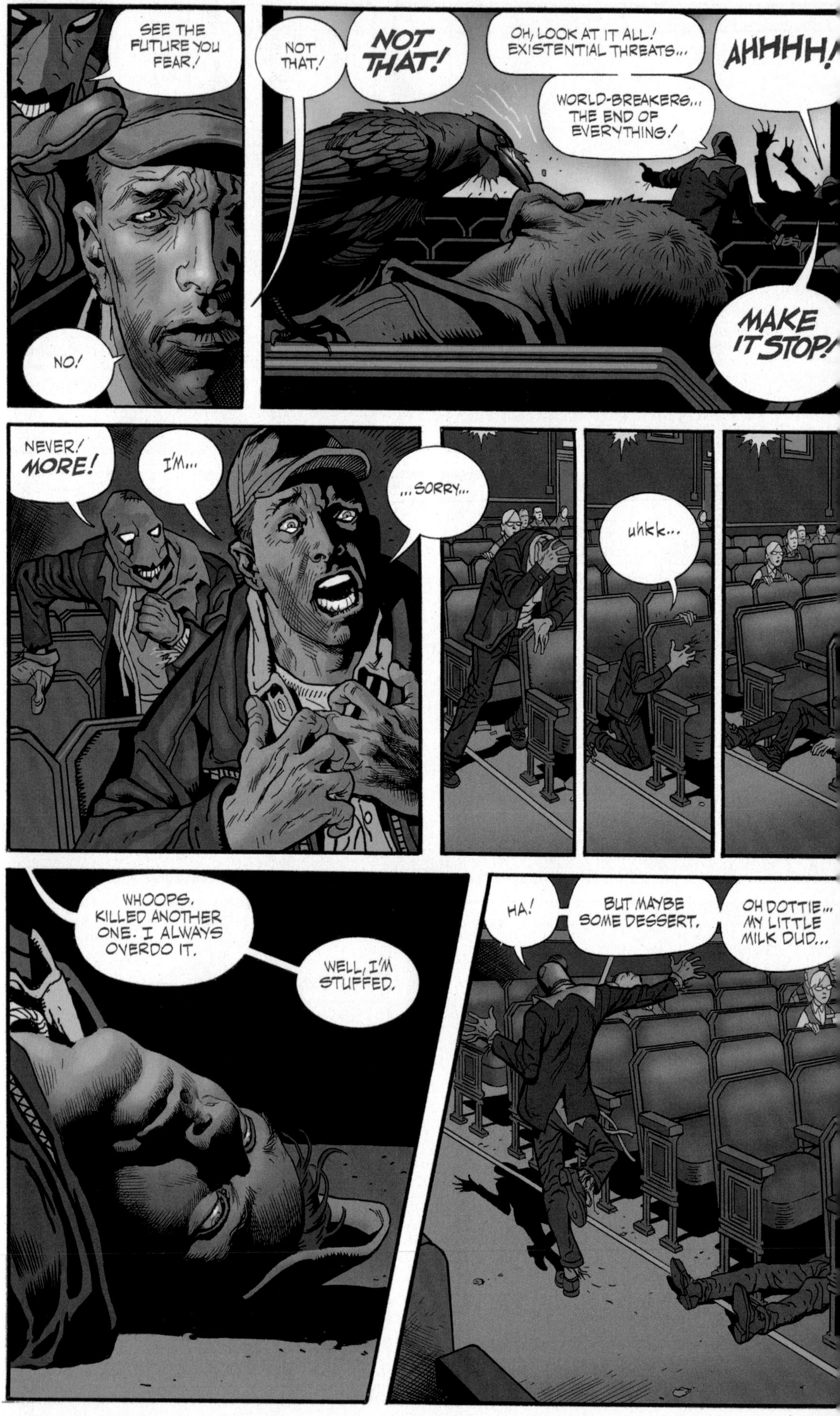
SEE THE FUTURE YOU FEAR!
NO!
NOT THAT!
NOT THAT!
OH, LOOK AT IT ALL! EXISTENTIAL THREATS...
WORLD-BREAKERS... THE END OF EVERYTHING!
AHHHH!
MAKE IT STOP!
NEVER! MORE!
I'M...
...SORRY...
uhkk...
WHOOPS. KILLED ANOTHER ONE. I ALWAYS OVERDO IT.
WELL, I'M STUFFED.
HA!
BUT MAYBE SOME DESSERT.
OH DOTTIE... MY LITTLE MILK DUD...

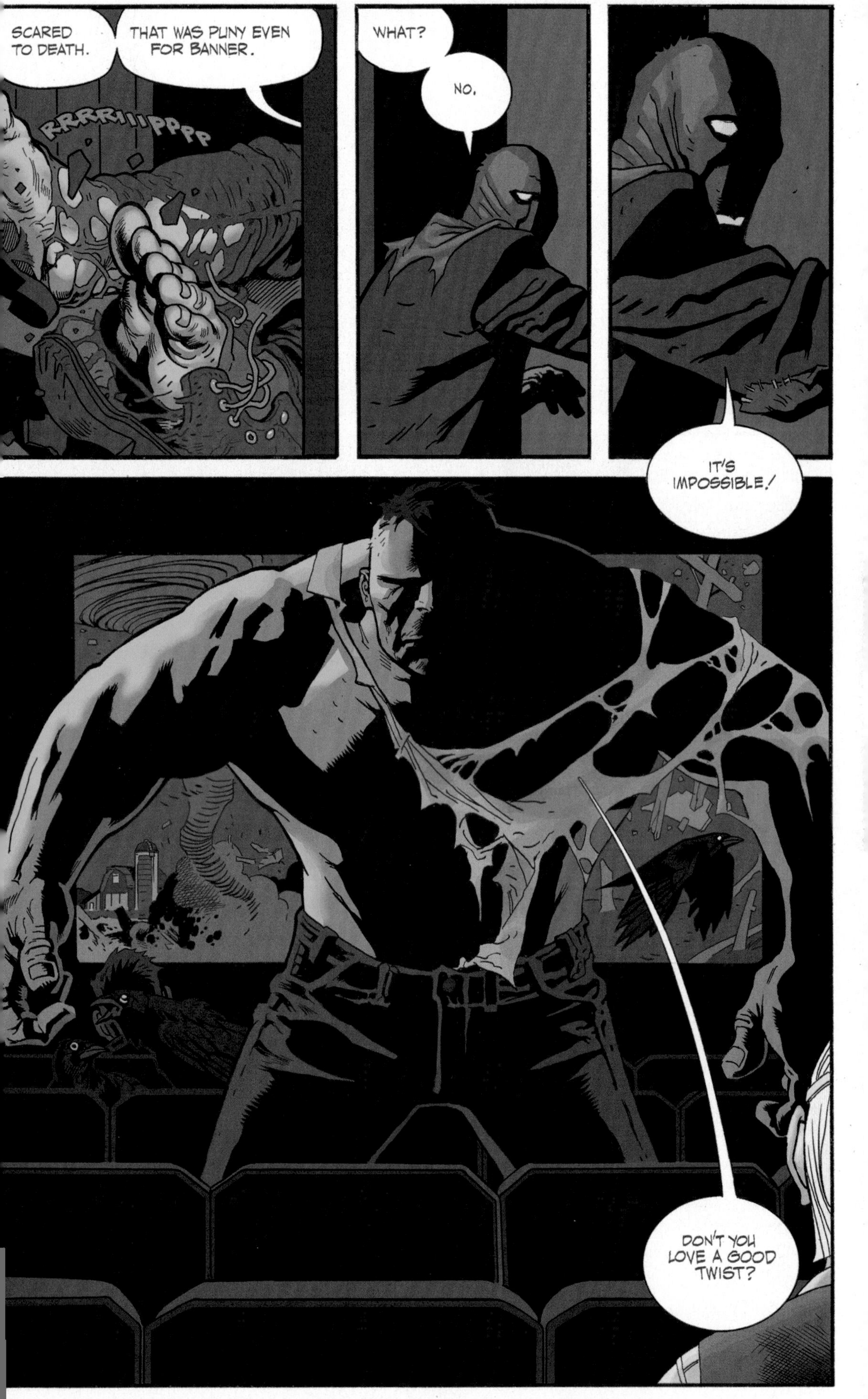
SCARED TO DEATH.
THAT WAS PUNY EVEN FOR BANNER.
RRRRIIIPPPP
WHAT?
NO.
IT'S IMPOSSIBLE.!
DON'T YOU LOVE A GOOD TWIST?

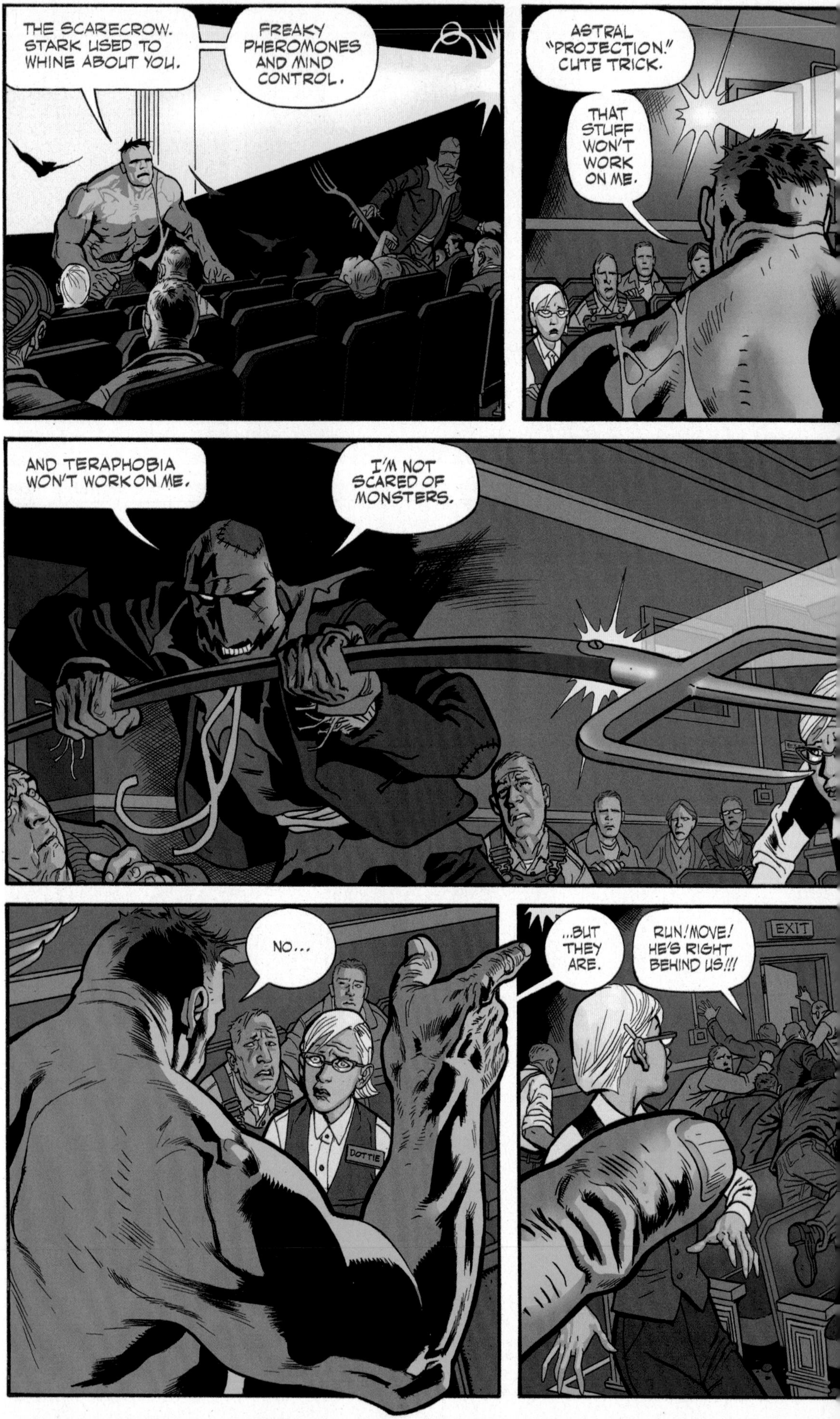
THE SCARECROW. STARK USED TO WHINE ABOUT YOU.
FREAKY PHEROMONES AND MIND CONTROL.
ASTRAL "PROJECTION." CUTE TRICK.
THAT STUFF WON'T WORK ON ME.
AND TERAPHOBIA WON'T WORK ON ME.
I'M NOT SCARED OF MONSTERS.
NO...
DOTTIE
...BUT THEY ARE.
RUN! MOVE! HE'S RIGHT BEHIND US!!!
EXIT

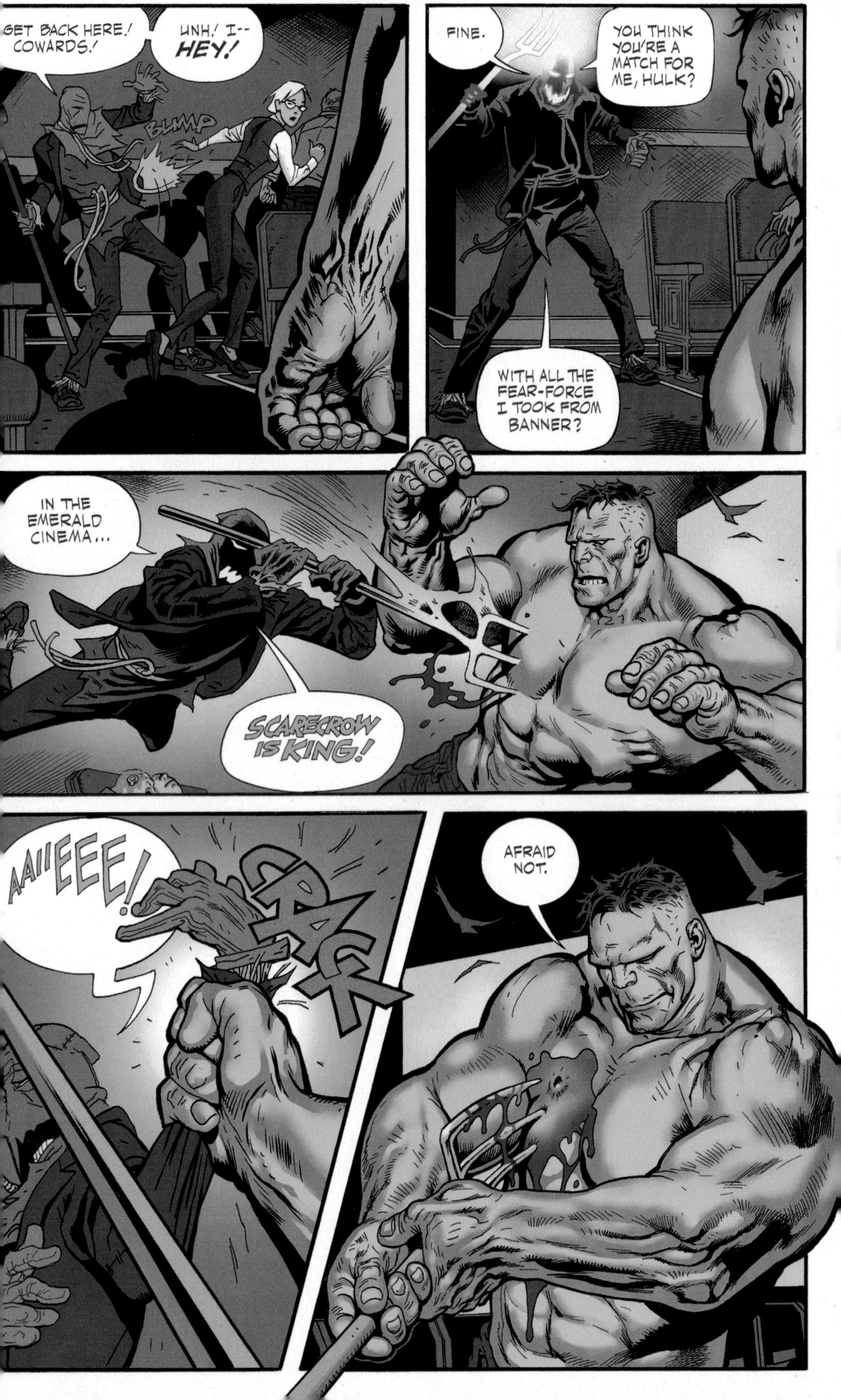
GET BACK HERE! COWARDS!
UNH! I-- HEY!
BUMP
FINE.
YOU THINK YOU'RE A MATCH FOR ME, HULK?
WITH ALL THE FEAR-FORCE I TOOK FROM BANNER?
IN THE EMERALD CINEMA...
SCARECROW IS KING!
AAIIEEE!
CRACK
AFRAID NOT.

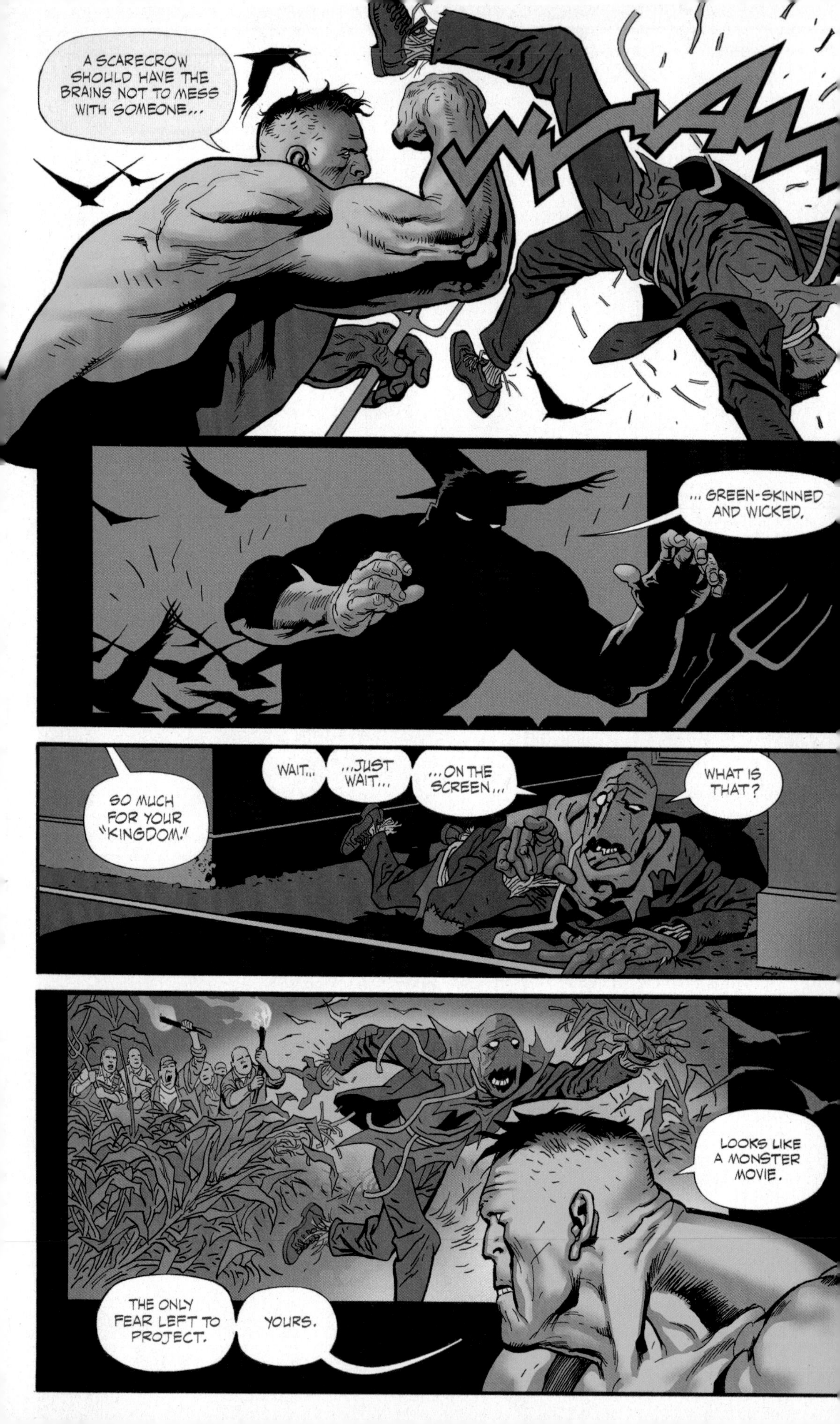
A SCARECROW SHOULD HAVE THE BRAINS NOT TO MESS WITH SOMEONE...
... GREEN-SKINNED AND WICKED.
SO MUCH FOR YOUR "KINGDOM."
WAIT...
...JUST WAIT...
...ON THE SCREEN...
WHAT IS THAT?
LOOKS LIKE A MONSTER MOVIE.
THE ONLY FEAR LEFT TO PROJECT.
YOURS.

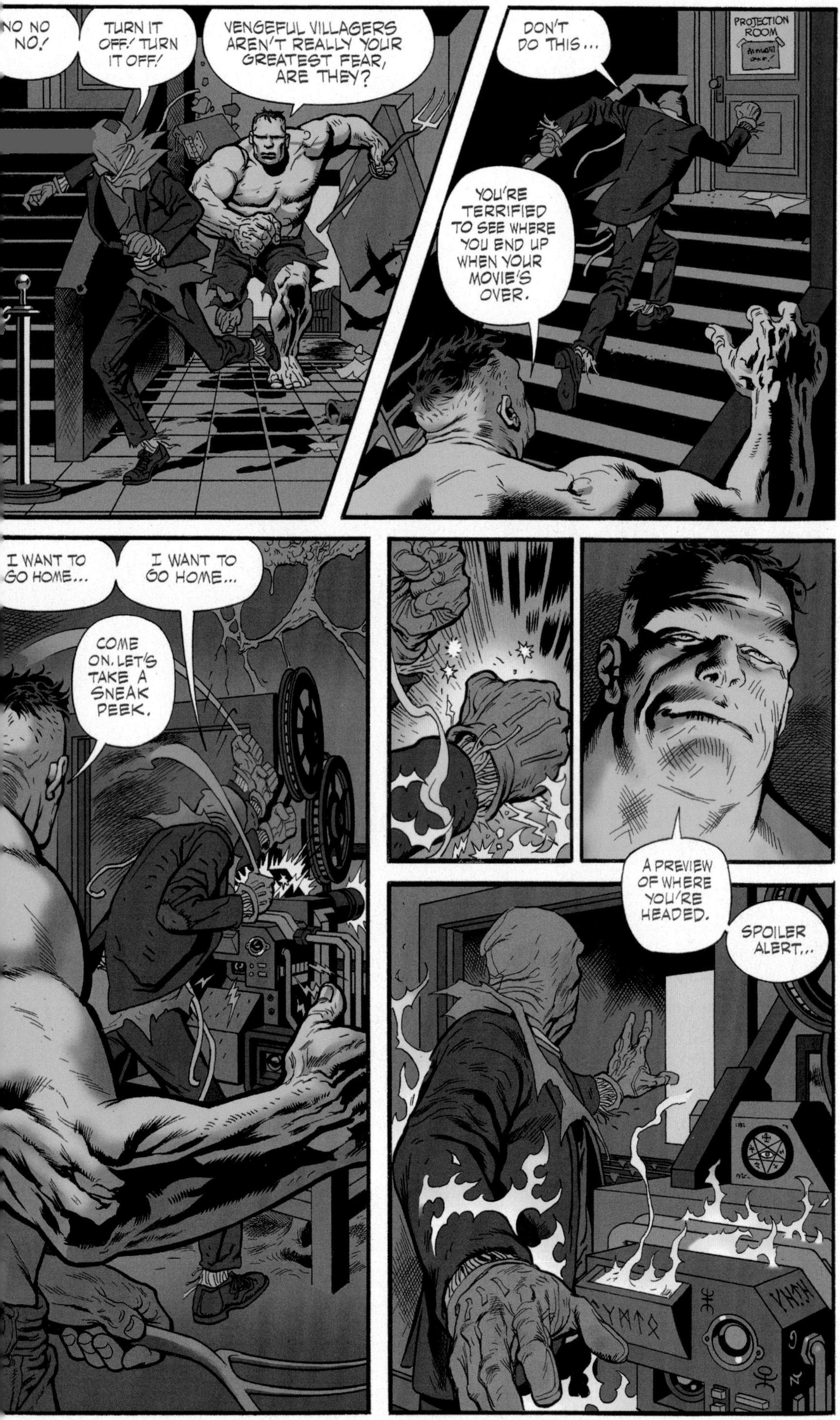
NO NO NO!
TURN IT OFF! TURN IT OFF!
VENGEFUL VILLAGERS AREN'T REALLY YOUR GREATEST FEAR, ARE THEY?
DON'T DO THIS...
PROJECTION ROOM
YOU'RE TERRIFIED TO SEE WHERE YOU END UP WHEN YOUR MOVIE'S OVER.
I WANT TO GO HOME...
I WANT TO GO HOME...
COME ON. LET'S TAKE A SNEAK PEEK.
A PREVIEW OF WHERE YOU'RE HEADED.
SPOILER ALERT...

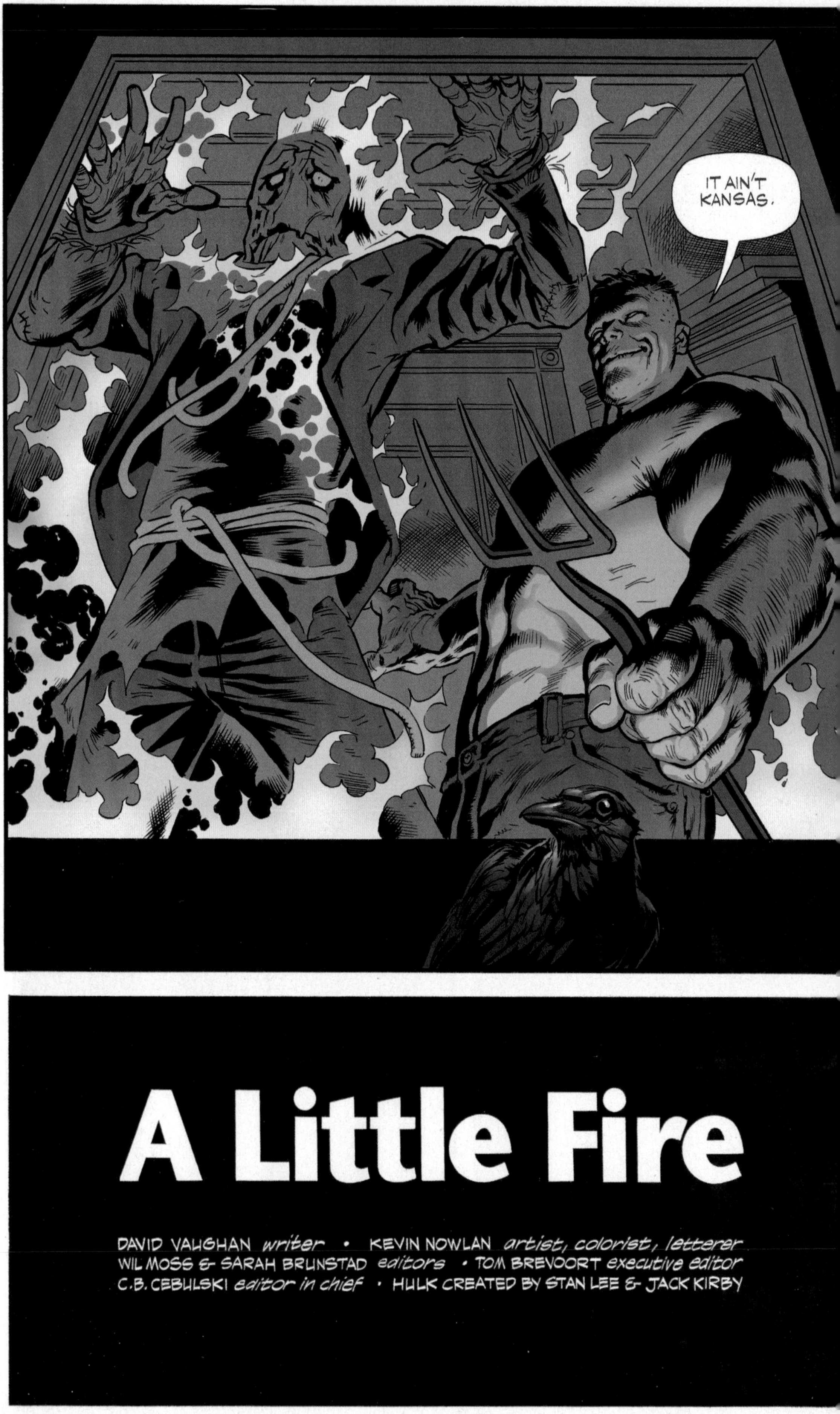
IT AIN'T KANSAS.

A Little Fire

DAVID VAUGHAN *writer* • KEVIN NOWLAN *artist, colorist, letterer*
WIL MOSS & SARAH BRUNSTAD *editors* • TOM BREVOORT *executive editor*
C.B. CEBULSKI *editor in chief* • HULK CREATED BY STAN LEE & JACK KIRBY